DAOIST NEI GONG
FOR
WOMEN

of related interest

White Moon on the Mountain Peak
The Alchemical Firing Process of Nei Dan
Damo Mitchell
Foreword by Jason Gregory
ISBN 978 1 84819 256 0
eISBN 978 0 85701 203 6

The Four Dragons
Clearing the Meridians and Awakening the Spine in Nei Gong
Damo Mitchell
Foreword by Ole Saether
ISBN 978 1 84819 226 3
eISBN 978 0 85701 173 2

Heavenly Streams
Meridian Theory in Nei Gong
Damo Mitchell
Foreword by Robert Aspell
ISBN 978 1 84819 116 7
eISBN 978 0 85701 092 6

Daoist Nei Gong
The Philosophical Art of Change
Damo Mitchell
Foreword by Cindy Engel
ISBN 978 1 84819 065 8
eISBN 978 0 85701 033 9

The Yellow Monkey Emperor's Classic of Chinese Medicine
Damo Mitchell
Art by Spencer Hill
ISBN 978 1 84819 286 7
eISBN 978 0 85701 233 3

DAOIST NEI GONG
·········· FOR ··········
WOMEN

The Art of the Lotus and the Moon

RONI EDLUND
AND DAMO MITCHELL

FOREWORD BY SOPHIE JOHNSON

SINGING
DRAGON
LONDON AND PHILADELPHIA

First published in 2016
by Singing Dragon
an imprint of Jessica Kingsley Publishers
73 Collier Street
London N1 9BE, UK
and
400 Market Street, Suite 400
Philadelphia, PA 19106, USA

www.singingdragon.com

Library of Congress Cataloging in Publication Data
Names: Edlund, Roni, author.
Title: Daoist Nei Gong for women : the art of the lotus and the moon / Roni
Edlund and Damo Mitchell ; foreword by Sophie Johnson.
Description: Philadelphia : Singing Dragon, 2016. | Includes bibliographical
references and index.
Identifiers: LCCN 2015038739 | ISBN 9781848192973 (alk. paper)
Subjects: LCSH: Qi gong. | Exercise. | Medicine, Chinese. | Women--Health and
hygiene.
Classification: LCC RA781.8 .E35 2016 | DDC 613.7/1489--
dc23 LC record available at http://lccn.loc.gov/2015038739

British Library Cataloguing in Publication Data
A CIP catalogue record for this book is available from the British Library

ISBN 978 1 84819 297 3
eISBN 978 0 85701 247 0

Printed and bound in Great Britain

CONTENTS

FOREWORD

Hooray hooray for a book dedicated to women's development in the internal arts! This fantastic book is a serious, comprehensive exploration of female cultivation – full of treasures to practise and information that addresses the glaring lack of feminine understanding in the internal arts.

I have the privilege of regarding Damo and Roni as my finest teachers and true examples of dedicated, insightful practitioners. The teachings presented in this book and in their courses are of phenomenally high calibre. This, when accompanied by the ethics by which they both live, is a rare thing.

As a young woman trying to find teachings within the energy arts, it made sense to me that my energy and body moved in a completely different way to those of a man. Surely, I thought, there must be some core differences in the way we women need to practise. I began studying internal energy work from the age of 15, working with Daoist, Tibetan and Sufi internal practices, and discovering common yet shocking experiences of misogyny. At worst…oh dear, I've been reincarnated as a woman, my bad – no chance of enlightenment for me then! Or simply a total lack of understanding that a woman's body has a different type of energetic makeup to a man's.

So I kept looking and explored many approaches and traditions while trying to find a serious, female-friendly approach…without much luck. A shockingly common experience, I now understand from speaking to other female practitioners.

I soon found that the teachers I met undoubtedly had some Qi skill and knowledge, yet they lacked ethics and there seemed to be little work on the Heart-mind. Emotionally, many of them appeared distorted, particularly around their relationship to sexuality, power and money. I learned a great deal about the general attitudes we have towards spirituality and the feminine. Although this was frustrating, it also encouraged me to explore an experientially based understanding of what spiritual transformation as a woman is all about.

Eventually, I found a teacher who wasn't trying to rob me or sleep with me! I studied with him for many years. He developed an internal energy system that worked with the Heart-mind as well as the other aspects of the energy body, which was wonderful work. Yet I had an intuition that there were many missing links. After his death, the time came to find another teacher. Seeing a YouTube video of Damo moving, I found myself saying, 'I could learn a great deal from that man.' I was by now a woman in her 40s and a little resistant and dubious about re-entering the Daoist world. I sent Damo a somewhat rude and blunt email! That email began an ongoing training journey with this remarkably skilled individual and teacher.

As a serious female practitioner, finding teachings appreciative of and adaptive to our uniquely female expression and route to the Dao is difficult, even ignored by most teachers. As women, we are surrounded by images of male cultivation and transcendence. Within the body/energy/ tantric traditions there is very little available for women to work with purposefully with their body, with the confidence that their female energy makeup is understood and utilised for awakening. Why there are so few female teachers and teachings is a mystery, apart perhaps from the vast worldwide suppression and fear of women. This sits in the heart of every woman I know, whether she is conscious of it or not. In my experience, to 'step out' in society as a woman of wisdom, a spiritual figure of any sort, takes the courage to release ourselves from the vibrational inheritance/ memory that to do so will result in violent persecution. This book is making a huge and vital contribution to all women who want to reclaim their *true* strength. Not the imitation of masculine expression, but the deep valuing of our intuition, softness, heart-centredness and connection to the environment. *Daoist Nei Gong for Women* will support women to value this real, incredible, wild femininity more deeply.

Over the years of training and spending time in the crazy restaurants Damo likes, we had many conversations. It was becoming clear to him and Roni that teaching regarding Daoist female cultivation was virtually impossible to access, that women needed it and, in typical Lotus Nei Gong fashion, they were going to do something about it!

This book is the result of that deep exploration, undertaken by both of them, to 'right' the balance and present this material for women. These two will only teach what they truly know. Roni has diligently worked with these practices for many years, until they have become steeped into her system. I have seen her transform, her own development moving deeper and deeper. The material in this book is wonderfully comprehensive — both in describing practices relevant to various times in a woman's life and as a detailed and thorough theoretical overview to strengthen and contextualise the practice of female Nei Gong. There is great attention to practices for specific times in a woman's life, and I very much look forward to learning more of them from Roni!

So enjoy this wonderful book, all you women out there (and men teaching women). It's a passionate wish of mine for women to grow in spiritual confidence, to realise that if we dedicate the hours necessary, we can reach profoundly within to our depth, and thereby contribute not only to ourselves but also, and perhaps especially, to the children we raise. The material in this exceptional book makes a tremendous contribution to that wish.

So head for your mat/cushion/training hall, ladies! Get going on the exercises in this book, support your intuition and, importantly, give yourselves a voice — speak and live what you know. Begin the process of stepping forward and being seen within your softness, with the wisdom and strength that you are.

Sophie Johnson
Director, Bonhays Meditation and Retreats
Practitioner, mother and teacher

PREFACE

RONI EDLUND

Modern society rarely places any great importance upon a person's inner development. It saddens me that there is not a greater emphasis upon the importance of health, spiritual growth and self-realisation. Instead, we are taught from an early age to focus more on our outer appearance as well as the 'things' we may acquire over the course of our lives. This imbalanced way of looking at ourselves has been particularly pushed upon women. Societal pressures on woman begin from an early age, telling them that they need to aspire towards a level of physical perfection that few will ever attain. This leads to feelings of dissatisfaction, worthlessness, depression and countless other negative emotional states which hold women back in their personal growth. This could be avoided by placing more of an emphasis on developing your inner state, a virtuous nature and opening the Heart centre up so that it may lead a woman to higher states of being. This path is based upon transforming your inner state so that true beauty shines from the inside out.

There are few books currently in print looking at the practices of Qi Gong or Nei Gong from a female perspective. The focus upon men at all levels of society ensured that it was male-based practices that were commonly spread, and women's teachings were often passed on through oral transmission only. It was for this reason that my partner, Damo Mitchell, and I decided to put together a book looking at these so often overlooked aspects of Daoist inner training. In the early stages of practice, there is little difference between the manner in which a man and a woman should train; everybody needs to learn how to stand, sit, move and breathe properly. After this, the intermediate levels of development begin to take on distinct variations, though; women have several aspects of energetic practice that are unique to them.

From the very first moment I started training in energy work through Nei Gong practice, I knew that this was something that I had to continue with. I could immediately feel the deep-reaching effects of the training. Since meeting my partner, I have been studying the Daoist arts in an effort to fully embrace the teachings of this ancient tradition. What struck me the most in those early days was the positive power that the practice had to change me physically, energetically and mentally. It was so fascinating to me that almost everything else in my life fell by the wayside as I focused myself solely on this one study. Even for somebody like me who was new to internal work and certainly not naturally sensitive to energy, I could engage with a deep inner transformation process very quickly. I continue to move deeper into Daoism with each day of practice, and it is my wish to make these teachings available to others so that they can also derive the same benefits from Nei Gong that I have.

Another factor that I considered when compiling this book was the life processes of a woman and in particular the issues surrounding menstruation and menopause. It is a shame that so many women consider it inevitable that they will suffer from negative physical and emotional symptoms attached to menstruation and the onset of menopause. Daoist and Chinese medical principles consider the shifts of energy taking place at these times to be potentially beneficial to a woman's inner growth; negative symptoms arising during these times are said to be signs of imbalance in a woman's health that need to be addressed. The truth is that many women simply don't know how to work with their own energy in an efficient manner because there is a lack of information on this subject. I know that I personally wish I had been given access to this information when I was younger, and I am sure that many other women who now practise the internal arts also wish the same.

I feel grateful and honoured each day to be able to practise the Daoist art of Nei Gong as well as to be involved in the spreading of these teachings to other women. I know that saying thank you is usually a part of the acknowledgements in a book, but I would like to express my gratitude to my partner, Damo Mitchell, for teaching me. Thank you for the light, inspiration and the huge amount of personal energy you put into teaching people and helping them come closer to some kind of personal 'truth'. I have enjoyed working with you on this book and I am hopeful that we will help to benefit the practice of women in the internal arts community.

Roni Edlund
Sweden Retreat Centre, Linköping

PREFACE

DAMO MITCHELL

O ver the last ten years I have been teaching Nei Gong. During this time I have seen a large increase in the number of women engaging in this powerful and fascinating practice. Initially, my classes had mainly male students, but then, as time went by, more and more women started on the path of internal change. Now, I am happy to say that in our classes and on our courses we have an even split of male and female students. This is how I like it to be. A class should be like a microcosm of the rest of life; a group is always the most satisfying to teach when there are people of all ages, cultures, backgrounds and of both genders.

With the even division of male and female students, it has become increasingly important for more information on women's practices to be openly shared. Essentially, male students are well catered for; many teachers focus solely upon male methods of training, and almost all of the written sources of information, both contemporary and classical, are written from a male perspective. What writing there is on the Daoist arts for women is generally focused on the medical aspects of the arts. Although there is nothing wrong with this, we felt that we (my partner, Roni, and I) wanted to put together a book for female practitioners that focused more on the internal process of development than solely on how to be healthy according to Chinese medical principles.

It has been interesting to speak with women who have studied Qi Gong or Nei Gong for a long time. In many cases they have been to a number of schools and generally been taught from a male-based perspective. A great number of them have voiced their frustration about an intuitive knowing, which they have had for some time, that they have been practising in a slightly incorrect manner. Women are the natural sensitive 'intuitives' of our species and as such have often felt that their internal process should be different from that practised by men. In more than a few cases women have told me that they have stumbled spontaneously upon energetic processes that they are taught in our classes, only to be told by male teachers elsewhere that they are doing it wrong and they should go back to doing the same as the rest of the class. Of course, this is not the fault of the teacher either – you can only teach what you know – but the truth is that women should indeed be practising slightly differently from men due to the particular nature of their energetic systems.

In writing this book, I have been involved in the layout and structuring of the book as well as writing many of the more technical sections. For obvious reasons I have stayed away from writing any of the experiential sections of the book based upon how a practice should feel for a woman who is working her way through the Nei Gong process. My partner, Roni Edlund, who has been far more pivotal in the creation of this book than I have, has put these sections together.

I met Roni while travelling through Thailand in late 2007. We quickly became friends and then partners, and shortly afterwards she began her own practice of the Daoist arts. Since this time she has studied full-time with me in Europe and then with some of my teachers in Asia. She has spent long periods in retreats on mountains, in temples and in the forests of Sweden, developing her internal practice through Nei Gong, Daoist alchemy, Chinese medicine and the martial arts. Throughout this time I have watched her move deep into the internal arts, working her way through the various stages of internal growth inherent in the Daoist tradition. Her own internal process has been quite different from mine, even though I have been her primary teacher, as she has moved through many of the woman-specific practices outlined in this book. The first-hand experience she has drawn from this practice has placed her in a perfect position to introduce these practices to women in this book. I am nowhere near able to convey these teachings. I am stuck purely on the intellectual and theoretical level in the case of Nei Gong for women, although I do know just how much positive development I have seen in women switching to these methods in their practice.

When planning this book project, Roni and I looked at what were the most important elements of women's practice that we thought we should discuss. After much deliberation we decided that we wished to introduce the individual nature of the female energy body, the concept of working with the moon, the life phases for women and then the importance of working with the middle Dan Tien. In doing this we have tried to produce a book that is accessible to beginners of Nei Gong training. For this reason we have attempted to stay away from any overly complex aspects of the practice as well as discussions that are only relevant to those with an in-depth understanding of Chinese medicine. An overview of female-specific training should help to inform those new to the practice, and those with prior experience should be able to see how this fits in with any methods in which they are already well versed.

In my opinion, even if female practitioners of the Daoist arts do not take on board anything else from this book, they should read closely the section on working with the moon. I never cease to be surprised at just how effective moon practice is for women and how quickly they connect with what at first appears to be a very esoteric and abstract practice. I have seen time and again how women's naturally intuitive nature gives them an ability to connect with environmental energies such as that given off by the moon, whereas the majority of men take a long time to reach a stage of being able to do the same. The connection between the moon and women is often drawn upon in Daoist art and folklore, as in the case of the moon deity Yue Guang Pu Sa (月光菩薩), who is shown here holding the moon itself.

THE MOON DEITY

I hope that this book will serve to answer many of the questions women may have about their practice and guide them in their training. I also hope that many male teachers of the internal arts who have women in their classes (I would guess most of them) may find something useful in this book which will help them to enable women fully in their school.

Damo Mitchell
Sweden Retreat Centre, Linköping

ACKNOWLEDGEMENTS

First, we would like to thank all of the people who have transmitted through to the modern age the wisdom of the Daoist tradition – teachings as relevant today as they were in ancient times. We would also like to give thanks to Sophie Johnson for writing the foreword to this book: a great teacher and a wonderful woman. Thank you to our good friend Lauren Faithfull for taking the time to go through each word of this book and help make it into something presentable. Thank you to our great student (and fellow author) Susan Casserfelt for sharing her spiralling energetic practice in photo form for the images in Chapter 8; she also entertains us on courses with her inner singing as well! Thanks to our usual artist, Joe Andrews, for helping out with line drawings and the ever-helpful Jason Smith for helping with photography. Much appreciation to Julie Qin once more for assistance with some of the Chinese characters. A final thank you to the students who appear in the photos from Chapter 6: Milka Nykanen, Ellie Talbot, Annabelle Herter, Clara Hendley, Linda Hallet, Colleen Mason and Cheryl Mandryk.

I (Roni Edlund) would also like to thank my mother for helping me to stay in tune with nature and myself while I was growing up.

DISCLAIMER

The authors and publisher of this material are not responsible in any way whatsoever for any injury that may occur through reading or practising the exercises outlined in this book.

The exercises and practices may be too strenuous or too risky for some people and so you should consult a qualified doctor before attempting anything from this book. It is also advised that you proceed under the guidance of an experienced teacher of the internal arts to avoid confusion and injury.

Note that any form of internal exercise is not a replacement for conventional health practices, medicines or any form of psychotherapy.

Notes on the Text

Throughout this book we have used the Pinyin system of Romanisation for the majority of Chinese words. Please note that much of the theory in this book differs greatly from Western science. The classical Chinese approach to understanding the organs of the body, for example, is based around the function of their energetic system rather than their physical anatomy. To distinguish the two understandings from each other, we have used capitalisation to indicate the Chinese understanding of the term. For example, 'Heart' refers to the classical Chinese understanding of the organ, whereas 'heart' refers to the physical organ as understood in contemporary Western biological sciences.

In addition, we have had a lot of correspondence from native Chinese speakers who have been reading our books. This, combined with an increase in the number of Chinese students, means that it is wise for us to put the Chinese characters next to each Pinyin term that we use in our writing. In order not to overcrowd the text, we have included the Chinese character on the first occasion each Pinyin term is used. The only exception to this is if it seemed relevant to include the Chinese character on another occasion, such as when listing Pinyin terms. There is also a full glossary of Chinese terminology at the rear of this book.

Chapter 1

WOMEN AND
NEI GONG

A t the spiritual heart of human existence there is no such thing as differentiation between genders. The higher states of spiritual awareness are neither masculine nor feminine in nature; both poles exist as a unified whole. This is a truth indicated by the depiction in the majority of Eastern traditions of deities who, though they may be declared as either male or female in form, are usually shown as being somewhat androgynous in appearance. These are the more advanced states of awareness that the majority of internal practitioners are attempting to connect with through dedication to a path of practice. In the meantime, while we flounder away in the lower vibrational states of existence, we must learn how to recognise and work with the differences that are inherent in male and female energetic systems.

The issue of gender impacts upon every facet of what we do and who we are. More than just a classification based upon biological differences, men and women have unique energetic and spiritual qualities that are a manifestation of the powers of Yin (陰) and Yang (陽). In the Eastern arts it has long been understood that men and women have individual traits that must be worked with in the correct manner in order to successfully progress towards a higher state of conscious transcendence. Although the ultimate aim of such practices was to rise above any sense of division, the path to this point was through embracing differences and learning how to work with them. For this reason there have long been individual nuances in the way in which men and women practitioners of the internal arts should approach their training.

Classically, Daoism was a tradition that did not relegate women into a secondary role, nor did it see female practitioners of the internal arts as any less likely to attain Dao (道) than their male counterparts. A whole pantheon of female immortals exists in philosophical and tantric Daoism. In religious Daoism (a later development) there are various female deities including such eminent beings as Xiwangmu (西王母), who is often known as the 'holy mother of the west', and Shengmu Yuanjun (聖母元君), who is the 'supreme sovereign mother'. Both of these important figures were venerated by practitioners of Daoist Nei Gong (內功) and Nei Dan (內丹) as symbols of what was possible through consistent alchemical practice. Sadly, this situation changed over time and Daoism became increasingly male-orientated. This took place as society became increasingly steered by the actions and desires of men. As women were relegated to secondary citizens, they took on a more subservient role – a situation that still exists for many women today. There are numerous ancient accounts of women who had to practise their arts in secrecy so that their husbands did not find out and punish them. As a result, many of the female-specific practices were ignored in favour of male-orientated training and this situation is only just starting once again to turn around. Although it is often the case that a Qi Gong or Nei Gong class is made up of roughly 50 per cent female students, the vast majority of writings and teachings of energetic practices are written with men in mind. As women had to hide their teachings, they often had to rely on oral transmission of the techniques and consequently many teachings have been lost. This has resulted in a situation where the practices will still work for women but they are not as efficient as they could be for harnessing the natural energetic strengths that women inherently have within them. Thus the entire process of spiritual growth through the Daoist arts is slowed down for female practitioners who could develop more effectively if only they had more informed knowledge on the nature of their energetic makeup from a Daoist perspective.

When starting out in the Daoist arts, it is wise to look at what you hope to get out of your practice. Your individual goals will dictate to what level you will need to study the underlying theories of Daoism. If, for example, you wish to practise the internal arts to help relax your mind and body, then there is no need to look at the differences between male and female practice. These levels of attainment can be achieved through simply learning to breathe deeply, stand correctly and move the joints in a slow and gentle manner. The practice will be the same whether you are a man or a woman. If, however, you wish to move deeper into the internal arts, towards the stages of awakening the energy system and refining various energetic substances within the body, then it is wise to understand the nature of your own energetic system. Women especially should look to understand their own energetic nature because the deeper levels of training are often reached through methods quite different from those commonly taught – those that are generally purely from a male-biased point of view.

This book aims to give an overview of the nature of training in the Daoist internal arts as a woman. In particular, the focus will be upon Nei Gong, although, of course, many of these principles can also be applied to other aspects of the Daoist tradition.

THE DIFFERENCES BETWEEN QI GONG AND NEI GONG

Many people these days will have heard of Qi Gong (氣功) but fewer will have heard the term Nei Gong (內功). A simple translation of Nei Gong would be 'internal skill', but this is an overly simplistic view of what is involved in Nei Gong training. A more complete definition of the term might be 'the process by which a person may condition their physical body, cultivate their internal universe and elevate their consciousness'.

If Qi Gong exercises are 'tools' – exercises with a defined goal – Nei Gong is the internal process inherent within Daoism if people choose to immerse themselves fully in the practice. Nei Gong is the energetic basis for the 'path' of Dao. Travel along this path is accomplished through the use of various vehicles including standing practices, moving exercises and sitting meditation.

Nei Gong teachings were classically held back from the general public and remained hidden long after Qi Gong became widely known. It was considered a higher-level practice because it effectively serves as a bridge between pure, energy-based practices and the alchemical meditation systems of the Daoists. It is worth noting here that teachers may use terms in different ways. Some may say they are teaching Qi Gong when in fact, by this definition, they are actually teaching Nei Gong and vice versa. One of the first important things you must ascertain when meeting a new teacher is how exactly they define certain terms because there is a great deal of variation from lineage to lineage.

The key process of development in Nei Gong training begins with working initially with the physical body, which provides the foundation necessary for moving towards working with the energy body. Once there has been a considerable amount of work with the energetic system, then direct work takes place with the consciousness. Classically, this was termed as working with the three treasures of Jing (精), Qi (氣) and Shen (神), as shown in Figure 1.1.

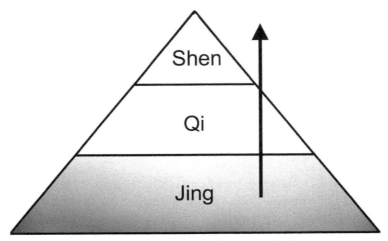

FIGURE 1.1: JING, QI AND SHEN IN NEI GONG

At each stage a solid foundation must be built in order to guarantee smooth and systematic progression towards increasingly higher states of development. Although this underlying theory is the same for both male and female practitioners of Nei Gong, it is important to understand the unique nature of these substances within both genders.

MALE AND FEMALE PRACTICE DIFFERENCES

The actual differences between male and female Nei Gong practice can be found primarily in the intermediate stages of training. At the very beginning of your practice, it does not matter whether you are a man or a woman, as you essentially have to work through the same body alignments and principles of learning how to breathe and relax. After this, the lower energy centre must be woken up and it is from here that the practice for men and women should begin to differ. Sadly, it has long been the case that teachings on the internal arts were recorded by men and passed on with a very male-heavy bias. Women's practices are seldom discussed, and consequently many women are having a 'glass ceiling' placed upon their development simply because they do not have access to the same level of information as their male counterparts. Although this does not mean that women have not been able to progress in practices such as Nei Gong, they have been slowed down by not working as efficiently as they can with their own internal environment.

In brief, we can summarise the key differences between male- and female-based practices, as shown in Table 1.1. This table provides an overview of male and female internal differences. Many of the terms in the table will be discussed in greater detail throughout the rest of this book.

TABLE 1.1: MALE AND FEMALE PRACTICE DIFFERENCES

	Men	Women
Foundation built in	Sexual fluids	Blood
Quality of Qi	Forceful	Soft
Energetic movement	Centrifugal	Centripetal
Focal energy centre	Lower Dan Tien	Middle Dan Tien
Celestial energy	Solar	Lunar
Key hurdle	Base desires	Emotional leakage

Understanding the differences between these facets of male and female energetic anatomy enables us to see the differences between how the two genders should approach their practice. Each of these differences is discussed in brief below.

Sexual Fluids and Blood

The classical sequence for working through the key substances of the body in the Daoist arts is to begin with refining the Jing, working up to refining the Qi and then finally developing the Shen. Although there is a large degree of interdependence between these substances, it is understood that, in order to develop effectively, a solid foundation must be built at each 'stage' before moving on to the next. Consolidation of Jing to a certain level is required in order to ensure that a practitioner's health is at such a stage that it can provide a high-quality base from which to begin moving deeper into Nei Gong. The Jing also serves as the primary fuel for the conversion of the three treasures into more refined spiritual substances.

It is the case for men that their Jing is lost through the natural life and ageing cycles, but also through the loss of sexual fluids upon ejaculation. This is why many classical schools of Daoism had guidelines that restricted sexual activity for male students or, in many cases, completely forbade it.

For women, their Jing is lost to a large degree through the monthly menstrual cycle. A woman does not lose Jing in the same way as a man during sex due to the more internalised nature of her orgasm. Although female Daoists still had guidance about the most efficient manner in which to engage in sexual intercourse in order to work with their Jing, the degree of restriction was not as high. Instead, women need to learn to refine the process of menstruation by aligning their energetic cycles with the phases of the moon. Once this foundation practice has successfully been worked with, it will ensure a solid foundation upon which to develop further.

Forceful and Soft Qi Quality

Of course, when discussing the relative qualities of Qi flow, there is a large amount of individual variation in each one of us. No two people have the same quality of energy; each of us has unique information stored within our energetic system which is made up of our life experiences, persona and countless other influences. That being said, we can generalise to a certain degree and understand that male energy tends to have a slightly more forceful quality to it than that of women. In the case of men, their Qi moves with a power that is directed by their naturally more Yang mind-state. Women tend to have more softly moving Qi that is directed by a more gentle Yin mind-state. What this means is that men will naturally use more assertion when they engage with internal arts such as Nei Gong, whereas women will have a tendency to come at their practice from a more passive direction. While both genders should adopt a gentle intention in their practice, men will be able to use more directed focus in their training to progress, especially in the earlier stages of working with the lower Dan Tien (丹田). By the time they move on to working with the more psychologically based middle Dan Tien, they must have learned how to soften the quality of their Qi; otherwise, they run the risk of damaging the fragile information field of the Heart, a common problem arising from Qi Gong training which leaves a practitioner with a feeling of depression and low energy levels.

In contrast, women's energy tends to flow more softly, which is far more in line with the Daoist ideal. Women can actually develop much more quickly if they learn how to harness the natural softness of their Qi by directing it with a gentle but focused intention and then simply sitting back and observing what is taking place. In this way they use their intention as a sort of catalyst to start a process of change, but then allow the natural softness of their Qi to continue the work for them. If a woman tries to use an overly powerful intention or direct her energy too forcefully, she will find that instead of developing she actually hinders her progression.

Centrifugal and Centripetal Energy Movement

Male energy tends to rotate outwards from the core, which means that it tends to have a stronger effect on the surrounding environment. It is also the basis for the very male-orientated interpersonal qualities of domination and control.

Female energy moves in the opposite way; it tends to move centripetally inwards towards the core of the energetic system. This means that there are a couple of key qualitative differences in the way that a woman relates to the outside environment. First, women will find that they naturally have a higher degree of energetic sensitivity to what is taking place around them. Your energetic field exchanges information with the world around you, and Qi carries with it a great deal of information that is then accessed once it interacts with your Shen. In the case of men, their naturally outwards-moving energy means that they are usually giving information out into the surrounding environment, whereas women are always absorbing. If a woman is able to locate the stillness at the centre of her consciousness, she will find that she naturally begins to interpret that information, giving her heightened intuitive skills. The second key advantage of centripetally moving energy is that women can use the environment's energy to fuel their practice to a far higher degree than their male counterparts. For women, there is a far greater benefit to practising in a healthy, natural environment because the Qi of these areas will bring her on in her practice very quickly.

Lower and Middle Dan Tien

Although both men and women begin their practice by working with the lower Dan Tien, women should be much quicker to move on to the higher-frequency energy centres. The lower Dan Tien is more physically based. It is connected to a person's root, their motion and their centre of gravity. It is the Earth-based energy centre, which males use in their training to anchor the rest of their energetic system into the physical world. Even when male practitioners develop beyond the lower Dan Tien, they still return there, as this is always the basis for their skill. Women practise in a different manner to this, and once they have progressed past the foundation of the lower Dan Tien, they rarely return to work at this level. Instead, they move on to the middle Dan Tien, situated within the chest at the height of their Heart. This is the emotionally powered centre of Qi, compassion and connection. Once a woman has reached the stage of working with the middle Dan Tien, all of her focus is put here because this is the basis upon which her internal skill is developed.

Solar and Lunar Influence

Male energy is very much connected to the sun. There are many practices in classical Qi Gong for working with the energy of the sun. Some of this training involves performing exercises while facing the rising sun, whereas others are more meditative in order to help the student absorb and benefit from the sun's energy. Although these practices are still useful for a woman, she will not gain anywhere near the same amount of energy from them as a male practitioner will. Instead, women should learn how to practise with the moon's energy, as this is the main celestial body of Yin energy in our sky. The moon's energy is primarily used to connect a woman to the Heavenly cycles and build a foundation within her menstrual Blood. Even when this has been accomplished and a female practitioner moves on to the more advanced stages of her practice, there is still a great gain to be had from practising any moving exercises or sitting meditation when the moon is high in the night sky.

Base Desires and Emotional Connection

The biggest hurdles to a person's practice come at different stages for men and women. In the case of men, it is their base desires that prove a problem. Each aspect of a person's psyche is rooted within either a physical aspect or an energetic element of their body. A person's base desires are rooted in the Jing, particularly in the case of men. If a male cannot overcome his base desires and convert the nature of his psyche to a higher state, then he will never refine the Jing to a high enough state to move on. Sadly, this is the earliest hurdle a person can come across in their practice and the reason why so many male practitioners become stuck right at the beginning of their spiritual development.

Women do not have such a huge connection to their base desires. Although they obviously still have such desires, these are not such an overpowering aspect of their acquired mind. A woman's natural state is to have desires arise but then fade into the background where they are not an issue. In contrast, the male psyche will have base desires arising but never fully fading away; this means that the desires are always there, influencing many aspects of the man's behaviour and development.

Consequently, women can usually progress beyond work with the lower Dan Tien much faster than men, and so begin working with the Heart centre and the middle Dan Tien. On the other hand, women will usually find that they can lose a lot more of their Jing, the essence stored in the region of the chest, through emotional connection to others, mainly in the case of emotional connection that is not returned. Women require an equal emotional exchange with those they care about in order to ensure that their Heart-centred energy is not weakened.

THE DEVELOPMENTAL PROCESS OF NEI GONG

Nei Gong is a very individual path of study. Although there are set steps that should be taken in a person's practice, each practitioner will have their own set of experiences as they develop further through their training. In the early stages of practice it is generally the case that a person begins to notice physical changes to their health. As they go deeper into the process, there are clear signs of transformation in their psychological nature. At the higher levels there are various stages that can be quite surprising at first. These are the stages of moving into the alchemical transformation of Daoism. Below is a brief outline of a few of the key stages of development commonly experienced by students of Nei Gong.

- The earliest stages of change through the Nei Gong process involve the melting of tension from the body's muscles. At first it is the large muscle groups that relax, but with time older, habitual tensions are released from deep within the connective tissues of the body. For many people, this brings a new-found level of bodily comfort as years of stored-up tightness begins to fade away. This largely happens early on through embodiment of a principle known as Sung (松), which can be understood as a form of energetic release based on increasing levels of relaxation.

- Old injuries can begin to repair themselves as the body is given enough 'space' to begin moving back into a healthier state. It is often quite surprising just how effective this kind of practice is at repairing old damage.

- The third stage of development involves the restoration of your internal health. As the transformation of Nei Gong moves deeper into the body, it is normal for organ-based imbalances to begin to improve. Conditions with a person's lungs or digestive system, for example, begin to change as the flow of the person's Qi becomes more efficient. This often happens as old toxins are removed from the energetic system. For women, there are often great changes with regard to their menstrual cycle if they have not yet entered the menopause. The timing of their periods usually goes through a large shift, and negative symptoms associated with menstruation begin to lessen.

- The more the body relaxes, the more a person's mind begins to still. Many of us live in a constant state of mental hyperactivity, largely brought on by an over-preoccupation with the external world. By learning how to relax and develop the energetic system, a practitioner's mind begins to grow increasingly quiet. This is an important foundational stage for further meditative training on top of having a positive influence upon a person's overall wellbeing.

- The deeper stages of softening through Nei Gong usually involve large changes taking place in a person's physical structure. The body is essentially a manifestation of the state of a person's mind; as a greater level of balance is reached, this starts to generate transformation within the body. It is normal to start hearing 'clicks and cracks' coming from a Nei Gong practitioner's body, even though they may not be making any large external movements. These are shifts taking place in the alignment of the bones as the body moves into better postural alignment. If this happens, do not worry; it is quite healthy for you. Most importantly, at this stage the spine starts to open up, creating more space between the vertebrae. This helps to ensure a healthy flow of energy up into the brain, but also has the added side effect of adding a little extra height to the majority of practitioners.

- Beyond here, practitioners of Nei Gong move into the more advanced stages of waking up the usually dormant energy system. This takes place through rotation of several key cycles of Qi through the body. Female Nei Gong practitioners have several important cycles that male practitioners don't have. This is due to the manner in which Jing and Qi is shifted through the body, which is quite unique for women. As the energy movement starts to increase, it begins the purging of pathogenic Qi from the meridian system as well as various levels of emotional release. These stages are required in order to help develop the energy body to a high enough level to provide a foundation for direct work with the consciousness. Although the actual process of having an emotional release can initially feel somewhat unpleasant, it generally leaves a person feeling somehow 'lighter'.

- The basic levels of Nei Gong training are complete when a person has moved through these stages. Beyond these are the more alchemical elements of Daoist internal training, which are explored in brief towards the end of this book. This list is included just to give a short introduction to what a person can expect when they start out along the path of Nei Gong.

WHO SHOULD NOT PRACTISE NEI GONG?

It should be recognised that Nei Gong training is really only for those people who wish to go deep into the transformational aspects of Daoism. It is a deceptively simple system but can be very powerful due to the strong shifts that can take place during the training. For this reason we advise that only those wishing to go beyond a 'casual' study of the internal arts consider working with Nei Gong. Those simply wishing for a form of relaxation should remain working only with Qi Gong exercises. In addition, there are several groups of people who really should not train in Nei Gong.

The first group is those who are under the age of 18. Children or young teenagers should never engage with Nei Gong training of any sort because of the powerful effect it can have upon a person's emotional state. Younger people are still going through a period of emotional turbulence. Their emotions are still moving towards some kind of stability and so any internal work at this time runs the risk of preventing them 'finding their own level'. This should also be the case for intense meditative or internal work of any kind. Simple sitting and breathing exercises are fine for children, but anything more intense should be avoided. It is more prudent to focus on external movements for younger people because this will help to establish a high degree of health at a young age – health that will stay with them as they grow older.

Women should never train in Nei Gong if they are pregnant. During those nine months the body is going through a great deal of energetic change; the last thing you should do is put yourself through the transformational process of Nei Gong as well. During pregnancy it is wise to focus on gentle stretching and breathing exercises in order to keep energy flowing, but powerful internal exercises should be avoided.

Those with a psychiatric illness should not train in Nei Gong as the shifting of the energy within the body can heighten extreme psychological states. In the same way, Nei Gong should never be started by anybody while they are experiencing an emotionally difficult time in their life. Periods of personal challenge are not good times to begin transformational work. Save it for when your life is more settled.

STAGES OF FEMALE NEI GONG

Although it is always difficult to fully systemise a process, it is useful to have a basic structure to follow. The modern, Western mind is particularly fond of having a set structure to work through. There is nothing inherently wrong with this at the beginning, but after a while such a structure can become somewhat limiting. For this reason the sequence below should be seen as a rough outline based around the order of stages that the vast majority of women move through when they engage with Nei Gong practice. You should find that you naturally begin to move around within this sequence in a more fluid manner once the foundation stages have been completed. The stages of development in female Nei Gong are as follows:

1. Conditioning and preparation of the physical body

2. Regulation of breath and mind

3. Regulation of the menstrual cycle

4. Extraction of Jing from Tian Gui

5. Awakening the energy system

6. Awakening of the Heart centre

7. Attainment of internal vibration

8. Conversion of Qi to Shen

9. Conversion of Shen to Dao

These nine stages are described below in brief and then explored in greater detail throughout the rest of the book.

1. Conditioning and Preparation of the Physical Body

The first thing to be taken into consideration is the health and condition of the physical body. As already discussed, the physical body is the workshop in which all of our practice takes place. Quite simply, if the workshop is in a poor condition, then we will only produce poor-quality results from our training.

A woman engaging with Nei Gong should aim to work on her alignments and the level of relaxation throughout her body, maintain a healthy level of flexibility and establish a healthy diet to optimise her physical health. It is only if we can build a solid base in the physical realm – by building as healthy a foundation in the physical body as possible in the earliest stages of Nei Gong – that we can be sure of moving effectively into the energetic level of our development.

2. Regulation of Breath and Mind

Regulation and control of our breath is a crucial aspect of any internal training. The quality of our breath is a direct result of the health of our emotions. By regulating the breath, we help to bring the mind towards a more centred point. In addition, our breath also directs a great deal of energy flow through our system. Improving the quality of our breathing therefore helps to smooth out the manner in which our Qi runs through the meridian system.

Because of the intimate relationship that exists between our breath and our awareness, it is possible to use the breath as a kind of intermediary between the three bodies (explored in depth in Chapter 2). By regulating our breathing patterns, we can literally adjust the frequency of the mind's awareness so that tangible experience of the energy body can be had. This is an important skill, particularly for women, who should aim to develop their internal sensitivity once they begin working at the level of Qi. In Chapter 3 we explore breathing in Nei Gong and attach it to a sound-based practice, which can be particularly useful for female Daoists.

3. Regulation of the Menstrual Cycle
A unique aspect of internal work for women is the effect that the training has upon their menstrual cycle. Any energetic transformational work is likely to create shifts in a woman's monthly cycle if she is below the age of menopause. A key concern for women should be to try to harmonise their menstrual pattern with the environmental changes taking place with the shifting of the moon's phases. This will help to minimise premenstrual symptoms and lessen the decline of a woman's Jing. There is also a powerful cleansing effect to be had from correctly managing menstruation.

4. Extraction of Jing from Tian Gui
The extraction of Jing from menstrual Blood is an important part of the 'small water wheel' training for female Nei Gong practitioners. In order to consolidate the Jing, female practitioners must learn how to cycle the energy in the Conception meridian along the front of their body. This begins to extract vital essence from the menstrual Blood, essence that would otherwise be lost through menstruation. This is one of the key stages of working with the rotations of the 'small water wheel' that are unique to female practice.

5. Awakening the Energy System
The process of waking up the usually dormant energetic system is a lengthy, but not particularly complex, aspect of the Nei Gong process. This is the stage of working through the various elements of the meridian system in order to purge pathogenic energies from the body and restore

a healthy flow of Qi. This is a natural advancement on the earlier 'small water wheels' which will have been initiated through work with the lower Dan Tien.

6. Awakening of the Heart Centre

Once a solid foundation has been established in the previous stages of the Nei Gong process, a female practitioner of Nei Gong will find that she is naturally led towards contact with the Heart centre and the associated Dan Tien. This is the key energetic focal point for women engaging in the Daoist arts and the strongest stage that brings about transformation of the consciousness.

7. Attainment of Internal Vibration

This is the stage of uniting mind, energy and body into a single unit. It is here that a person can begin to experientially understand the deeper energetic aspects of human existence. It is here that the meridians are said to be 'open' as they transfer the vibrational force of the mind throughout the entire body.

8. Conversion of Qi to Shen

Although this conversion happens all of the time via the functional activities of the three Dan Tien, the Nei Gong practitioner begins to increase the efficiency of the process. At this stage, the practitioner has worked through a great deal of the beginner and intermediate stages of Nei Gong practice. The conversion of the internal three treasures, Jing, Qi and Shen, serves to nourish the mind and so bring a person closer to a state of conscious transcendence. Here, a person is moving beyond pure Nei Gong into the alchemical Nei Dan meditative practices of Daoism.

9. Conversion of Shen to Dao

The highest stages of internal development through the process of Nei Gong involve the conversion of spiritual energy back towards the original state of Dao. This is a complex stage which can only be achieved by the most diligent of practitioners. This is the point at which a female practitioner learns how to reconnect to the original spirit from which true human consciousness was born. To fully understand this stage of training, it is necessary to look at the practice of Nei Dan.

YIN AND YANG

When looking to understand the nature of existence through Daoist philosophy, it is important to understand the initial generation of the two poles of Yin and Yang. Collectively known as Liang Yi (兩儀), Yin and Yang are seen as two opposite, yet complementary, forces which are the basis for all of existence. They are two points of manifestation born from the stillness of Wuji (無極). This is the underlying philosophy for all of the Daoist arts as well as the rationale for the process of development inherent in practices such as Nei Gong. Figure 1.2 shows the process of Yin and Yang being born from the stillness of Wuji.

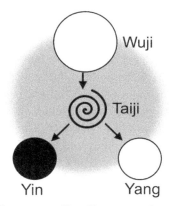

FIGURE 1.2: YIN, YANG AND WUJI

Wuji can be translated as meaning 'without extremities' or 'without projections'. It is said to be the extreme emptiness that existed at the absolute origin of all manifested phenomena. Wuji is the state prior to the formation of the cosmos, as well as the still-point at the centre of human consciousness, which is said to have given birth to life. The importance of this stillness is greatly emphasised in the Daoist tradition, as it is the vessel of true potential.

An underlying tenet of Daoism states that stillness cannot exist for long without it beginning to manifest the opposite force of movement. This is the inevitable nature of change which permeates all of reality. In the case of the stillness of Wuji, a single point of movement came into being. This single point is known as Taiji (太極), which can be translated as 'great pole' or 'great extremity'. Taiji is the motive force for the creation of reality, because through Taiji, which manifests in life as a spiral, the undifferentiated stillness of Wuji began to divide into Yin and Yang.

Yin and Yang can be understood as two points of extreme between which there is a sliding scale, as shown in Figure 1.3.

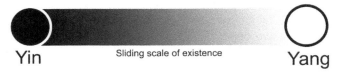

Yin   Sliding scale of existence   Yang

FIGURE 1.3: YIN, YANG AND EXISTENCE

The 'shades of grey' that exist between Yin and Yang give us the potential for movement of energy in cycles and developmental processes. These are the movements that create life, movements that are in general simply named Qi in Daoist literature. So if Yin is the darkness of night and Yang is the brightness of day, the shades of grey between these two extremes manifest as the cycling between night and day.

Because Daoism recognised the inherent importance of both extremes, Daoists traditionally placed equal emphasis on the reverence of both Yin and Yang. In the realm of humanity, Yin and Yang are primarily reflected in the energies of femininity and masculinity – women and men. Therefore, both sexes were seen as being of equal standing, both socially and spiritually. This was in contrast to the other great philosophical tradition of China, Confucianism, which saw women as inferior to their male counterparts in society. The Daoists recognised that both genders were required in order for balance to exist; a society that over-emphasised character traits usually associated with just one of the two genders would quickly fall into a state of disharmony. Sadly, this original ethos was lost in the Daoist tradition and so historically we can see a development over time of over-emphasising men and masculine traits. Male-based practices became the norm and women were relegated to being of secondary importance. Despite this, several key writings and traditions on women's internal practice survived through to modern times, largely through the oral tradition kept alive by Daoist nuns across the generations.

THE DAOIST WOMAN

Daoism saw women as having several innate strengths over men, strengths that were important for their spiritual development. These are as follows:

- Women are naturally more in tune with their Heart centre and so therefore more in line with the vibrational frequency of Qi. This makes them naturally more sensitive to the fluctuations of energetic information within the cosmos.

- Women naturally find it easier to separate themselves from the base desires that tend to shackle male practitioners of the internal arts to the lower levels of attainment.

- Women are said to be able to attune themselves with the spiritual realms more easily than their male counterparts, making them effective channels for the teachings of the immortal spirits.

- Women are the manifestation of the ability to bring forth life. This brings them naturally closer to the state of the universe which serves to generate existence.

These aspects of female spirit mean that it is women who should be society's natural mystics, spiritual teachers and guides. For this reason the majority of internal arts teachers should really be women. It is often said that men have to learn how to 'become like women' in order to progress in the internal arts. This refers to the requirement that men reverse the natural outward expansion of their Qi field and subdue their more masculine psychological traits. In alchemical teachings, it was said that a diligent female Nei Dan practitioner could attain realisation within six years, whereas a male would take nine years. The exact number of years is metaphorical – six being the sacred number of Earth or Yin, and nine the number of Heaven or Yang. What is important, though, is that women are said to be able to reach such a high state of awareness much faster than men.

YIN AND YANG IN WOMEN AND MEN

Although women are primarily a manifestation of the essence of Yin and men of Yang, both genders contain aspects of both poles. With regard to areas of the body, women are Yang above with Yin below, whereas men are Yin above with Yang below. This is shown in Figure 1.4.

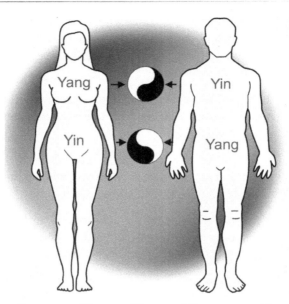

FIGURE 1.4: YIN AND YANG IN WOMEN AND MEN

In order to understand the reason this is relevant to our practice, we need to look at a few of the key resonances of the terms Yin and Yang. As two comparative poles, they exist in relation to each other and manifest many principles which, at first, appear to exist in opposition to each other, but on further exploration are shown to exist as complementary forces. Table 1.2 shows some of the resonances of Yin and Yang.

TABLE 1.2: YIN AND YANG RESONANCES

	Yin	Yang
Gender	Female	Male
Movement	Decreasing	Increasing
Direction	Inwards	Outwards
Position	Lower	Upper
Power	Earth	Heaven
Temperature	Cold	Hot
State	Storage	Leakage

These resonances become very important for understanding the nature of Nei Gong training, especially with regard to building an effective foundation. If these resonances are developed in the wrong way, then a solid foundation cannot be built and so progression along the Nei Gong process will be slowed or even halted altogether.

If we want to understand the state of Yin and Yang in men and women physically, then it is fairly simple. In the case of women, their lower body is Yin, a quality that is manifested in the woman's sexual organs which extend inwards. The upper body is Yang, manifested in the breasts which extend out from the chest. Men are the opposite: the lower body is more Yang than in women, an aspect of their being that manifests in the male sexual organ which protrudes outwards. The chest and upper body of men is Yin; compared with women, it is very flat and does not extend outwards.

Energetically, the important focal points for both women and men exist within the more Yang regions of their body. For women, the Heart centre of the middle Dan Tien is the key energy centre. It is here that the greatest advancements in their development take place. When women can reach the stage of working with the (more Yang) middle Dan Tien, they can bring about huge transformations in the state of their consciousness. For men, the focal point of their training remains with the (more Yang) lower Dan Tien. It is here, at this lower energy centre, that a large change in their nature has to take place. This shift happens when the Jing is consolidated and the base desires are therefore brought under control.

The greatest challenge to any practitioner of Nei Gong seeking to build a foundation in the Daoist arts is control of energetic leakage. This leakage takes place within the more Yang regions of the body because the nature of Yang is to move outwards, to disperse and to be difficult to store. As energetic leakage takes place, it has a draining effect upon the Jing, or essence, which in turn weakens the base upon which alchemical transcendence is based.

In the case of men, this leakage takes place within the lower aspects of the body, as Jing is lost through sexual intercourse. Male practitioners often receive a great deal of guidance about reversing this issue when they begin studying the internal arts. There are already a great many books discussing this issue from a male perspective, so we will not look at it here.

What is not considered so frequently is the nature of leakage for women. The nature of women's sexual energy is such that they do not lose any great amount of Jing through sexual intercourse or orgasm. Instead, they lose Jing each month through menstruation, though nowhere near the amount that men lose through orgasm. It is said in the Daoist classics that 'the loss of one drop of semen is worse than one hundred drops of menstrual Blood'. Curiously, one of the largest energetic ingredients of menstrual Blood is considered to be the Jing that resides in the region of the chest for women. This ingredient moves downwards into the Uterus just prior to a woman's monthly bleed. This in turn draws essence down away from the Yang region of the chest. In addition, women have a higher degree of essence connected to their emotional centre than men. This means that excessive emotional states can be a lot more draining for women than they are for men. Although both genders may struggle with their emotional makeup, men will find that the biggest issue with this is that it further distorts the layers of the acquired mind, whereas for women it will result in a draining of their essence. These concepts are explored in greater detail when we look at working with the middle Dan Tien and the Heart's energy in Chapter 8.

ALIGNMENT WITH THE FORCES OF HEAVEN AND EARTH

The ultimate manifestations of Yin and Yang energy are, respectively, Earth and Heaven. These are the two poles of manifestation between which all of existence takes place. Heaven resides above and Earth below. Heaven, according to Daoist thought, is a reference to the shifting energies of the planets, stars and other celestial bodies as well as the various immortal planes which a person can only visit once they have attained realised states of awareness. The Earth below is the planet we live on as well as the numerous energetic influences that it exerts upon us on a daily basis. The saying in Daoism is that humanity exists between Heaven and Earth and that we are an integral whole of the spiritual relationship between them.

The harmonious relationship between Heaven and Earth can only exist when both are in their right place. In order for human beings to rise towards spiritual elevation, they must become 'conduits' for these two forces and so align themselves with these two great poles. In the case of men, Yang is below and Yin is above. This is in direct opposition to the alignments of Heaven and Earth. Consequently, men must work to reverse this energetic state in the foundational stages of their training. Their essence must be conserved through elimination of their base desires and then the congenital nature must be brought forth. In the case of women, Yang is already above and Yin is below; this is directly in harmony with the power of Heaven and Earth, meaning that the foundation stages of Nei Gong for women do not involve such arduous attempts to change their nature. Consequently, the early stages of internal development can be attained much earlier, providing that women practise correctly. This will bring them into line with the powers above and below them fairly quickly. The advantage of this is that women can soon begin to use the surrounding Qi of the universe in their training, a stage that men progress to much later on in their Nei Gong training.

Chapter 2

THE FEMALE BODY

The Daoist tradition takes a very different view of the human body from Western biological sciences. According to Daoist philosophy, everything exists as various layers. These layers result from the three key vibrational states that make up reality. The three layers are a manifestation of the three treasures of Jing, Qi and Shen. With regard to the human body, these layers concern the three prime bodies of humans, which are the physical body, the energy body and the consciousness or spirit body. These then exist as one integrated unit, each anchoring into another via the three Dan Tien. This concept is shown in Figure 2.1.

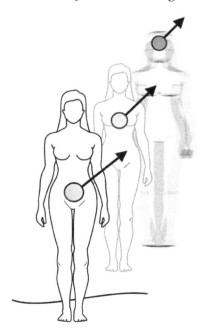

FIGURE 2.1: THE ANCHORING OF THE THREE BODIES

Progression along the path of Nei Gong is, in part, an ability to refine your awareness to such a point that you are able to become aware of each body in turn. Once you can shift your focus on to higher vibrational frequencies, your tangible experience of the body jumps upwards towards a higher state. This connection to the three bodies then enables you to begin working with and improving the qualitative state of each body in turn.

There is already a large range of literature on the various aspects of the energetic system. These books include Qi Gong titles, alchemical books and Chinese medical texts. Almost invariably, though, they discuss the nature of the internal environment from the position of men. In this chapter we look at the three key bodies of humans with an emphasis upon the differences for women. Where information is the same for both men and women, we have provided a brief overview.

THE THREE PRIME BODIES OF HUMANS
The Physical Body
The physical body exists as the densest level of vibration, the level of manifestation. It is the body that we can easily 'tune in to' and the form through which we generally interact with the external world. The definition of the physical body includes all of the aspects that we would usually associate with the body from a Western biological standpoint – from our tissues and bones through to our physical organs, body fluids, blood and so on. The health of the physical body is closely linked to the state of our Jing, the aspect of the three treasures that exists furthest from the realm of Dao, at the very borderline between potential and the manifestation of form. It is the internal treasure associated with nourishment, birth, development and the inevitability of decline.

In Daoist thought, the development from Jing through to physical form takes place as a direct result of the movement of spirit, followed by the interaction of the Jing of both parents in its male and female forms. Human development within the womb then takes place over a period of ten lunar months while the three key bodies of humans fully develop. Summarised below are the ten lunar months of development in utero. Included here is only the inner process of foetal development. Alongside this, there is an outer process. The outer process is more to do with how an unborn child's health is established prior to entering the external world. Appendix 2 includes a brief discussion of this aspect of human development.

- Prior to conception the spiritual pathways of Heaven begin to extend through the doorway of Dao into the realm of potential. This is the movement of Ming (命), or 'pre-ordained destiny', which brings with it the immortal spirit of seed consciousness. This 'seed' is the basis of your true self, that which a person is trying to reconnect with through internal practices. This aspect of human consciousness exists above any such concepts as male or female.

- Over the duration of the first lunar month there is an interaction that takes place between the poles of Yin, Yang, female essence and male sexual fluid. Each of these four agents is required for conception to take place; the development of gender will vary according to the sequence the four agents come together. If Yin arrives prior to female essence and male sexual fluid, then Yin will reinforce female essence. This will then embrace male essence and so the potential is there for a female child. If Yang arrives first, then female essence is weakened, meaning that male essence is dominant. The result is the potential for a male child.

- Over the course of the second lunar month stabilisation of these four elements is said to continue, further reinforcing the gender of the developing child. The four aspects of creation become the four divisions of Yin and Yang: Tai Yang (太陽) or 'greater Yang', which is the pole of Yang; Tai Yin (太陰) or 'Greater Yin', which is the pole of Yin; Shao Yang (少陽) or 'lesser Yang', which is male essence; and Shao Yin (少陰) or female essence. These form the philosophical 'four directions' of Daoism – that which is required to formulate the potential for three-dimensional development. At the centre of these four directions is formed the lower Dan Tien, the basis for energetic life.

- During the third lunar month the Dan Tien begins to develop the two key congenital channels known as the Governing and Conception meridians. These extend around the foetus as a circuit, enabling Yin and Yang original energy to flow into the rest of the body. This sets up the two poles that will later become the extreme Yin and Yang meridian points of Hui Yin (會陰) (or CV 1) and Bai Hui (百會) (or GV 20). With the two poles in place, the original spirit or Shen can enter the body and begin to manifest as the three Yang souls.

- Over the course of the fourth lunar month the rest of the congenital meridians develop and form the energetic cage. The original Qi begins to root the Yang souls into the material realm, and this in turn gives birth to the seven Yin souls.

• In the fifth lunar month the five lights of creation are divided outwards from the unified light of original spirit. These lights match the five elemental energies which form a major part of Chinese medical theory. They enter the body in order, beginning with Wood and moving through the sequence of Wood, Fire, Earth, Metal and finally Water. These five lights sit within the core of the energetic cage and begin to breathe conscious life into the developing child.

• During the sixth lunar month the five lights condense downwards to create the five Qi of the organs, the five Zang (臟) and the six Fu (腑) organs of the body. These organs then form the physical anchor for the spiritual components of human awareness.

• During the seventh lunar month it is said that the seven points along the length of the central channel of the Thrusting meridian open up, including the remaining two key energy centres of the middle and upper Dan Tien. These seven energies are then said to energise the seven orifices of the head, which are the two eyes, the two ears, the two nostrils and the mouth. These seven orifices are seen as seven spiritual windows through which the developing human awareness may interact with the world. Though necessary for human awareness to take place, they are also seen as the 'seven thieves' because our sense functions, via the seven orifices, are responsible for the distortion of the acquired mind.

• The eighth lunar month sees the original Jing beginning its developmental process of converting to acquired Jing. Even at this early stage in human life, the inevitability of eventual decline has been set in motion. This is representative of the eight key forms of Qi moving into place. These are the eight Qi depicted in the classical text of change, the *Yi Jing* (易經).

• The ninth lunar month is nearing the stage of birth; here the various aspects of spirit start to form into their congenital state. These are dependent upon the information contained within the parents' combined essence, the nature of the pregnancy, the astrological alignments at the time of conception and the pre-ordained nature of the line of Ming which extended through into the realm of manifestation in the first place.

- The final lunar month sees the focal point of the energetic system beginning to switch from the congenital to the acquired meridians. The child is getting ready to be born. During this final month the energetic nuances individual to men and women begin to manifest within the child. This is the energetic fruition of the initial combining of Yin and Yang essence that took place during the first lunar month of pregnancy.

All of this obviously takes place within a woman's body when she is pregnant. This is an aspect of female biology that was highly valued by the Daoist tradition. Having the ability to create life in this way was said to place women closer to the nature of Heaven and Dao than men.

The Energy Body

Daoism is certainly not the only tradition to map out the human energy body, but it is arguably the most complete with regard to the level of detail in its teachings. The Daoist canon of classical writings has a wealth of detailed information on the nature and movements of Qi through the meridian system. The nature of the various meridian pathways that make up the energy body, along with the Dan Tien and various other energetic components, is explored in greater detail in the remainder of this chapter.

When they begin Nei Gong training, the majority of people cannot feel their energy body very clearly, although it is more common for women to be naturally sensitive to its movements than men. It is for this reason that so many students of the Daoist arts only study the meridian system in a theoretical manner. It is necessary to understand the theory behind what you do, but you should also strive to gain an experiential understanding of your art. For women in particular, it is important to begin moving towards conscious connection with the energetic body. It is only at this stage that clear work with the Heart centre can be engaged in.

The energy body is 'anchored' into the physical body via its connection to the lower Dan Tien. This is why correct focus upon the lower Dan Tien gradually begins to convert a person's awareness up towards the frequency of Qi and the energy body.

The Consciousness Body

Furthest from the physical realm of manifestation is the vibrational frequency of spirit or Shen. The interactions of the various facets of human spirit make up the consciousness body. Although human consciousness is beyond the three-dimensional limitations of exact form, it is generally termed one of the 'bodies' because it is rooted into the energy body via the middle Dan Tien.

The formative substance of the consciousness body is Shen, or 'spiritual energy', which is the highest-frequency and most ethereal manifestation of the three treasures. Contacting this level of awareness involves moving from the physical, through the energetic, into the realm of spirit. At this stage the level of refinement of a person's Shen will dictate to what degree transformational work with the consciousness can take place. Direct work to any deep level relies on being able to understand and practise alchemical meditative techniques.

THE THREE TREASURES

The three treasures of Daoism – Jing, Qi and Shen – are an aspect of Daoist theory that anybody who picks up a Daoist textbook will come across. Each practitioner will have their own idea of the definition of these treasures. To define exactly what the substances are would be impossible due to the broad manner in which Daoism applies any definition. On the other hand, to have no definition at all can also be difficult because you end up working with something so abstract that it hinders your development. The most effective way to develop in an art such as Nei Gong is to have a definition that serves as a conceptual framework within which you can work. At later stages these frameworks can be dropped in favour of more abstract understandings which generally develop through experiential learning. In Daoist study, this is known as 'learning and then forgetting'. It is useful to develop in this manner because at the level of working with the physical or energetic bodies you are still practising within realms of manifestation that have 'form'. When working within the level of form, defined conceptual frameworks are useful. Beyond these stages are the alchemical levels of work with the consciousness body. At this stage you are moving beyond manifested form into formlessness. This is the stage at which frameworks can give way to more abstract understanding. That being said, discussed here are the conceptual frameworks for the nature of Jing, Qi and Shen based on classical teachings as well as tangible experiences that can arise during practice.

The basic translation usually given for Jing is our 'essence', Qi is generally known as 'energy' and Shen is translated as 'spirit'. Although these may be great over-simplifications, it can help us to begin to develop an understanding of how the internal environment of the human body functions.

A Further Look at Jing

Jing is the densest of the three treasures; it sits at the borderline between potential and manifestation and so is always on the cusp of becoming form. Many practitioners think that Jing is sperm or sexual fluid, but this is simply not the case. Sexual fluid is one substance that Jing can become upon the point of manifestation, but the truth is that all manifested matter is a form of Jing. Figure 2.2 shows the Chinese character for Jing.

FIGURE 2.2: THE CHINESE CHARACTER FOR JING

The Chinese character for Jing is comprised of two key parts. The first is the character for grain or food in an uncooked state. The second shows the potential for growth. When put together, we can ascertain that Jing provides us with our 'fuel' as well as the potential for the developmental processes of birth, growth and decline. Usually, when beginners look at the nature of Jing, they are taught that we have a finite amount which will at some point run out. When this happens, we die. This is a simple concept that can help to develop a working understanding of the preservation of Jing, but in actual fact Jing does not quite function in this manner. Instead, Jing has an inbuilt 'timer' that ticks down throughout the course of our life. This 'timer' carries out the developmental process we know as ageing: its main function is to carry you from birth through to death. Through the quality of our lifestyle and our ability to embrace healthy living, we can either slow down or speed up this process, thus either prolonging or speeding up our physical demise.

Jing exists in two key forms. The first is our original Jing, which was given to us at birth primarily through our parents. The second form is our acquired Jing, the transient form of Jing which is subject to the passing of time. It is the acquired Jing that we are primarily concerned with when practising Nei Gong. This is the aspect of Jing that manifests as various substances within the body. It is also easier to connect with than original Jing.

Jing governs the manner in which we develop, and it does this according to numerological patterns which vary for men and women. Men operate according to an eight-year cycle, meaning that key events take place every eight years, whereas women operate to the celestial number of seven, meaning that at seven-year intervals changes take place within their system. The seven-year cycles for women are summarised below:

- At age seven a woman's essence should begin to consolidate around the region of the Kidneys. As a result, her energy reaches high levels, her permanent teeth come through and her hair grows thick and long.

- At age 14 a woman's Jing starts to produce menstrual Blood and so menstruation begins. The Governing and Conception meridians become active with regard to procreation and so it becomes possible to conceive a child. That being said, it takes a few more years before the procreative energy within the two meridians stabilises enough for it to be healthy for her to become pregnant.

- At age 21 the Kidney energy is strong and abundant, wisdom teeth appear in the mouth and the body is full of vitality. The Shen should be nourished through the growth of Jing at this stage, resulting in a stabilisation of the emotions and the beginning of 'adult-type' thought processes.

- At age 28 the bones and tendons are said to be strong and fully developed. This is the peak of Jing development for a woman and so the strongest point in her life with regard to levels of abundance of energy and essence. Her body at this age should be fully formed as this is seen as the height of female development.

- At age 35 the digestive-based meridians begin to move into decline. This in turn causes the face to lose some of its essence due to the pathway of the Stomach and Large Intestine meridians. This means that wrinkles can start to appear on the face and a woman's hair can begin to grow thinner.

- At age 42 many of the meridians begin to grow more depleted, meaning ageing becomes more obvious and the hair starts to turn grey.

- At age 49 a woman has reached the culmination of the developmental processes of her Jing, which matches the numerical pattern of seven multiplied by seven. At this age her Conception and Thrusting meridians often cease to function to any major degree. The menstrual Blood ceases to flow and menopause is entered. This prevents a woman from being able to conceive. It is also said to be the beginning of a woman's spiritual age, a period known as the 'second spring' in Daoist medical literature.

Of course, these ages are only guidelines and, as such, a woman can find that she reaches these milestones within a year or so in either direction. It is natural for the Jing to take a woman through this process, and if there is too much of a deviation from these numbers, then it is said that there has been a disturbance in the progression of the Jing from either physical sickness or emotional imbalance. This is particularly true with regard to the ages of commencement of menstruation and menopause, which are key manifestations of the quality and movement of Blood (Blood being the key internal substance for a woman to seek to regulate).

In order to understand the nature of Jing, it is wise to look at its movements through the body. Figure 2.3 summarises the progression and movement of Jing through the body in diagrammatic form.

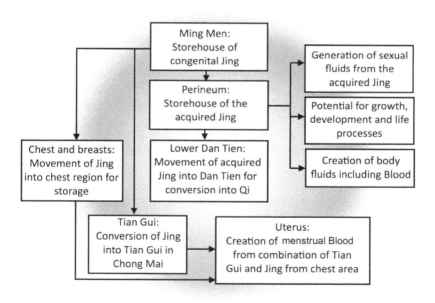

FIGURE 2.3: THE MOVEMENT OF FEMALE JING

The starting place for a woman's Jing is between her Kidneys at a meridian point known as Ming Men (命門) (or GV 4). This is the point where her congenital Jing is stored. From this 'storehouse' a woman's Jing moves in three different directions.

- The first movement of Jing from the region of the Kidneys is down into the perineum, where it transforms into acquired Jing. It is the Jing in this region of the body that then goes on to become a woman's sexual fluids, vaginal secretions and body fluids. In addition, it is this aspect of Jing that controls the seven-year cycle and a woman's developmental processes. This is the aspect of a woman's Jing that is commonly written about in the majority of books on Qi Gong or Daoism. This is because the Jing for men also operates in the same manner. From this area of the body some of this Jing moves upwards into the lower Dan Tien where it is gradually converted into Qi, the next transformational state of the three treasures within the human body.

- The second movement of Jing from the region of the Kidneys takes place as acquired Jing transforms into a substance known as Tian Gui (天癸). The term 'Tian' literally means Heaven, which denotes a connection between Tian Gui and the movements of the Heavenly bodies, in particular the moon. 'Gui' is a term taken from a classical system of categorising the five elemental phases into Yin and Yang divisions. Gui is the Yin Water phase of this system, which connects menstrual Blood to the Water elemental organ of the Kidneys and in particular its Yin substance of Jing. This shows us that Tian Gui is generated from the Jing of the Kidneys. The Tian Gui travels through the body via the vertical branch of the Thrusting meridian.

- The third movement of a woman's Jing is from the Kidney region upwards into the chest where it is stored in the breasts. This is a major storage area for Jing in the female body and an aspect of female energetic anatomy that is often overlooked in Daoist teachings. Over the course of a woman's monthly cycle the Jing from the breasts moves downwards through the Thrusting meridian, where it combines with Tian Gui to become menstrual Blood, which then enters the Uterus.

THE BREASTS, STORAGE AND CONVERSION OF JING

A woman's breasts begin to develop during puberty as a result of the energetic activity of the Governing and Conception meridians. From this age a woman's Jing begins to move, in part, up from the Kidney region through the vertical branch of the Thrusting meridian towards the chest and the breasts where it is stored. The movement of Jing into the breasts is shown in Figure 2.4.

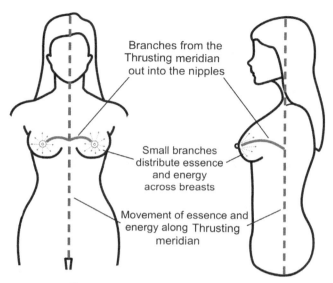

Branches from the
Thrusting meridian
out into the nipples

Small branches
distribute essence
and energy
across breasts

Movement of essence and
energy along Thrusting
meridian

FIGURE 2.4: JING AND THE BREASTS

The Jing that moves upwards into the region of the breasts serves to strengthen the function of the Heart centre and the middle Dan Tien (this is explored in greater detail later in this chapter). It also has the potential to form breast milk, which is seen as a powerful alchemical agent and necessary fuel for a baby's growth. From the region of the breasts, some of this Jing converts into Qi, which is one of the natural evolutionary developments of Jing. This Qi is situated at the nipples where it is said to become stimulated as the female nipples become erect. Excess Jing from the region of the breasts then moves down to combine with Tian Gui to become menstrual Blood which is then lost through a woman's monthly bleed.

All of these transformational processes take place within the breasts, which are seen as major alchemical centres within women, every bit as powerful as the three Dan Tien. Interestingly, if we analyse the Chinese character for breasts, Ru, it can give us extra insight into their functions. Figure 2.5 shows a breakdown of the character for breasts.

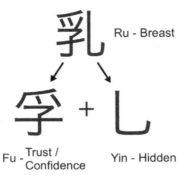

FIGURE 2.5: THE CHINESE CHARACTER FOR BREASTS

The first part of the character for breasts is made from the character Fu, which is generally translated as 'to have trust or confidence'; it actually depicts a mother bird's claw holding her eggs, a symbol of safety and reassurance. Sometimes this character is even used to denote a bird brooding over its unborn chicks. The second character is Yin or 'hidden/ concealed'.

If we examine the meaning behind the formation of the character, it shows us some of the deeper aspects of a woman's energetic anatomy. First, the depiction of the mother bird holding her young or unborn chicks is symbolic of the level of caring that a woman has for her young when she is breastfeeding. Second, the meaning of trust or confidence is important as this is the emotional aspect that can generate imbalance in the health of a woman's breasts. Every physical part of a person's body reacts to different elements of their psyche, and so each emotion you have will resonate and affect a different area of your body. A woman's breasts are strongly affected by her ability to have trust, faith or confidence in those around her. If a woman's faith in those close to her is detrimentally affected, it can disturb the delicate energy around this area of the body and so lead to imbalance. In cases of acute disturbances the result is a weakening of the Jing and Qi in the breasts. In more serious cases stagnation can develop which can manifest as cysts or lumps. Emotionally based Chinese medical treatments for lumps on the breasts may focus on dealing with damage that the patient has suffered to her confidence in those around her, which she has kept hidden or buried deep inside. It is not always a definite rule, but in the majority of cases lumps to the right breast are a result of emotional hurt caused by male figures in a woman's life, whereas the left breast relates to hurt caused by female figures. It is quite normal when energetic movement begins to take place around the region of the breasts for women to start releasing trapped emotions related to these types of emotional hurt. If this happens, do not worry; just allow the emotions to pass you by, as they are all a healthy part of the Nei Gong process.

A Closer Look at Qi

Qi is a complex term with many different meanings. The simple translation of 'energy' is partially accurate, but Qi is also responsible for many of the functional activities of the organs of the body. It sits at a higher range of frequency than Jing, so is further from the physical realm of manifestation. Beginners can rarely access the vibrational range of Qi, which makes it completely unperceivable to newcomers to the internal arts, but this can change with time and internal development. Figure 2.6 shows the Chinese character for Qi.

FIGURE 2.6: THE CHINESE CHARACTER FOR QI

The character for Qi is comprised of the characters for 'grain' and 'vapour'. It depicts the grain being cooked to produce vapour or steam that is rising upwards. There are a couple of meanings behind this. From a medical perspective, it shows the two main ways in which we can generate or improve the quality of our acquired Qi: through the food we eat and the air we breathe. If we wish to keep our Qi flowing efficiently, then we need to breathe well or practise breathing exercises and we need to eat healthy food. Looking at this, we can already see the basis for many people's states of internal disharmony. A second meaning involves an advancement on the character for Jing. The same character of uncooked rice or grain appears in both the characters for Jing and Qi, but now in Qi the rice is being cooked so that steam is produced from it. In this case the uncooked rice is Jing, while the process of heating the rice produces steam, heat and energy – Qi.

Interestingly, Qi is generally experienced during Nei Gong training as internalised movement or a vibration/shaking. This vibration begins to change over time until you generally get a clear idea of a wave moving along lines through the body. These lines carry information throughout the whole of your body via the meridian pathways. For this reason it is simple to think of Qi as a form of 'information' when you practise.

This information can be related to the functional activities of the body, emotional information or information related to pathogenic imbalances.

As well as these lines of information flowing throughout the meridian system, there are also other aspects of the energy body that are made up of the energy of Qi. We will explore some of these other aspects of the energy body in the remainder of this chapter.

The Nature of Shen

Shen is the highest vibrational element of the three internal treasures. It is the 'substance' of the consciousness body and the most ethereal energetic aspect within our internal environment. The model of the Shen is divided up into various aspects of human consciousness. These are the (little) Shen (神), the Hun (魂), the Po (魄), the Zhi (志) and the Yi (意). These are explored in more detail later in the book. For now it is enough to know that the Shen is responsible for the overall state of a person's mind. The Shen is something of a double-bladed weapon; it has the potential to lead a person towards enlightened realisation, but at the other end of the scale can bog them down in trivial concerns and mundane thinking. The division between these two states was said to be based in the problem of the apparent division of human consciousness into two key aspects, the congenital and the acquired mind. The congenital mind is that which is true, constant and all-knowing, whereas the acquired mind is transient, subject to change and heavily fuelled by the emotions. Ultimately, there is no such division between these two aspects of consciousness, but this is a realisation that has to be achieved through advanced inner practice rather than something a person can understand intellectually. Although we return to these two aspects of mind in the final chapters of this book, they are also referred to throughout. As a summary, it is enough to understand that when discussing the congenital mind we are referring to the innate state of unity contained within each living creature, and when we refer to the acquired mind we are discussing the layers of emotionally charged cognitive 'self' which are built up around the congenital mind throughout the course of our lives.

Three Aspects of One Substance

The most important thing to understand about Jing, Qi and Shen is that although they are discussed individually, they are essentially one and the same. They are a single thread of energetic information which exists as three different states. In order to understand this concept, the comparison is made between Jing, Qi and Shen and ice, water and steam. When Jing or ice is warmed up, it becomes water or Qi, which is more fluid than Jing. Further warming of water or Qi causes it to convert into steam or Shen, the most ethereal of the three states. In the same manner, cooling the substances will take them back through the process of steam to water to ice. The act of 'heating' or 'cooling' depends on the functional activities of Yang and Yin within the human body.

It is also in part the role of the three Dan Tien to serve as converters for the three treasures of Jing, Qi and Shen throughout the body. These Dan Tien function much like 'step-up transformers' in an electrical circuit: they enable the conversion of energy to increase as it moves from Jing to Qi to Shen. The lower Dan Tien is primarily responsible for the conversion of Jing to Qi, the middle Dan Tien for the conversion of Qi to Shen, and the upper Dan Tien has the potential to convert Shen into undifferentiated potential spiritual information which can connect a person to Dao itself.

BLOOD AND FEMALE SPIRIT

It is stated in classical texts from both the Daoist and the Chinese medical traditions that regulation of the health of the Blood is vitally important for women. In part this is discussing the health and flow of menstrual Blood as discussed above, but it is also pointing towards the important link that exists between Blood and Shen.

Ultimately, Blood is understood to be something of a crystalline substance which takes the form of a liquid. It is also the root or the 'anchor' of the spirit. Every aspect of consciousness has a root within an element of the physical body, but the basis for the overall state of a person's spirit or Shen lies in the health of the Blood. In Chinese medicine, it is often stated that if the Blood is weak or deficient, then the spirit becomes unrooted. The result of this is that a person can lose their sense of 'grounding' psychologically. This can lead to emotional swings, illogical thought patterns or behaviour and, at its most extreme, mental illness.

In the case of men, Blood is still the root of the spirit, but male Blood is not so prone to flux. Women have the combined effects of the cycles of the moon and the loss of menstrual Blood prior to menopause, both of which contribute to a weakening of the root of the spirit. For women to stabilise their consciousness and govern their emotional centre, they need to focus on the health and flow of the Blood within the body. This will then enable them to find a higher degree of harmony within the spirit, which will assist with work at the level of the middle Dan Tien. The practice of moon gazing from Chapter 4 of this book, combined with a regular Nei Gong practice and a healthy diet, will help to maintain the strength of the

Blood. There are many Chinese dietary books with comprehensive lists of Blood-building foods; these are sensible foods for women to include in their diet in order to help the overall state of their health.

Returning to the concept of Blood being a crystalline substance, we can use this to understand exactly how the Shen moves through the Blood. As unified spirit moves into the Blood, it refracts into manifestations of the five spirits of Shen, Hun, Yi, Zhi and Po. These aspects of spirit then carry with them the various aspects of emotional information that make up the human mind. It is this emotional information that contributes to the shedding of emotional pathogenic information during the course of menstruation.

TUNING IN TO THE THREE BODIES

Progressively working through the three main bodies during your Nei Gong practice is the key to ensuring that you build a solid foundation in each stage of your development. When beginning a practice such as Nei Gong, most people find that they require a great deal of work with the physical body. Habitual tensions need to be let go of, alignments need correcting and then the structure of each of the postures needs to be studied. On top of this, women then have to work with physical substances such as the Blood through practices such as moon gazing and regulation of the diet. At the border of the physical and energy bodies sits the breath, and this is why regulation of the breath is also required from an early stage in the training.

As discussed previously, the three bodies are anchored into each other via the key energy centres of the Dan Tien. The lower Dan Tien is concerned with the conversion of Jing to Qi, the middle Dan Tien converts Qi to Shen, and the upper Dan Tien converts Shen back into unified spiritual light. This high stage of conversion manifests itself as a bright white or golden light that can be perceived in the mind's eye of the practitioner.

Progression along the process of working with the three bodies largely revolves around connecting with and efficiently utilising the three Dan Tien during your practice. Almost every system of internal arts requires you to work with the lower Dan Tien in the early stages of your training. As well as consolidating various energetic substances in the lower abdominal region and awakening the various small water wheels of Qi (discussed in Chapter 7), it also helps with the conversion of our awareness. If our attention can be placed within the region of the lower Dan Tien, it begins a conversion of the frequency at which we are able to perceive ourselves. As this perception rises in frequency, it enables a person to begin tangibly feeling the movement of the energy body. In this way the lower Dan Tien has assisted in the conversion of our awareness in the same manner that it controls the conversion of Jing to Qi.

The same process takes place in the middle Dan Tien, which enables a person's awareness to shift towards the spiritual energy that sits behind the movement of the emotions and acquired mind. It is here that much of the Nei Gong process can be carried out for female practitioners. The upper Dan Tien is saved for very advanced stages in the training because it has the potential to bring a person completely out of sync with the physical world. Instead, their connection moves upwards into the realm of pure spirit. This is usually carried out during seated alchemical training under the close guidance of an advanced instructor. If this stage is worked on too soon, then it runs the risk of firing too much Qi upwards into the region of the skull, which can lead to serious energetic sickness. Symptoms of this imbalance can range from tinnitus and migraines through to pain in the eyes and psychological disturbances. It is neither a pleasant nor an advisable state to be in.

THE ENERGY BODY

There has been a great deal written about the energy body and in particular the meridian system. Many Chinese medical textbooks have detailed descriptions of the pathway of the meridians and the various points that sit along their lengths. In this book we will focus on some of the information that is often lacking in other literature. We can divide the various aspects of the energy body into three main parts – the acquired energy body, the congenital energy body and miscellaneous aspects of the energy body.

The acquired components of the energy body are:

- Fire element meridians

- Earth element meridians

- Metal element meridians

- Water element meridians

- Wood element meridians

The congenital components of the energy body are:

- the congenital meridians

- the congenital cage

- the five pulses

- the three Dan Tien

The miscellaneous components of the energy body are:

- the Wei Qi field

- the auric field

- the Uterus

The Acquired Energy Body

The acquired energy body is essentially comprised of the 12 key paired meridians, which anybody will have seen if they have opened an acupuncture textbook. It is along the line of these meridians that most Qi is circulated after a person is born. Prior to this time they are of secondary importance as the congenital aspects of the meridian system are dominant.

There is much debate about whether or not the meridian system really exists. Many practitioners of Chinese medicine and even Qi Gong do not believe in meridians and instead say that the ancient Chinese were talking about blood vessels, lymphatic pathways or the nervous system. In a similar manner, the existence of Qi itself is questioned. All we can do as authors and teachers is give you our own opinion based on our experience through training in both Chinese medicine and Nei Gong. By going deep enough into the internal aspects of Nei Gong, it is possible to develop both a heightened connection to your own internal environment and even visual perception of the energetic matrix. It is our experience that the meridian pathways are lines of vibratory information which move through the body and control various functions related to the organ systems associated with each meridian. Although this information, Qi, is moving throughout the whole body, there are certain lines that are clearly stronger and provide a definite pathway of moving energy. Unrelated to any of the physical systems of the body such as the nervous system, this flow of information provides the energetic blueprints for all of the body's activity. It also connects the emotional aspect of the mind into the body, providing the mind/body link that is so important in any internal practice. It seems that these lines of information flow within long lines of semi-fluid connective tissue known as fascia. It is our belief that many of these lines of fascia correspond to the Jing Jin (經筋) lines of Chinese medicine, which are generally translated as the 'musculo-tendonal regions' in Chinese medical literature. These lines of connective tissue essentially serve as the 'riverbeds' for the flow of Qi in the meridian system. Perhaps a better way of understanding what is taking place is to say that the fascia lines 'conduct' the information of the meridian system throughout the body.

For those interested in working towards directly experiencing the flow of energetic information along the meridian pathways, please refer to *Heavenly Streams: Meridian Theory in Nei Gong* by Damo Mitchell. In this book is a step-by-step method for working with and feeling the meridians for yourself.

Figure 2.7 shows the pathways of the 12 acquired meridians. As you can see, they flow throughout the entire body. More detailed diagrams may be found in any Chinese medical textbook. Note that in the image the meridians are drawn on one side of the body. In actual fact, the 12 acquired meridians appear on both sides of the body, making this aspect of the energy body bilateral.

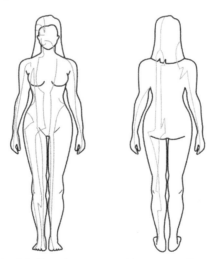

FIGURE 2.7: THE ACQUIRED MERIDIAN PATHWAYS

Each of the meridians is named after an organ of the body, with the exception of the Triple Heater meridian, named after three chambers of the torso which act to regulate the temperatures and internal pressures of the body as well as Qi, Blood and body fluid circulation. In addition, the Pericardium is seen as an organ in Chinese medical thought and is important in the energetic 'protection' of the delicate Heart.

Throughout the course of our lives, it is these meridians that pick up pathogenic information from the external environment, the food we eat, our emotions and various other sources. As these pathogens build up, they generate blockages, stagnation and, ultimately, disease. Through the practice of arts such as Nei Gong, we seek to clear this information from the meridian system, which should in turn improve our health. Practically, though, the vast majority of work in Nei Gong is actually carried out with the various circulations of the congenital energy body. These circulations then generate change within the acquired meridians and so cleansing of the acquired meridians takes place as a by-product of Nei Gong training. This is in contrast to many systems of medical Qi Gong which aim to work directly with and clear the acquired meridians, while placing less of an emphasis upon the congenital pathways.

In Daoist thought, the 12 acquired meridians are often categorised according to one of five elemental phases, as shown in Table 2.1.

TABLE 2.1: ELEMENTAL ASSOCIATIONS OF THE 12 ACQUIRED MERIDIANS

Acquired Meridian	Elemental Phase
Heart, Small Intestine, Pericardium, Triple Heater	Fire
Spleen, Stomach	Earth
Lungs, Large Intestine	Metal
Kidneys, Bladder	Water
Liver, Gall Bladder	Wood

The model of the five elemental phases or Wu Xing (五行) is a model that applies to Chinese medical thought, Qi Gong, Nei Gong and even some martial arts. It is a way of categorising phenomena and understanding their interrelations in accordance with the key energetic movement that takes place 'beneath' them. These five elemental energies are very tangible aspects of the congenital energy body known as the five pulses. These pulses serve to govern the energetic quality of the rest of the meridian system and, as such, the 12 organ meridians are a reflection of the state of these pulses. For Nei Gong training, it is not required to have as intimate a knowledge of the theory of the five elemental phases as you would need for Chinese medicine, for example. It is enough to understand the basis of the model and to be familiar with an understanding of how the five elemental phases work together to create balance and harmony. This concept is shown in Figure 2.8.

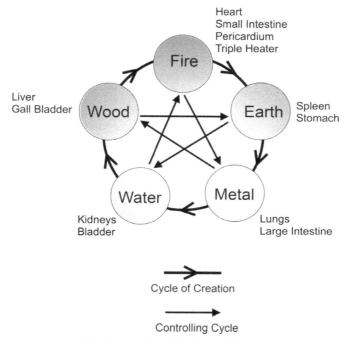

FIGURE 2.8: THE WU XING MODEL

In short, the outer ring of arrows represents the cycle of creation. According to this concept, each of the elemental phases is responsible for the generation of the next phase and is in turn generated by the preceding phase. This perpetual cycle of creation ensures that the five energies flourish. The inner star-shaped group of arrows is the controlling cycle. This concept shows how each of the phases is held in check by another phase and at the same time controls a phase. This relationship ensures that none of the phases becomes overly forceful.

This model is applied to the relationships of the body's energies, physical organs and also the five key aspects of human consciousness. If this cycle is thrown into a state of imbalance, as is often the case, then it starts to create shifts in a person's mind, energy system and physical health. As the acquired meridians begin to shift through Nei Gong training, they move back towards a state of wellbeing and the five elemental phases may begin to reharmonise themselves. While in a state of imbalance, it is classically said that one of the elements will likely be in either excess or deficiency; this will in turn adjust the quality of Qi flowing through the 12 acquired meridians.

THE BALANCE OF THE FIRE ELEMENTAL MERIDIANS

Fire elemental energy is naturally expansive and warm. People with healthy Fire energy will 'glow' with an abundance of warmth, both physically and emotionally. This is the energy that governs our desire to connect with people on an emotional level, and so a healthy Fire energy within the body helps a person to be socially capable.

If there is an excess of Fire elemental energy in a person, it is normal for the energy, which is essentially directed from the region of the Heart, to become sputtering and erratic. This is then reflected in the person's emotional behaviour, which is likely to be slightly manic and overly excitable. Physical symptoms can include a reddening of the face and a feeling of heat and pressure around the chest, neck and head. In the case of women who have entered the menopause, the Fire element energy is often imbalanced in an excessive manner and this becomes the basis for symptoms such as hot flushes. This is partly due to a natural weakening of the Water element during this phase of a woman's life. This Water element is supposed to be controlling the Fire in order to keep it in balance, but due to the Water's weakness the Fire becomes too excessive.

When Fire elemental energy becomes too deficient, it can lead to a sinking of the Heart's energy, which will in turn result in a low mood. People with deficient Fire elemental energy will struggle to become excited about anything and consequently their lives will often lack joy. In extreme cases this can lead to depression. One of the most important things for women to do in their lives is help the Fire elemental energy to 'fire up' and glow. This can be achieved through tapping into the Fire element's natural desire to express itself. It is for this reason that artistic outlets such as singing, painting, dancing and Taijiquan are particularly important for women. However, if the Fire elemental energy has become deficient, it can be difficult to drum up the motivation to find this self-expression.

As a woman moves deeper into her Nei Gong practice, it should be the case that the Fire elemental energy moves into balance. Any fluctuating moods will gradually move towards a centred state of contentment, artistic expression will come more naturally and a glowing, warm energy should emanate from within her energy body.

THE BALANCE OF THE EARTH ELEMENTAL MERIDIANS

Earth elemental energy governs a person's ability to change and evolve. If Earth elemental energy becomes imbalanced, then the energy of evolution is often hampered. This energy flows mainly within the Spleen and Stomach meridians and is closely linked to the digestive system. Many women suffer from imbalances in the energy of their digestive system and this is in part due to a restriction of Earth elemental energy caused by societal norms, which prevent a woman from tapping into the energy of evolution. Women are the gender that has the capability to produce life within themselves; they are caring, sensitive and expressive, and also the natural spiritual teachers of the human race. The energy of a woman is at its healthiest when it is in a constant state of evolution and connection to a higher purpose, all while growing through spontaneous artistic expression. This is not to say that these traits are not available to men as well – of course they are – but they are inherently important to a woman's health. If women are constrained into a life of drudgery or existence as second-class citizens to their male counterparts, then disease will always manifest.

An excess of Earth elemental energy will cause a woman to worry and overthink as her mind moves into a hyperactive state. Every little thing can become an issue and in extreme cases obsessive-compulsive behaviour will appear. Alongside this, a woman's natural capacity as a mother/carer can move out of balance, resulting in her manifesting 'over-smothering' tendencies. This is usually projected on to her family but can also appear when dealing with her friends.

In the case of a weakness of Earth elemental energy, a woman will begin to suffer from great amounts of self-doubt. She will often worry a great deal about her own actions as well as what others think of her. The Earth's desire to nourish itself produces overly 'needy' behavioural tendencies and a paranoia that she is not loved or appreciated. This is not a logical need, and so often no amount of emotional reassurance will help to alleviate these worries.

These psychological traits begin to move into harmony as a woman moves deeper into Nei Gong training. In this manner, self-doubt will fade away and a natural trust in the spontaneous evolution taking place will manifest itself. This is highly important for all women on the path of Daoism.

THE BALANCE OF THE METAL ELEMENTAL MERIDIANS

Metal element energy is a slightly contracting energy. It is generated within the core of the energy system and flows most strongly through the Lung and Large Intestine meridians. If the Metal element energy is healthy, then this contraction feels kind of like a reassuring hug; when out of balance, it can feel somewhat constrictive.

An excess of Metal element energy will result in a tightening of energy around the region of the chest. This generally affects the health of the Lungs but also comes with feelings of low mood and sadness. The ability to connect with others becomes hampered by a need to keep putting up defensive shields, so a person with excessive Metal energy can become shut off from those around them. This results in the person often appearing quite emotionally cold. This can be quite an important imbalance to tackle for women, as it will prevent them from connecting with the innate power of the energy of their Heart.

Deficient Metal elemental energy will lead to depression and sadness. It will lead a person to feeling as though they are sinking into a large hole within the centre of their being. They can become emotionally shut off from the rest of the world.

As a woman moves deeper into her Nei Gong training, it is normal for these experiences of sadness to become a thing of the past. Her mood will lighten, and she will open up to those around her and be able to see things more objectively, without the veil of depression making everything seem hopeless.

THE BALANCE OF THE WATER ELEMENTAL MERIDIANS

Water elemental energy is the most versatile of the five elemental energies. It is the quickest to shift and is the energy that circulates through the system to the highest degree. It is related strongly to the health of the Kidney and Bladder meridians.

If a person's Water elemental energy is in an excessive state, it will force itself upwards with too much power. This results in a person becoming too highly strung. For many women it can lead to slightly neurotic behaviour. Over time this will burn out the nervous system and drain the Kidneys. Both of these issues will often lead to sudden collapse of a woman's health.

A deficiency of Water elemental energy will cause the Kidneys to feel weak, resulting in low vitality and energy levels. The natural drive behind a person's actions becomes weak and in its place we often find fear and nervousness. These aspects of the psyche get in the way of every action a woman may wish to undertake, and so progress through life becomes very difficult. Physically, this will generally manifest in back pain, weak knees and premature ageing.

As the Water elemental energy is balanced through Nei Gong training, a woman's sense of wellbeing should increase and any fears should fade away, allowing for a higher degree of confidence.

THE BALANCE OF THE WOOD ELEMENTAL MERIDIANS

Wood elemental energy is the most direct and straightforward of the elemental phases. It shoots through the body in very direct lines, providing the impetus behind both planning and actions. It is closely linked to the Qi of the Liver and Gall Bladder meridians.

Excessive Wood elemental energy generally results in outwardly directed feelings of anger, rage, competitiveness and jealousy. Somebody in this state will find many things in life annoying and seek to blame those around them for every little thing that goes wrong. Physically, it tends to tighten the body and produce symptoms such as migraine headaches.

Deficient Wood elemental energy also results in feelings of anger, but these tend to be directed inwards. This energy becomes tight and pent-up inside a person, resulting in feelings of inner frustration. Blame for everything that happens is often placed upon the self and this in turn damages a person's sense of self-worth. Rarely does a person with this kind of imbalance allow their anger to show outwardly; when it does, it is often explosive. Women are not naturally governed very strongly by the energy of Wood or the Liver. Although excessive Wood energy can manifest within women, it is nowhere near as common as the more inwardly directed frustration of deficient Wood elemental energy.

As the Nei Gong training begins to rebalance the Wood elemental energy, it should lead a person towards a calmer state. Anger and frustration become less frequent and an overall feeling of patience becomes the norm. This is very useful for Nei Gong training, which requires a great deal of patience in its later stages!

The Congenital Energy Body

The congenital energy body is made up of the eight key congenital meridians which work together to cycle various energetic substances throughout the body. Contained within a kind of 'energetic cage' of these meridians are the five pulses, which form the basis of the five elemental energies within the body. As well as these components are the three Dan Tien, which serve to direct information through the system and convert Jing to Qi and then to Shen.

The congenital meridians tend to be deeper within the body than the acquired meridians, with the exception of the Governing and Conception meridians. The congenital meridians are also not directly related to any of the organs. Arguably, the exception to this last rule is the Conception meridian within women, which is closely linked to the Uterus.

In Nei Gong we are primarily working with energetic flow and circulation in the eight key channels of the congenital meridian system. It is through these channels that we learn to direct information utilising the motivating power of the lower Dan Tien and this is in part what separates Nei Gong from many systems of Qi Gong.

Daoist theory states that, while in the womb, we operate energetically according to the function of the congenital meridians. Through these pathways circulate the three key internal substances of Jing, Qi and Shen. The conversion process is twofold, first generating the potential for physical manifestation of a body and, second, setting in place the physical anchor of human consciousness. All of this is largely motivated by the steady rotation of the lower Dan Tien which generates the necessary power to create human life.

After we are born, we begin to use the congenital meridians to a lesser degree. Instead, the acquired meridians become active and our health and development is controlled by the relationship of the organs of the body. The lower Dan Tien naturally begins to slow down its rotation, and by the time we are in our early teens it is moving hardly at all. For women, the menstrual cycle starts and thus the foundation of Jing is governed largely by their menstrual flow. Although this is a natural aspect of human development, it also has one major disadvantage. As the lower Dan Tien slows down, it stops being so effective at nourishing human consciousness. Shen stops being generated as a natural by-product of human evolution and instead the intellect of the acquired mind takes over. At this time the congenital meridians switch their key function over to serving as a series of 'energetic reservoirs' which store Qi, Blood, Yin and Yang within the body.

Through the reawakening of the lower Dan Tien, one of the earliest internal phases of Nei Gong training, we seek to reverse this gradual decline. This takes us back towards a state closer to when we were in the womb, a state that we require in order to generate the change process of Nei Gong.

As the lower Dan Tien awakens, it begins to start the various small water wheels of Qi circulation, which are pretty well known in Daoist esoteric literature. Commonly, you will see writings on only one circulation of Qi – the rotation that moves up the centre of a person's back through the Governing meridian and then down the front of the body through the Conception meridian. This is the circulation shown in Figure 2.9.

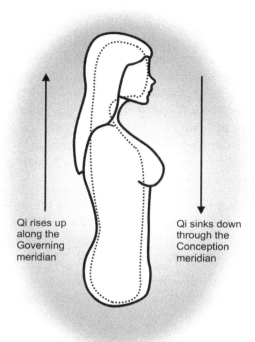

Qi rises up
along the
Governing
meridian

Qi sinks down
through the
Conception
meridian

FIGURE 2.9: THE FIRST SMALL WATER WHEEL OF QI

Although it is true that there is the need for a strong, unobstructed flow
of Qi along the length of this cycle, there are other rotations that are
equally important. Furthermore, there are slightly different qualities for
the rotations of Qi for women within the small water wheel. The various
rotations of energy as well as the women-specific details are as follows:

•   The first small water wheel of Qi takes place along the length of
    the Governing meridian and then down through the Conception
    meridian. This is the initial rotation that we must achieve if we wish
    to progress safely and efficiently in our Nei Gong training. It is driven
    by the initial awakening of the lower Dan Tien.

•   Women then need to understand the nature of the reverse cycle of
    the initial rotation. This cycle is required in order to extract essence
    from the menstrual Blood and draw it up towards the chest region
    where it nourishes the breasts and Heart centre. This rotation is rarely

discussed for women who practise the internal arts to any level beyond the basics, but it is essential in their development.

• A second rotation needs to take place around the length of the Girdling meridian which sits around the waist like a belt. This rotation is important for both men and women as it serves to set up the extension lines for the opening of the central branch of the Thrusting meridian. On top of this, women require a healthy flow through this rotation in order to consolidate the health of the Uterus and lower abdomen. The horizontal driving force of this circulation helps to generate the baseline force through which the Heart's Qi can meet with the essence contained within the Uterus.

• A third rotation needs to take place within the torso between the two side branches of the Thrusting meridian. This helps to generate healthy energetic conversion within the body and stabilise the essence stored within the breasts.

• Further movements generated by these rotations then circulate energy along the length of the arms and legs via extending branches of the Thrusting meridian.

Once these various circulations of the small water wheels have opened up, a kind of energetic cage will be formed, as shown in Figure 2.10.

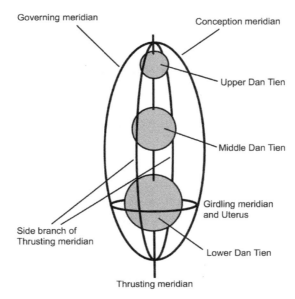

FIGURE 2.10: THE ENERGETIC CAGE

Consolidation of this 'cage' is required in order to work effectively with the three Dan Tien and to guarantee smooth progression into the deeper stages of Nei Gong training. As teachers, we have met many practitioners from different Nei Gong schools who have developed imbalances through their training. These imbalances have ranged from mildly uncomfortable to completely debilitating. In many cases these issues developed because the practitioners did not work effectively with the rotation of the small water wheels of Qi. The result is that blockages will occur within the body. Such blockages occurring deep within the congenital energy body will always lead to the development of problems and in many cases they can be very challenging to correct. For this reason we urge practitioners to make sure they fully understand the training and the function of the small water wheels. Ideally, you should work with an experienced teacher to ensure that these rotations are successfully opened up before moving further into energy work. Please do not underestimate the importance of opening these circulations.

THE MERIDIANS
THE GOVERNING AND CONCEPTION MERIDIANS

These two energetic pathways form a linked orbit along the centre front and back lines of the body. Essentially, they can be seen to be one channel in charge of regulating the flow of Yin and Yang information throughout the acquired energy body. This happens because over the course of a day the circulation of Qi through these channels causes more energy to be distributed into the 12 acquired meridians. Figure 2.11 shows the Governing and Conception meridians.

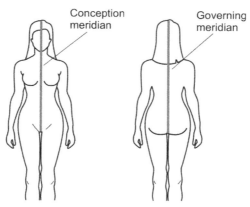

FIGURE 2.11: THE GOVERNING AND CONCEPTION MERIDIANS

In Nei Gong practice we use these channels for various reasons. The first goal of our practice is to free them up from any blockages that may exist along their length and increase the efficiency of energy flow. This energy flow should move unimpeded as a circular rotation of information throughout the body. This initially increases the amount of energy and movement within the 12 acquired meridians, which has the advantage of improving our health. In addition, it is these channels that we will use in our practice to serve as a kind of energetic 'safety net'. The job of this safety net is to ensure that any energetic transformation taking place in an upwards direction has the space to flow downwards again. Without this orbit, any alchemical transformation could be risky. If too much pressure is built up anywhere, there will be no route for this pressure to escape and sink back downwards again. Many practitioners of the internal arts have fallen foul of energetically based disease by not successfully opening this circulation.

The standard direction of Qi flow in Nei Gong is up along the back of the body and then down along the front. For male practitioners, this is the direction they would practise with for the vast majority of their time. Women differ in this way because they need to learn how to work with both directions of energy flow from an early stage in their training. This reverse flow is to assist in the extraction of Jing from the Tian Gui, a concept discussed in greater detail in Chapter 7.

The Conception meridian is of particular importance for women, and part of the reason that the flow is reversed on occasion within the orbit of these two channels is so that the Conception meridian dominates. In the 'regular' direction, the Governing meridian dominates and this results in very different instructions being sent out into the energy body. Table 2.2 shows the different factors involved in the two directions of the orbit between these two meridians.

TABLE 2.2: THE TWO DIRECTIONS OF THE SMALL WATER WHEEL

	Regular Direction	**Reverse Direction**
Dominant meridian	Governing meridian	Conception meridian
Secondary meridian	Conception meridian	Governing meridian
Dominant function	Invigorating energy	Extracting essence
Secondary function	Safety mechanism	Strengthening Uterus
Effect on Jing	Circulates	Delivers to chest
Strengthens	Spine and back	Abdomen and breasts
Dan Tien connection	Lower Dan Tien	Middle Dan Tien

The Conception meridian can be considered to be the meridian associated with the organ of the Uterus within women. This is a major part of the reason the reverse direction of circulation through these two meridians is important for female practitioners. The flow of energy in this direction begins to connect the Uterus to the energy of the Heart centre.

THE PATHWAYS OF THE THRUSTING MERIDIAN

The Thrusting meridian is a complex channel that has a number of pathways. As well as the commonly known branch that runs through the centre of the spine, there is also a vertically aligned branch that runs through the core of the body. Either side of this are two side branches that run through the middle of the torso, and then finally there are deep internal branches that travel through the middle of the arms and legs. Figure 2.12 shows the various pathways of the Thrusting meridian. Note that the appendicular branches are bilateral; we have included them on only one side of the body in this diagram for reasons of neatness.

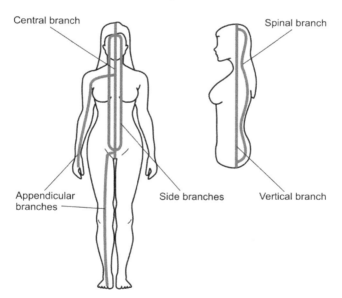

FIGURE 2.12: THE THRUSTING MERIDIAN

The Thrusting meridian is the key channel through which a great deal of energetic transformation takes place. This happens as the conversion of Jing, Qi and Shen is initiated by correct work with the three Dan Tien during Nei Gong practice. It is also the key meridian connecting a practitioner into the higher spiritual realms once they have reached advanced stages in their training.

For women, it is the Thrusting meridian, and in particular the vertical branch of this meridian, that is closely connected to the cycles of the moon. When looking to regulate menstruation, it is this meridian that is primarily being worked with. It is a slight oversimplification, but not inaccurate, to say that the Conception meridian is linked to the energy of the Uterus, while the Thrusting meridian is connected to the flow of Tian Gui and menstrual Blood.

THE GIRDLING MERIDIAN

The only meridian to travel horizontally through the body is the Girdling meridian. It encircles the waist like a belt and dips down slightly on the front of the body, as shown in Figure 2.13. This is an important meridian for female Nei Gong practitioners.

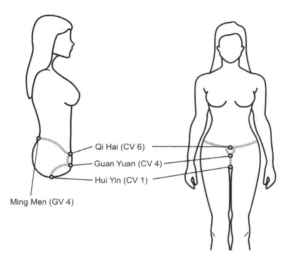

FIGURE 2.13: THE GIRDLING MERIDIAN

This meridian is in part responsible for the correct direction of rotation for the lower Dan Tien when it is left in a 'neutral' state of being. The combination of the rising of energy along the Governing meridian and the dipping down of the Girdling meridian at the front of the body encourages a vertical roll of the Dan Tien which moves energy into the base of the spine. The horizontal pathway of the Girdling meridian then creates a second directional force which stabilises the lower Dan Tien, forming a kind of energetic gyroscope within the lower abdomen.

At later stages in Nei Gong training it is this meridian that extends out in both directions, upwards towards the head and down towards the feet, generating spiralling lines of energy. For men, this is vitally important as it takes their naturally centrifugally moving Qi and binds it into a column of information which assists in the final stages of the opening of the Thrusting meridian. Women's internal energy naturally moves inwards in a centripetal manner, making it much easier for them to open the Thrusting meridian in their practice.

A more important function for the Girdling meridian in the case of women is its connection to the circulation of Jing around the region of the lower abdomen. The Girdling meridian has a strong governing effect upon the health of the Uterus and its ability to 'store'. If the Girdling meridian is weak, then this 'storage' function can become weakened, meaning that imbalances in the menstrual cycle can take place. Usually, this results in overly heavy bleeds. In addition, if the Girdling meridian becomes weakened, it can lessen a woman's fertility levels and be a possible cause of miscarriage. A clear sign of the Girdling meridian being weak is that the body can almost look as though it is 'unbound' around the abdominal region. A woman may be of normal build all over her body but carry extra weight on the lower abdomen. As the Girdling meridian awakens through Nei Gong practice, it is normal for this area of the body to tighten.

As shown in Figure 2.13, several meridian points are also involved in the pathway of the Girdling meridian for women. Although these points are also a part of a male practitioner's Girdling meridian, they are nowhere near as important and so are rarely indicated in diagrams of this energetic pathway.

The meridian point of Qi Hai (CV 6) governs the health of a woman's energy in the lower abdominal region, in the Uterus and around the lower Dan Tien. If there is an imbalance in the flow of information within the Girdling meridian, it is possible for the Qi of the Uterus to become compromised.

The second meridian point is Guan Yuan (關元) (CV 4), an important point for controlling the flow of Jing within the Uterus. The Girdling meridian brings information to Guan Yuan in order to ensure that the Uterus serves as a solid location for the Jing to move into. If there is an imbalance in this region of the energy body, then it does not take long for a woman to develop menstrual issues or experience feelings of exhaustion.

The point of Hui Yin (CV 1) is connected to the Girdling meridian in women via an internal branch which runs off the Girdling meridian deep into the body. If this point is weakened through an imbalance within the Girdling meridian, then a woman can start to develop issues with her Uterus and her genito-urinary system, as well as her sex drive. In many women, there is a weakening of energy in this region of the body, which in turn leads to small leakages of urine, especially when engaging in light exercise. Many Chinese medicine practitioners would attribute this to a weakness in the Kidneys, when in actual fact it is more likely to be a deficiency in the energy flow of the Girdling meridian.

The final point involved in the health of the Girdling meridian is Ming Men. This point controls many of the Yang warming functions of the body and is an important driving force for energy along the length of the Governing meridian. If the Ming Men point becomes weak for any reason, it is common for the Girdling meridian to become compromised in women.

THE YIN AND YANG LINKING MERIDIANS

These meridians run along the length of the body, as shown in Figure 2.14. They serve to connect together all of the Yin and Yang acquired meridians of the body.

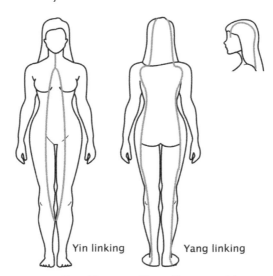

Yin linking   Yang linking

FIGURE 2.14: THE YIN AND YANG LINKING MERIDIANS

These channels ensure that if there are any excesses or deficiencies within the acquired meridians of the body, they equalise these amounts. If there is any excess energy left after this redistribution, they will help to send this energy back towards the congenital energy body where it is stored. They are also in charge of regulating the balance of energetics across the upper, lower, left and right sides of the body. These channels are not used so much in Nei Gong practice but are included here in order to give a complete picture.

Also included here for the purpose of giving a comprehensive picture are the Yin and Yang heel meridians, shown in Figure 2.15.

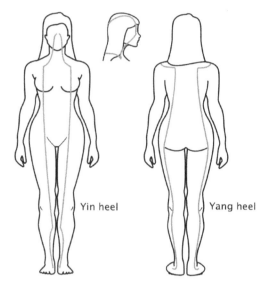

Yin heel   Yang heel

FIGURE 2.15: THE YIN AND YANG HEEL MERIDIANS

These meridians can be thought of as similar to the 'earth wire' in an electrical circuit. They ensure that if any sudden excesses occur within the body, they drop down towards the planet. These meridians will open naturally of their own accord during training and are not focused on to any great extent in this system of Nei Gong training.

THE ENERGETIC CAGE AND THE FIVE PULSES
The meridians of the congenital energy body connect together to form a kind of energetic cage, as discussed earlier. This cage is where all of the rotations of orbiting energy take place during Nei Gong practice. Within the centre of this cage are five pulses of congenital energy, which are rarely discussed but are clear to feel by anybody who has moved beyond the foundation stages of their internal practice. These five pulses are different movements of information corresponding to the five elemental energies of Daoism. They work together as a cycle to generate the basis for our

emotional and energetic health. As we open up the various circulations of the energetic cage, it becomes much easier to regulate the five pulses. Table 2.3 summarises the nature of the five congenital pulses.

TABLE 2.3: THE FIVE CONGENITAL PULSES

Element	Movement	Effects
Fire	Expansion	Generates warmth and nourishment
Earth	Division	Generates change and evolution
Metal	Contraction	Generates stability and connection
Water	Cycling	Generates life and growth
Wood	Driving	Generates power and planning

There is little direct work to do with these five pulses, but you can expect to connect with and feel them during your practice. At these times there will be a clear tangible sensation of these five directional energies moving through your body. As this happens, there are shifts starting to take place within the energy body, shifts that will then have an effect upon the health of your body and organs.

THE THREE DAN TIEN
The three Dan Tien sit within the core of the body and are connected together via the vertical branch of the Thrusting meridian. They are spherical fields of information which vary from person to person with regard to their degree of consolidation. In the vast majority of beginners, you could say that the Dan Tien are there but have the potential to be a great deal more powerful. This strengthening process generally takes place as the practitioner's awareness interacts with the energy in the vicinity of the Dan Tien. The mind begins to reinforce the strength of the information field and so the function of the Dan Tien becomes stronger.

The key role of the Dan Tien is to convert each of our energetic substances either up or down: the Dan Tien are conversion centres for vibrational states. This conversion takes place as the hollow centre of each Dan Tien receives one of the three key energetic substances before transforming it into the next. This conversion process is shown in Figure 2.16.

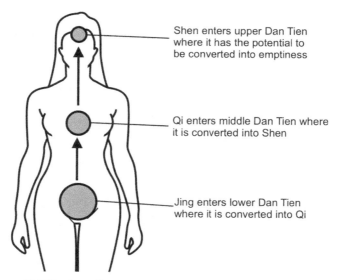

Shen enters upper Dan Tien where it has the potential to be converted into emptiness

Qi enters middle Dan Tien where it is converted into Shen

Jing enters lower Dan Tien where it is converted into Qi

FIGURE 2.16: CONVERSION THROUGH THE DAN TIEN

A great deal of work in Nei Gong is centred upon the efficient use of the three Dan Tien. As we carry out this work, the conversion functions of the Dan Tien also have an effect upon our awareness, which gradually begins to be able to tune in to deeper levels of internal sensitivity.

THE LOWER DAN TIEN

The lower Dan Tien serves as the main driving force for energy throughout the rest of our body. It sits within the lower abdomen, below the navel and in line with the vertical branch of the Thrusting meridian. In Nei Gong training, our initial task is to awaken this energy centre, and this is largely accomplished through aiming for a smooth and steady rotation. The lower Dan Tien is in charge of driving energy as well as the conversion of Jing to Qi; as such, it is the energy centre most responsible for dealing with the denser aspects of the energy body. It is generally the simplest to connect with and the focal point for the majority of men's Nei Gong training. In the case of women, the foundation stages are still with this centre but they should aim to progress upwards into direct work with the middle Dan Tien instead.

THE MIDDLE DAN TIEN

The middle Dan Tien sits within the centre of the chest at the height of the Heart. For this reason it is often known as the Heart centre. The middle Dan Tien is the location for conversion of Qi into Shen, the spiritual energy that governs all aspects of mind, from the most mundane thought through to divine comprehension. It is the energy centre most closely connected to our emotions and this is why the heart has been linked to the emotional mind in almost every culture. This is the energy centre that dominates women's practice once they have moved beyond the foundation stages of their training. For women, there is a unique challenge at this level of training as the middle Dan Tien tends to lose energy through being subject to constant emotional fluctuations. This loss of energy causes a weakness in the rising of Shen upwards towards the upper Dan Tien. This is shown in Figure 2.17.

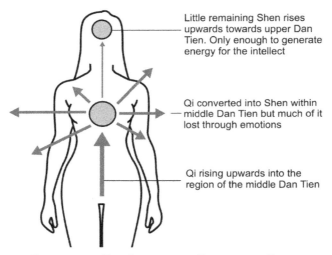

Little remaining Shen rises upwards towards upper Dan Tien. Only enough to generate energy for the intellect

Qi converted into Shen within middle Dan Tien but much of it lost through emotions

Qi rising upwards into the region of the middle Dan Tien

FIGURE 2.17: THE LEAKAGE OF EMOTIONAL ENERGY

The emotions cause a great deal of energy to leak away from the middle Dan Tien. What remains is only enough to empower the strength of the intellect. In order to move towards heightened states of realisation, a practitioner needs to build enough internal energy to strengthen the deeper aspects of human consciousness. This is the way towards connection with Dao and the reason why so much importance is placed upon centring the emotions in the majority of Eastern traditions.

Although, of course, this leaking of emotional energy is a concern for both genders, it carries particular importance for women due to the housing of their essence around the region of the chest and breasts. As women experience emotional shifts, this has the added effect of draining the essence, which has a detrimental effect upon a woman's health, mental wellbeing and overall vitality. By boosting the middle Dan Tien and centring the mind, it becomes much easier for women to gain the benefits to be had from consolidation of their essence.

THE UPPER DAN TIEN

The upper Dan Tien sits within the middle of the skull. It has an exit point which extends outwards to between the eyebrows, a point corresponding to the concept of the 'third eye'. The upper Dan Tien is the conversion point of Shen into emptiness and the seat of all of the higher-level attainments in the Daoist tradition. To be honest, work carried out with the upper Dan Tien should take place in a practice such as alchemical meditation. In this book, the only practice we will discuss with regard to the upper Dan Tien is a sound practice in Chapter 3. This exercise will help to tonify the health of the upper Dan Tien. Any more complex work than this with the upper Dan Tien should be carried out under the supervision of an experienced teacher.

Miscellaneous Components of the Energy Body

As well as the Dan Tien and various meridians of the acquired and congenital energy bodies, there are also various other energetic elements of the body that do not easily fall into either category. Two of these components are the Wei Qi (衛氣) field and the auric field. These two components are important to understand in Nei Gong training.

THE WEI QI FIELD

The Wei Qi field is a protective field of information which serves to guard us from externally based pathogens. If the Wei Qi field is weak, then a person will be more susceptible to becoming sick if they spend periods of time in cold or damp weather. Our Wei Qi field is rooted in the skin and extends a few centimetres out from our body, as shown in Figure 2.18.

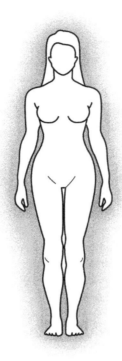

FIGURE 2.18: THE WEI QI FIELD

The Wei Qi field is comprised of a combination of Qi and Jing, meaning that its strength depends on the quality of both of these substances. The Wei Qi field is interesting as it is entirely dependent upon the local health of the energy system. What this means is that a person rarely has an even distribution of Wei Qi around the exterior of their body. Although it may be strong over the majority of the body, it can still have several holes or deficiencies through which elemental information can get into the body. The result of this is that people will often have specific areas of the body that they do not like to have exposed to the elements.

Alongside this elemental protection is an emotional layer of the Wei Qi field which tends to extend a little further out from the body. This layer of the Wei Qi field protects a person from emotional information that can be passed from person to person. If a person's emotional Wei Qi layer is weak, they will often find that the emotional states of other people affect them strongly. They may spend time with a person suffering from depression only to find that their mood is low afterwards. Strengthening this layer of the field is particularly important for women, who should ensure that they are robust enough to avoid taking on the emotional imbalances of others. This will help them to strengthen the energy of the middle Dan Tien.

THE AURIC FIELD

Extending further out from the body like a bubble is the auric field. This field expands and contracts as we breathe, resulting in a continuous exchange of energetic information with our environment. This interchange also takes place during every interaction we have with another person and this information is then stored within the auric field. The information within the auric field takes the form of Yin and Yang waves which store every little facet of our existence in energetic form. It is this field that skilled energy workers are able to palpate and read from.

Many people will have experienced the nature of the auric field without being aware of it when they meet people. This takes place most obviously when you instinctively take a dislike to somebody on your first meeting for no obvious reason. In many cases what is happening is that your own auric field is drawing in information from the person you are meeting and your subconscious mind is finding something to which it takes offence. It is a great boon of continuous internal training that the majority of practitioners begin to connect their awareness to this field to a greater degree, which in turn gives them increased powers of intuition.

Contained within your own auric field is a record of your emotional standpoint as well as a history of every little hurt or past trauma you have suffered. As you move into the Nei Gong process, you should naturally begin to shed this information. As practitioners go through this process, they often state that they feel lighter in some way.

THE UTERUS

We have included the organ of the Uterus here in this miscellaneous section as it does not fit neatly into either the congenital or the acquired categories. It is an organ that has a physical structure and yet has strong energetic properties which make it an important aspect of the female body to understand for practitioners of the Daoist arts.

When discussing the physical organ of the Uterus, it is important to understand that the ancient Chinese were discussing not only the uterus as we understand it in Western physiology but also other physical aspects such as the fallopian tubes, the ovaries and even, in part, some aspects of the sexual organs. This is because the Chinese medical model always refers to organ systems rather than isolated physical body parts.

There are several names for the Uterus in Chinese medical literature but the most commonly used term is the Zi Bao (子胞), which can be translated as 'to contain a baby', and thus refers more to the energetic matrix which sits within the region of the Uterus than to the physical structure. Within this region all of the various energetic and spiritual components may come together to form the congenital basis of new life. Interestingly, men are also said to have a Bao (胞) within their lower abdomen, just not a Zi Bao. In the case of men, the power of the Bao is said to help consolidate the essence that will later go on to form the material basis for their sexual fluids.

The Zi Bao for women and the Bao for men are related to the storage of different substances. Both of these structures are then associated with the lower Dan Tien and its various aspects. Understanding the difference between the male and female Bao is key to seeing exactly why women do not require the same level of work with the lower Dan Tien region of the body as men; this in turn becomes the basis for why they should progress more quickly than men through the Nei Gong process. Table 2.4 summarises the differences between the Zi Bao and the Bao.

TABLE 2.4: THE ZI BAO AND THE BAO

	Zi Bao	Bao
Present in	Women	Men
Primarily related to	Blood	Jing
Storage of	Tian Gui	Sexual potential
Psychological need	Reproduction	Base desires
Key organ connection	Heart and Kidneys	Kidneys

As stated above, the Tian Gui is stored within the Uterus. It is generated from a mixture of Jing and Blood. This substance is then shed from the body during menstruation. This is a key loss of essence for women that takes place on a monthly basis. In the case of men, it is sexual potential that is 'stored' within the Bao region. This then goes on to combine with their Jing to produce semen which is lost through ejaculation.

Psychologically, the Zi Bao connects a woman to her desire to reproduce and become a mother. This inbuilt psychological need then includes the desire to bring up a child and be the pivotal person within a functioning family. Although, of course, this is not a psychological need that every single woman has – many go through their lives without this desire – the vast majority of women will find that at some point a deep inner wish for this to happen kicks in. According to Daoist thought, this is a spiritual function of the Uterus. At a certain age, it causes women to seek out the potential for having a child. For those women who have a healthy connection to their inner nature, having a child at this time can be a greatly beneficial spiritual process. The connection between the Heart and the Uterus ensures that the requirement for warmth and compassion (a psychological aspect of the Heart) is there, and it will assist a woman in seeking out a sensible partner with whom to have a child. This should be a partner who fulfils her needs on a level of personal growth.

When this psychological desire to have a child develops within women, it can be a powerful force which takes over a great deal of their acquired mind. In the case of women, though, this only happens at certain times in their life. It is rare, and considered an imbalance, for a woman to wish for a child right from hitting puberty through to old age. It should happen at certain times in accordance with the natural rhythms set up by the numerological cycles contained within her Jing.

Conversely, the psychological aspect of men linked to the Bao and Jing is that of base desires. With regard to reproduction, it is the act of sex and sexual stimulation that drives them, rather than the desire to have a child. Although there are times in many men's lives when they desire to have a family, it is generally far less of a powerful force for them than it is for women. In the same way, women desire sexual stimulation just as men do, but this desire rarely sits at the back of their mind all of the time as is the case for the majority of men. This all means that male sexual desires are having an effect upon their mind far more often than the equivalent desires of women. The result is that women need to work with the lower Dan Tien to consolidate the health of the various organs and substances in this region of the body, whereas men have to remain here until a key instinctual desire is changed. Men literally need to evolve beyond their base psychological programming in order to progress on to work with the middle Dan Tien – a very difficult task which actually prevents the majority of male internal arts practitioners from ever moving beyond the basics.

The male Bao is closely connected to the Kidneys. This is to do with the movement of Jing through the body. The female Zi Bao is connected, via two internal channels, into both the Heart and the Kidneys. This means that there are two strong organ influences taking place upon the organ of the Uterus. This is shown in Figure 2.19.

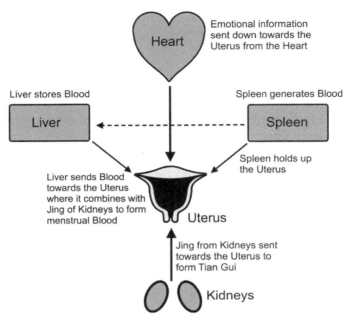

FIGURE 2.19: THE UTERUS, THE HEART AND THE KIDNEYS

The Heart to Uterus is an important organ connection to understand. In one way, it is beneficial because it represents the pathway through which emotional pathogenic debris is moved into the menstrual Blood ready for expulsion from the body (see Chapter 4); on the other side of the coin, this connection also explains the disruptive effect that women's emotions can have upon their menstrual cycle. The circulations of Tian Gui within women are largely dependent upon the cycles of the moon but can be disrupted by any large experiences of stress, emotional hurt, sadness and so on. This brings us back once again to the importance for women to regulate their emotional state and thus the health of the Heart centre during their training.

Also included in Figure 2.19 are the organs of the Spleen and the Liver. These two organs are also important in the health of the Uterus even though they are not a part of the Heart/Uterus/Kidney axis. The Spleen is important because one of its energetic functions in Chinese medical theory is that it 'holds up' organs within the body. This means that it generates a form of information that literally suspends the organs correctly within the body cavities. If the Spleen becomes weakened for any reason, then it can cause the Uterus to prolapse. The Liver is included because one of the key roles of this organ is to ensure that the energy of the body flows smoothly. This has an effect on the Uterus because the Liver is required to keep the menstrual Blood flowing smoothly. If the Liver becomes imbalanced for any reason, then it is common for the Qi flowing through the region of the Uterus to become stagnant. This can result in clots in the menstrual Blood as well as symptoms of frustration just prior to the onset of menstruation. In addition, the Blood that flows through a person's body is generated through the actions of the Spleen. The Spleen then sends the Blood across to the Liver. In Chinese medical thought, it is the Liver that stores the Blood, where it becomes more active when we exert ourselves. Some of this Blood flows downwards towards the Uterus where it combines with the Jing of the Kidneys to form the menstrual Blood. Although essentially it is a different substance entirely from the Blood of the body, menstrual Blood is in part generated by the Blood that travels to the Uterus from the Liver.

THE CONSCIOUSNESS BODY

In the Daoist tradition, human consciousness is often considered to be a third 'body' that makes up human life. This is in part due to the concept of every aspect of spirit being rooted into a physical anchor, generally via an energetic connection. Different aspects of human consciousness are linked to very specific areas of the physical body, and yet despite this we can safely say that the consciousness body is beyond the realm of having a three-dimensional structure. Many Eastern traditions have engaged in complex studies of the nature of the consciousness body, and Daoism is no exception. Perhaps one of the factors of the Daoist concept of the consciousness body that makes the Daoist framework unique is the view that everything that exists in the realm of consciousness also exists in the energetic realm. This was the basis for the alchemical meditative practices of the Daoists that aim to lead a practitioner into direct contact with the energetic substances, Qi, which are the basis for various aspects of the human mind.

Being a pragmatic group of people, the Daoists recognised the strengths of other traditions they were exposed to rather than simply seeing them as rivals. From the Buddhist tradition they 'borrowed' the model of the Heart-mind which is a simple yet effective conceptual framework for helping us to understand the basics of the consciousness body. Figure 2.20 shows the model of the Heart-mind concept.

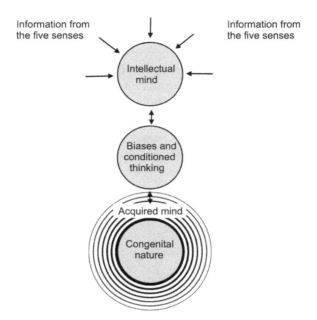

FIGURE 2.20: THE HEART-MIND MODEL

According to Daoist thought, it is only Dao that is permanent. Everything that is born from this state is subject to the laws of change which make up life and existence. The congenital nature that sits at the core of our consciousness body is a reflection of the stillness of Dao. When we touch upon this state of being, we are drawn into a profound inner stillness which becomes the basis for true union of spirit.

As we move through life, various layers of emotionally charged information build up around the congenital nature, obscuring it from the rest of our awareness. These layers are facets of the acquired mind, an aspect of consciousness that is constantly shifting. The acquired mind is responsible for the formation of our biases and conditioned thinking, which in turn generates the nature of our intellectual mind.

As human beings, we interact with our outside world primarily through the vehicle of the five senses. These senses bring in information which is processed by the intellectual mind. Our intellect passes this information down through the filter of our conditioned thinking where it then adds to the emotionally based layers of the acquired mind. Nei Gong is, in part, an attempt to shed these layers and bring ourselves closer to the source of our congenital nature. Ultimately, if we ever achieve this, we can experientially understand that these divisions are just a conceptual model created by the mind. As we touch upon congenital nature, we are able to experience unification of consciousness with Dao and this is the path to transcendence.

IN CONCLUSION

This chapter has been a brief overview and introduction to the various facets of the three bodies that make up human existence. There is a great deal more we could write about the nature of the three bodies, but much of it can be experienced first-hand when moving through the Nei Gong process. It is wise to ensure that you are familiar with the information from this chapter before moving on to any of the practical exercises outlined in the rest of the book. A sound theoretical basis is wise because it ensures steady progress as well as enabling you to recognise which aspects of your inner environment you are working with at any moment.

Chapter 3
_____

BREATH AND SOUND

A ny internal practice that you engage with will no doubt, at some stage,
require you to work with your breath. The various methods may
differ but the end result is nearly always the same: to regulate and improve
the efficiency of your breathing, which in turn will have a positive effect
on your mind-state, as well as smoothing energy flow. Accomplishing a
solid base with breath work is an invaluable tool for one simple reason:
you are breathing all of the time. This means that, whether your practice
is for spiritual growth or improvement of health, you have a way to ensure
that your practice becomes something that you are doing 24 hours a day,
even when you are sleeping.

Working with the breath is a foundation-level practice for both Qi
Gong and Nei Gong training, but it is also something that should be
returned to regularly in order to ensure that your evolution continues
in the right direction. This is because your breathing carries out several
important tasks, including:

- bringing oxygen into the body upon inhalation and expelling carbon
  dioxide when we exhale

- regulating the emotional aspect of our mind on a simple level

- increasing the efficiency of our acquired Qi intake and flow

- regulating the internal pressures of the torso

- translating mental awareness into conscious energetic connection.

Each of these factors is required for ensuring that a practitioner develops
a high-quality practice.

OXYGEN AND CARBON DIOXIDE EXCHANGE

On a physiological level, we require the oxygen absorbed upon inhalation to enter our bloodstream so that it may reach every tissue and cell of the body. This ensures that our body is functioning as efficiently as possible, not only for our practice but also over the course of our daily lives. Since we are breathing from the second we are born right up until the moment of our death, it would seem ludicrous not to turn it into a healthy practice. On top of this, the oxygen that enters our body also helps to relax the muscles, which will help us to soften the body and increase flexibility. Attempting to relax and open up the body with a poor state of breathing is almost impossible.

One of the greatest problems for people as they age is a gradual decline in mental faculties. This begins with a weakening in our ability to learn and remember information, and culminates in various imbalances with cognitive functioning. The brain absorbs huge amounts of oxygen, meaning that if we can regulate our breath over the course of our lives, we will help to maintain brain function at a higher level much later in life.

As we exhale, we remove excess carbon dioxide from the body. If this gas were to remain in the body in great amounts, it would lead to sickness. If there is too much in the body, then our breathing naturally speeds up to assist in its removal. Unfortunately, this causes the breath to become shallow, meaning that we never fully expel carbon dioxide from deep inside the lungs. For this reason we want our breathing to be as deep and relaxed as it can be.

REGULATION OF THE EMOTIONAL MIND

It is well understood by the majority of people how our breathing can be used to regulate our emotional state. If we become stressed or angry, we are often told that we should 'take deep breaths' which will help to calm us. Almost any acute or chronic emotional state can be observed in the breath, and so this means that by regulating the breath we can begin to change these emotional patterns. Although the root cause of a psychological issue is rarely dealt with purely in this manner, it does enable us to regulate the emotional content and experience of any imbalances as they may arise. It is a large part of the reason why practised meditators tend to have a very centred emotional state of being and a good level of control over how they react to external stimuli. Through prolonged observation or control of the breath, they have helped to regulate their emotional mind.

Especially in the case of women, it is important to regulate the emotional mind, as there is a greater risk of draining essence from the region of the chest if you are subject to a large amount of emotional swings. This essence is required for further internal development.

ACQUIRED QI INTAKE AND FLOW

One of the largest ingredients in the formation of acquired Qi is the air we breathe and the energy that it contains. Everything in life is essentially a source of information; Qi, and the air surrounding us, is no exception. Through deep, high-quality breathing, we can ensure that we absorb the maximum amount of energy from the environment, which is then combined with the food we eat to develop a healthy source of Qi for the body.

INTERNAL PRESSURE OF THE TORSO

The torso is divided into two main parts by the diaphragm, as shown in Figure 3.1. These two sections each have their own energetic pressure which is, in part, regulated through the movement of the diaphragm during breathing.

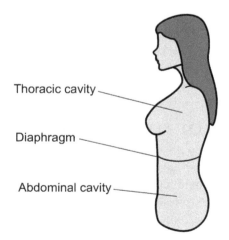

Thoracic cavity

Diaphragm

Abdominal cavity

FIGURE 3.1: TWO SECTIONS OF THE TORSO

According to Daoist teachings, there should be a healthy level of communication taking place between these two chambers. As the diaphragm moves, it serves to massage the organs sitting within these two sections of the body and then shift energy back and forth as the pressures alternate between Yin and Yang with your respiration. This movement of energy helps to set up a healthy level of communication between the lower organs such as the Uterus and the organs within the chest cavity, in particular the Heart. If the breathing is forced or uneven, then the exchange of information between these two key organs can become imbalanced and so problems can manifest. The key issue in this case is that the Heart will begin to send imbalanced emotional information down to the Uterus and this will begin to generate problems with a woman's menstrual flow. There will be an increase in emotional issues around this time of the month and the flow of menstrual Blood can be affected. In the case of women who have moved through into the menopause, there will be a prolonging of menopausal symptoms and the development of stagnation around the lower abdomen. In many cases, imbalances to a woman's health can be helped a great deal by working with the breath to ensure a healthy level of communication between the energies of the thoracic and abdominal cavities.

TRANSLATION OF MENTAL AWARENESS
One aspect of understanding the nature of breath that is often missed is its role as a kind of 'translator' between the physical and energetic realms. Although rarely discussed, it can readily be experienced by any meditation or Qi Gong practitioner who has spent long enough working with their breath. When we breathe, we cause a wave of energy to move through the meridians as well as the tissues and fascia lines of the body. This energy moves through us, nourishing various parts of our system. On top of this, our breath moves energy in and out of the body through countless energetic pores that serve to anchor our auric field into the rest of our energy body.

Because of the unique role of our breath as both a physiological and an energetic process, it can also help to adjust the level of our awareness. As we observe the breath through our work, it begins to 'translate' the level of our awareness and so with time we begin to be able to 'tune in' to the energetic realm. This helps to develop a heightened level of sensitivity which gives you conscious awareness of how your energy is moving within the body. This skill develops naturally with time but is usually developed much more quickly by female practitioners of Nei Gong than by men. Women's natural innate sensitivity helps them to develop awareness of energetic movement via the breath much more quickly. It is interesting to note, although this is only the personal experience of the authors, that male practitioners of Nei Gong who develop energetic sensitivity too quickly or with too much ease tend to be slightly imbalanced in that they are somewhat energetically 'ungrounded'. It often becomes an important aspect of their training to try to bring them away from direct work with their energy body and back into work with the physical body in order to build a solid foundation. They should return to the energy body much later. In the case of women, however, the sooner they can develop awareness of their energetic shifts the better, as it gives them access to the stages of working with the Heart centre and the middle Dan Tien.

BREATH AND SOUND WORK

When we began working on this book, we realised that there needed to be a chapter focusing solely on the breath. This is because it is one of the key areas that need to be regulated when beginning any internal practice such as Nei Gong. Also, we envisaged this book to be a version of the previous title by Damo Mitchell, *Daoist Nei Gong: The Philosophical Art of Change*, for female practitioners of the Daoist arts. In this book, Damo outlined a practice called Sung breathing which is essentially a way to use the breath to release tensions within the mind, energy system and body. This is a useful breathing technique for any practitioner of Nei Gong to get to grips with, no matter what gender, but we did not want to simply repeat the information from the previous book here as we know that many people reading this will have both titles. For this reason we are going to explore the breath in a slightly different manner and connect it to sound work. Although at first this may seem like a strange connection to form between two practices, it is not. If we look at the physical anatomy of how sound is produced, we can see that the quality and strength of our breathing is what provides the power for the production of sound. The breath moving out of the lungs on exhalation causes the vocal cords to vibrate and then the various shapes made with our mouth and throat, as well as the nose, cause this vibration to resonate in different ways. The end result is an externalised sound. From this we can see that the production of sound is an extension of the act of breathing.

Sound work is a very powerful tool and consequently there are many different forms of exercise utilising the voice. Several Qi Gong systems based upon the use of sound are in existence; there are also the more complex sounds that we commonly know as mantra. Part of the strength of this kind of work comes from the vibration generated by each sound and how it then resonates with different areas of the energy body. No matter what sound is used, there is also a strong connection to the Heart centre and so women often find that they connect with sound work very easily. In order to work with sound, we must first go back to its foundation, though, and regulate the motivating source for the sound: our breath.

When beginning to work with the breath, it is important first to understand the difference between two key terms, attention and intention. These are different states of awareness, but both can be applied to internal practices and often there is much confusion among practitioners as to which of these two states is required. Indeed, many times it can be difficult to even understand which of the two states of awareness you are using.

AWARENESS
The Use of Attention
The energy body should be fostered in much the same way as a small child can be encouraged to develop. Both require gentle attention that is neither too assertive nor restrictive. The ability to simply observe what is taking place in a focused yet not forceful manner is a surprisingly difficult skill when you first begin any form of internal practice.

The principle behind this kind of awareness is that once an internal process is taking place, by gently bringing our awareness to this process we give it what it needs to become stronger. This increase in efficiency takes place through simply taking the mind and keeping it gently resting on what is taking place without trying to force or change anything. It is said in Qi Gong circles that where the awareness goes, energy follows, and in this way we are using our awareness to enable an unfolding process to evolve in the right direction.

The challenge with this type of awareness is that many people will want to begin changing what is taking place or adding to it with their intention. The concept is that the body already knows what it is supposed to do; the process is already unfolding, and by giving it our attention for a while we are helping it to develop without the interference of our conscious mind.

The Use of Intention
The second key state of awareness we commonly utilise in a practice such as Nei Gong is focused intention. Unlike the previous use of attention, we now utilise the acquired mind either to assist or to strengthen the process through the assertion of a small amount of our willpower. When an internal process begins to take place, we may add to it through our intention; an example of this would be when working towards awakening the lower Dan Tien, as discussed in Chapter 7.

The skill in working in this manner is understanding exactly how strong our intention needs to be in order to ensure that we are working efficiently and safely. The most common mistake people make is to use far too strong an intention, which can be problematic because it can lead to internal stagnation. At the other end of the scale, if the intention is scattered and not focused enough, then the energy behind your practice will disperse and so your progress will be slowed.

Another great risk of the use of intention is that it engages the acquired aspect of our conscious mind, which is the same part of our awareness responsible for controlling our imagination skills. When they begin to use focused intention, many people end up initiating the imaginative mind and so many images and concepts will jump into their head. This will distract the mind from its role and run the risk of leading a practitioner towards a state of delusion. For this reason it is always wise to keep visualisation and other imagination-based skills to a minimum or cut them out of your training altogether.

OBSERVING THE BREATH

A great many spiritual traditions begin by having students sit and simply observe their breathing. Although it sounds like a simple process, it is actually a very difficult task at first, because the mind has difficulty focusing upon this one single thing. Some traditions have students focus upon a single area such as the nostrils, while others are based around observing the entire breathing process. As students become more proficient, they may be led into increasingly deeper states of awareness as the breath begins to bridge the connection between the external and internal worlds. For our purposes as Nei Gong practitioners, we are going to observe the breath as a foundation practice with only one real aim: to be able to use the breath as a translator for our awareness into the energy body.

This practice can be carried out standing, sitting or lying down; the posture does not matter too much, provided that you are comfortable and not 'crunched up' in any way. Relax the whole body as much as you can and then simply breathe naturally with your eyes closed and your attention gently focused inwards, observing the movements of your breathing. These movements will no doubt start purely physically as you feel the rising and falling of the ribs and abdomen. This is fine; wherever your awareness is led, go with it and simply observe.

Remain with this practice for a short session of 20 minutes or so, ensuring that your intention does not get involved; you are just a passive observer in the respiratory process.

This practice should be kept up regularly until you start to feel that your breathing begins to change of its own accord. It should naturally start to grow slower, deeper and smoother due to your focused awareness giving your breath the space and attention it needs in order to change. As this happens, you will find that the mind will become calmer and you will find increasing levels of satisfaction from this simple exercise. The 20 minutes you start with will begin to naturally increase in length until you can practise in this manner for up to an hour. This is the level of time required by most people in order to progress systematically through into the deeper aspects of observing the breath.

Ensure that throughout this exercise you use attention and not your intention. Although it is true that controlled intention is used at various times with Daoist breath work, for this practice it is better to stay with a more neutral mind so that your breathing can begin to evolve on its own.

Each person exploring this practice will have their own experiences which are individual to them. Despite the unique nature of everybody's practice, there are always going to be certain common experiences that many people have. For this reason we have outlined below some of the common stages of development that we have been through ourselves and witnessed in our students. We have tried to put them in a logical sequence, but it is normal to move through them in a different order.

THE RELAXATION OF BODY AND BREATH

The most common experience for beginners is that their body starts to become very relaxed. This takes place alongside a gradual slowing down and deepening of their respiratory process. At first this increasing level of relaxation will be within the large muscle groups, but with time it will move deeper into the tissues of the body to begin relaxing right through the body to the depth of the bones. This will begin a gradual 'unfurling' process within the layers of connective tissue and fascia lines of the body. It is often now that many people realise just how much habitual tension they have been storing in the body. Chronic tightness of this sort causes a great deal of energetic stagnation which is the basis for many weaknesses in the body, as well as internal disease. This relaxation usually takes place alongside a gradual deepening of the breath. Chronic tension in the body causes the breath to speed up, in part to assist with the expulsion from the lungs of noxious gases produced by this tension, but also as the tension stored in the body generates mental tension which then affects the breath.

Beginners will find that the relaxation they derive from this practice will usually end when they stop each session, but with practice you will find that the level of inner ease you have achieved will stay with you into the rest of your daily life. In addition, increased levels of vitality should become the norm as your body learns to take more vital energy from the air you breathe.

EMOTIONAL RELEASE
The Release of Physical Imbalance
As your relaxation moves deeper into the body, you will find that there are various physical imbalances that have been stored up by your body, usually for a very long time. You may not have been aware of these imbalances before, but as you start to peel back the layers of tension, they will become apparent. These tensions can be based in either physical injury or old emotions, but the effect is the same: they bind up the tissues and generate energetic stagnation, and this in turn leads to the gradual formation of disease.

As they begin to show themselves to you, they will give you the experience of a deep bruise. The exact location of these bruised sensations can be hard to pinpoint as they are not on the surface of the body, but there is no need to worry about this. Simply continue to observe the breath and the experience of the sensation without becoming mentally involved, and you will find that the body begins to release these stored-up tensions of its own accord. Sometimes this will come with the clear experience of the bruise 'moving' through the body towards your extremities where it is evacuated from the body or can begin to disperse. This is all a positive sign of the body moving deeper into a state of relaxation.

The Release of Emotional Stagnation
It is also quite normal for the release of stored tensions to come with the experience of an emotional release. This is due to the intimate nature of the mind and body's connection. As the feelings of deep bruises begin to shift, they can release the dormant information of an emotional blockage, which will result in a temporary experience of an emotion being let go of. It is normal to have brief experiences of sadness, anger, fear or jealousy, or even spontaneous fits of laughter. You do not need to concern yourself with these. Simply continue to observe your breath and pay no importance to the emotional content of your experience. In this way it will pass out of you and leave the body in a healthy manner. As pent-up emotional energy leaves the body, it has to move from deep within you up towards the surface where it can be expelled. As it nears the surface of your body, it reacts with your awareness; this is why it is normal for an emotion to arise up within you.

If any emotional experience becomes too strong or unpleasant, then simply relax, end your practice session and walk around, shaking your joints. It will quickly pass and you can return to your practice when you feel ready.

ENERGETIC SHIFTS

As you begin to move deeper into your practice, you will begin to contact the energetic nature of stagnation. Once you touch upon this level of your being with your awareness, it can generate energetic shifts which are positive for your development. As the information within your energy system moves, it is normal to experience small shakes, twitches or spasms in the limbs as the body reacts to the movement of internal energy. In some cases people experience an arm or leg suddenly straightening out or contracting. Do not worry about these experiences or place any great importance on them; simply continue to observe the breath with your gentle attention and you will progress in the right direction.

If your awareness manages to tune deeper into the body, then you may become aware of tangible sensations of energetic movement deeper within the body. These will usually manifest as sudden movements of hot or cold, feelings of inner vibrations or any one of countless sensations. These sensations are the result of the information contained within your moving energy body being read by your acquired mind. As the acquired mind processes the information within your Qi, it generates a direct experience of subtle energy movement. Once again, as interesting as these experiences can be, simply continue with your practice of observing the breath so that you may progress beyond them to the next stage.

THE CONNECTION OF BREATH TO ENERGY

The stage you are working towards is a clear awareness of how your energy system and your breath are connected. This stage can only be reached once you have managed to 'tune in' to the energetic realm. Realistically, a woman practising this method can often reach this stage within a few weeks of regular practice, whereas the majority of men seem to take a few months; of course, this is a generalisation and there are exceptions to this rule.

Figure 3.2 shows the movement of energy throughout your energetic field as you breathe in and out.

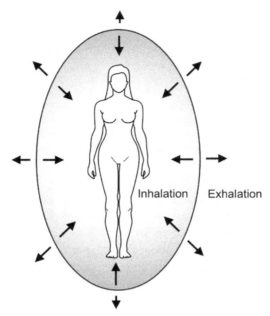

FIGURE 3.2: RESPIRATION AND THE AURIC FIELD

The energetic information contained within the auric field moves in and out as you breathe. Upon inhalation it moves inwards towards your body, reaching a depth just below the skin. Upon exhalation it moves outwards into the area surrounding you. For the majority of people, this field moves out to a few inches from your skin, but long-term practitioners will find that inhalation can lead this field right in towards their core and out to a much further distance from the body as they exhale. Whatever your experience of the movement of this field, you should not try to change or direct its movements with your intention; simply observe this field moving with your breathing. You will find at this stage that the movement of your auric field begins to replace any physical sensation you may have as your awareness 'tunes out' of your body and 'tunes in' to the energetic realm.

The early stages of this level of awareness usually revolve around the surface of the skin. The sensation you feel is the point at which the auric field moves in and out of this depth and so generates a response in your nervous system. It has often been described as feeling something like the tide washing up and down a beach as the energy moves over you. With practice and patience, though, you will find that your awareness no longer relies on the sensation on the skin and instead begins to connect with the auric field itself. This is a good stage because for the first time many people are able to experience a tangible sensation taking place outside their body completely independent of the physical nervous system.

The auric field is rooted into the body through the middle Dan Tien, making it an important aspect of the energetic body for women, who function mostly according to their Heart centre. The connection between the Lungs and the Heart is clear to feel in the movement of the auric field as the Qi of the Lungs generated through our breath causes the auric field to shift, while the emotional energy of the Heart governs the quality of information contained within this field.

As you begin to become more aware of the auric field, you will begin to feel how it helps to gently shift energetic pathogenic information out of your body via the pores. As your awareness remains with the movements of this field, you will naturally experience a purging process which goes much deeper than the previous stages.

Once you have reached this stage, you should remain here for some time – at least several weeks – allowing your awareness to connect as deeply as possible with the movements of the auric field. This will become the basis for the practice of effective sound work.

THE FLUCTUATIONS OF THE ACQUIRED MIND

Anybody engaging with a practice such as observing the breath will no doubt become aware of the way that the acquired mind becomes involved. The acquired aspect of mind is that part of our consciousness that incessantly produces mental chatter throughout the duration of our lives. Many people are blissfully unaware of the hyperactive state of their mind, but as soon as they enter into a kind of internal practice such as observing the breath, they become acutely aware of just how busy their mind is. Often likened to a playful monkey in Eastern schools, the acquired mind is constantly seeking sources of stimulation. Closely linked to the emotional aspect of consciousness, the acquired mind is never happy to just be; instead, it seeks out sense-based stimulation that usually takes the form of trivia and other pointless nonsense. Through this stimulation it assists in the building of a false sense of self which meditation practitioners across the world have been trying to work through since the dawn of time. As soon as your awareness is placed upon something that does not rely on externally based stimulation, such as the breath, then you will begin to experience just how hyperactive your mind can be. This is why all of a sudden your mind is filled with constant thoughts, concerns and mental activity unrelated to your practice. The longer you sit there trying to keep your mind quiet, the more mental chatter takes place.

Usually, a person new to this sort of quiet practice will move through the same series of mental challenges:

- First, trivial thoughts and concerns will start going through your head, which distract you from your task. If you allow yourself to engage in any of these thought processes, you quickly find that you have moved away from your task and instead are listening to the acquired mind.

- Upon realisation of the activity of the acquired mind, it is normal for a person to start trying to force this aspect of mind to become quiet. A second voice appears in your head, telling the first voice to be quiet. Before long you realise that you are arguing with yourself and all you have managed to do is generate even more activity within the mind.

- The third experience is that people start to realise that each thought they are having has some kind of emotional seed to it, and so the acquired mind can lead a person into increasingly emotive thought patterns which make the practice difficult.

- A fourth experience, though not necessarily in this order, is that the mind will create feelings of boredom. This can reach such a stage that it feels almost tortuous not to end the training and seek out some kind of mental stimulation. This is just an aspect of the acquired mind that will fade once it is not succumbed to.

These are all normal experiences to have during any internal practice and are nothing to be concerned about. Just remember that, where your awareness goes, energy flows, meaning that if you pay any attention to your thoughts, then you have instantly stimulated them into more activity and so given the mind fuel to become more active. If you try to force the mind to become quiet or start to 'argue' with yourself, this will have the same effect and so you will begin to work against yourself. Simply return to your breathing and do not worry if you are led away from this practice by the mind every now and then. Any emotions that come up within your mind are more difficult to leave alone, but again you should attempt to return to observation of the breath.

After doing this for some time, you will find that your acquired mind begins to grow more still. The level of activity of the mind will lessen and the result will be a feeling of peace while you are engaging with this practice. Although it sounds simple enough, this is one of the greatest challenges for anybody starting out in the internal arts. It is a hurdle that must be overcome if a practitioner wishes to move beyond the foundation stages of their training and so a solid foundation should be built here. Be patient with yourself and with your mind. Simply follow the breath and allow your mind to grow more quiet. This will lead you into connection with the movements of the energetic realm.

BEGINNING TO WORK WITH SOUND

Once you have established a strong connection to the movement of your auric field, you are ready to begin working with sound exercises. The important thing for gaining strong results from Daoist sound work is that the sound you produce should be seen as an extension of your breath, rather than an isolated noise that you simply issue from your mouth.

If you start to practise sound work prior to being able to connect with the movement of your own energy, then you will be limiting the effectiveness of the technique. There are countless variations in possible tones for a sound and each one produces a slightly different effect. It is the ability to directly experience how the sound affects your energetic system that enables you to adjust the sound to its most efficient state. It is for this reason that we decided to include sound work in a book written specifically for women. Women can connect with the feeling of their auric field a lot sooner than the majority of male practitioners. Although sound work is equally as effective for both genders, experience has shown us that women connect with it much faster and so gain stronger results from the practice.

The first sound to practise is the sound 'ah'. Though not classically placed into any particular sequence, the 'ah' sound tends to be the easiest to feel and work with for women because it resonates strongly with the Heart centre, more so than any of the other sounds. Through practice of this sound it is possible to help open up the middle Dan Tien and its connection to the external world. This begins to develop a harmonisation with the auric field, as shown in Figure 3.3.

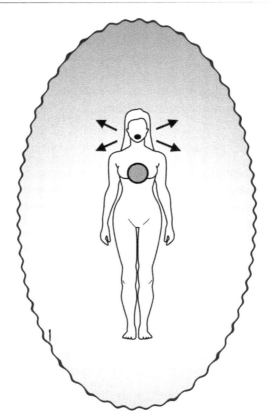

FIGURE 3.3: THE MIDDLE DAN TIEN AND AURIC FIELD IN SOUND WORK

The aim of the three sounds included in this chapter is to cause an awakening of one of the three Dan Tien and to help connect it into the movement of the auric field. This helps to encourage a stronger environmental connection and a strengthening of the various functions of each of these three energy centres. Figure 3.4 shows the three sounds discussed in this chapter with the corresponding Dan Tien.

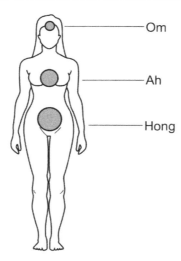

FIGURE 3.4: THE THREE SOUNDS AND THE DAN TIEN

When working with each of the three sounds, we move through the following process. Each of these stages should be practised and refined before moving on. Progressing gradually and sequentially in this manner is the only way ever to become proficient in any internal methodology.

- Any sound practice should begin with an awareness of the energetic relationship between your breath and the movement of the auric field. As you begin to exhale, this serves not only as the catalyst for the making of the sound but also for the start of the expansion of your internal energy. Begin by gently breathing out and connecting your awareness to the movement of your auric field.

- Once you feel the field begin to move, you should start to issue your sound. Keep the tone even and slow. Make sure that you do not force your breath out through overly squeezing the ribs or lower abdominal muscles, as this will generate too much force. Keep the exhalation and making of the sound slow, even and smooth.

- Practise this until you can feel a pull coming from the relevant Dan Tien outwards into the space surrounding you. This pull will be directed by the sound if the tone is correct and you have successfully built a foundation in the prior practice of observing the breath. In some cases a practitioner will find that this pull begins to move them forward or makes them take a step to keep their balance. This is quite normal and nothing to be concerned about. The Dan Tien are closely linked to the energetic aspect of your sense of balance, and the pulling motion can start to affect you in this way.

- Once this connection has been made, there will be a period of adjusting the tone of the sound higher and lower to find the optimum pitch. This pitch will vary from person to person. You should spend time looking for the point at which you feel a strong vibration coming from the relevant Dan Tien. For example, the 'ah' sound, if performed correctly, should cause the chest and region of the Heart to begin vibrating strongly, and this vibration will then move out into the auric field. These effects can be clearly felt.

All of this should be carried out upon exhalation and then you should return to silence when you inhale. When practising the sounds, set aside a minimum of 20–30 minutes in a practice session, making the sound on each exhalation.

Practising the 'Ah' Sound

In order to begin practising the 'ah' sound, you should stand in the position shown in Figure 3.5. Although the sounds can be made from any posture, including sitting, this position helps to focus all of the body's energy towards the region of the chest.

FIGURE 3.5: THE 'AH' SOUND POSTURE

You should stand with all of the correct postural details that you would apply to the early stages of Nei Gong training. These are the same principles that are applied to the Wuji standing position which is outlined in Chapter 6. The only difference in this case is that the hands are placed at the height of the heart in the Mudra shown in Figure 3.6.

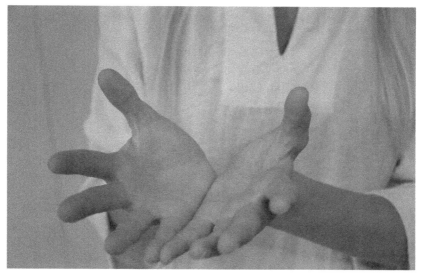

FIGURE 3.6: LOTUS MUDRA

Note that the edges of the hands and little fingers are lightly touching, and the hands are held a couple of inches away from the body. The fingers are then gently outstretched in a slightly circular fashion as if you are forming a loose bowl shape with your hands. The intention is for the tips of the fingers to be pulling outwards away from you in order to help facilitate the desired expansion of energy from the region of the middle Dan Tien.

Now, as you exhale and make the 'ah' sound, you should extend your intention out through the tips of the fingers into the distance as if you could touch the far horizon. Make sure you do not make the 'ah' sound too quietly at first. Open your mouth and make it nice and loud so that you have a clear physical vibration to work with. With practice, your awareness will move deeper into the energetic realm, meaning that the depth of subtlety you can pick up with regard to vibrational frequencies will increase. At this stage you will be able to be quieter with your sound work and still be able to move through the progressive stages outlined above.

When making the 'ah' sound, you should extend the 'ah' to make the sound 'aaaaaaaah' – that is, the same length as your exhalation. The exact sound is the sound in words such as 'far' or 'tar'. When you begin making the sound, you will first have to play with raising and lowering the tone in order to find the correct level that causes the vibration around the region of the Heart. A common error is to practise this vibration at the level of the throat; you should experiment in order to bring the tone's effects down to the chest region.

If you have the opportunity to practise this exercise in a group, you will find the results much stronger. It is not long before participants in a session start to harmonise with one another. At this level of practice the energetic vibrations become much stronger, which in turn helps to open a person up to heightened states of connection.

Practising the 'Om' Sound

The 'om' sound is used heavily in many different Eastern traditions as a powerful mantra. When used in the Nei Gong tradition as a vibratory sound, it is used primarily to connect with the upper Dan Tien. It is comprised of two main parts. The first aspect of the sound helps to raise awareness and energy up towards the centre of the head, and then the second aspect causes the upper Dan Tien to begin to vibrate strongly. It is generally a more difficult sound for people to connect with than 'ah', which is why we advise you to practise it only after you are used to working with 'ah'.

When practising 'om', you can stand or sit in any position, but it is generally most effective to stand, as shown in Figure 3.7. This posture assists the energetic movement that should accompany the sound.

FIGURE 3.7: THE 'OM' SOUND POSTURE

Those who are religious or do not like religions for any reason should not worry about the hand position used in this practice. It looks as if a person is engaged in prayer, but in actual fact the hands are placed together for two main purposes. The first is to seal two large energetic exit points that sit in the centre of the palms, and the second reason is because the stretching up of the middle fingers combined with the light pressing together of the palms helps the body to send its own internal energy towards the core of the body. This will then help the vibration force inside the body to move upwards into the Dan Tien.

All of the principles for the Wuji posture apply, apart from the raising of the hands in the position shown in Figure 3.7. The hands are then held in front of the space between the eyebrows, as this is the natural energetic exit point for information coming from the upper Dan Tien.

As before, use enough volume in your practice to gain a strong feeling of a physical vibration before beginning to make it quieter as you are able to connect deeper with the practice.

As stated above, the 'om' sound has two main parts. The first part is the 'o', which is the same as the sound in the middle of words such as 'fox' or 'box'. The second part is the 'm', held as an extended 'mmmmmm' sound, which always generates a clear feeling of vibration. The first part should be used initially to bring the vibration force up to the correct height and then the 'mmmmmm' sound is held in order to maximise the vibration within the upper Dan Tien. The resultant sound is 'ooooooooooooooommmmmmmmmmmmmm', which is held throughout your exhalation.

Note that this use of 'om' is different from other traditions, where it would be more accurately spelled phonetically as 'auhm'. Rather than focusing on its esoteric spiritual functions, in this practice we are simply utilising it as a force to generate internal vibration within the energy body.

Practising the 'Hong' Sound

The third and final sound discussed in this book is the sound of 'hong'. In the Daoist tradition there are countless sounds used. Many of the sounds used are single-syllable tones such as the three shown here. These simple sounds are used as discussed to generate internally based vibrations. Beyond this there are other variations including longer multiple-syllable sounds, esoteric phrases which contain empowered meaning and then personalised chants which can only be taught and passed on by a realised master. Whatever the function and 'mechanics' behind such exercises, the basis for all of them is becoming familiar with the single-syllable tones such as the ones described in this chapter.

The 'hong' sound is generally the most difficult sound for women to connect with as it is the sound that works with the lower Dan Tien. It is for this reason that we decided to include it as the third sound in this chapter, although there is not really a strict order in which they must be trained.

As with the previous sound, any posture can be used, but the most effective is the Wuji position shown in Figure 3.8. Exact alignment details for Wuji are outlined in Chapter 6.

FIGURE 3.8: WUJI FOR 'HONG' SOUND PRACTICE

When practising this sound, allow your awareness to rest gently in the lower abdomen so you can begin to 'listen' for the vibrations generated through the practice of 'hong'. As before, start fairly loud; the more you can vocalise the sound, the easier it will be to begin feeling the physical vibrations as they move through the body. Continue practising the sound and adjusting it until you can feel it resonating strongly in the region of the lower Dan Tien. As stated above, this can be quite difficult at first, but persevere and before long you will have an effective practice for vibrating the energy in the lower abdomen, which will then benefit the organs in this region, including the Uterus.

The 'hong' sound is made up of three main parts. The first is the clear 'h' sound at the beginning, which is the same sound as at the beginning of words such as 'hat' or 'hot'. It is said quickly in the same way as in these two words, so the 'h' sound is not held. Its function is to help engage the muscles of the lower abdominal region, so in order to do this you should say it fairly loudly. This engagement of the lower region of the abdomen helps to bring the vibration down into the lower Dan Tien. The second aspect of the sound is the 'o', which is the same as for 'om'. The difference is that with 'hong' there is less time spent with the sound as it is only used to generate the vibration. If you emphasise this sound for too long, you will end up raising the vibration too high within the body. The third aspect of 'hong' is the 'ng' sound. This sound is a little trickier to describe. It would be like making the sound at the end of 'ing' and then holding it as an extended vibrating tone.

When all of this is put together, the resultant sound of 'hooooongggggggggggggggggggggggggggggggg' should be made with the correct level of emphasis upon each aspect of the sound.

STAGES OF PROGRESSION FOR SOUND WORK

In order to move towards the deeper aspects of working with these three sounds, you must first have successfully completed the foundation-level attainments. You should continue to train regularly with observing the breath and making the three sounds until you can easily move through the progressive stages outlined earlier in this chapter. You should have managed to even out your breath, still the mind to a certain degree and then have connected the vibration produced from your sound practice out from the relevant Dan Tien into the auric field. We believe that anybody can do all of the above with little difficulty, providing that they practise diligently and are realistic with regard to timescales. You should expect all of this to take several months rather than several weeks. If you manage to do all of this on your first attempt, then you should seriously consider whether or not you really have attained everything you think you have. The results drawn from these practices should always be strong. If they are subtle and could possibly be explained away as autosuggestion or imagination, then put it down to just that. Keep practising until the results are so clear that there is no doubt whatsoever that you are ready to move on.

If you are sure that your foundation is successfully completed, then you will find that your sound can become progressively quieter until you are issuing no sound at all. For the majority of Westerners, we have seen that this stage is quite desirable, so many people try to rush through to this stage too quickly. There are obviously practical issues with standing in your front room shouting these sounds loudly, and then there is the other issue of many people being very shy. When we teach large groups of people together, it becomes one of our first tasks to move through the lines of people encouraging many of them to raise the volume. If you have ever been to a Chinese park in the morning, you may have had the good fortune to hear practitioners there working on their sound practice. There was one park in particular that we used to visit, to the East of Shandong province, where there were many women working on their sound exercises. It was so loud that it was sometimes more akin to primal screaming!

Once your body has learned how to connect the vibration to the various sounds, then you will find that even just thinking of the sound itself, or saying it in your head, starts the vibration without there being any need for externalising it any more. This is a high stage of practice, though, so be prepared to take some time before you reach it.

Each of the three tones outlined in this chapter is associated with one of the three Dan Tien. These key energy centres sit within different regions of the body and connect to the functioning of various organs within the body. As the vibrations move into the correct areas, they cause a 'repatterning' of the energetic information within the body. The result is that the sounds can be used to work with the health of the organs outlined in Table 3.1.

TABLE 3.1: DAN TIEN CONNECTIONS

Dan Tien	Dan Tien Associations
Upper	Brain, mental faculties, sense organs, sense of clarity
Middle	Heart, Lungs, breasts, emotions
Lower	Kidneys, Intestines, Bladder, Uterus, Liver, Spleen, Stomach, Gall Bladder, physical power, sex drive

In addition, sound practice can tackle a key issue that many women, but not all, suffer from. This is an inability to express themselves in some way. Societally, there has long been a history of oppression of women; sadly, this has taken place in the vast majority of cultures worldwide. Although, in many cases, things are starting to change, we are still far from being at a level of equality between genders. Even in cases where equality may be close to being achieved on a practical level, there are still deep imprinted scars upon the spiritual psyche of many women. One result of this is a difficulty expressing oneself in public. This can manifest in different ways, some more obvious to see than others. The more overtly clear expressions of this are the overly demure stereotypes by which many women still feel constrained. In social situations women are often expected to be quieter than their male counterparts, and many women subconsciously implant these societally based imbalances upon themselves, as well as suffering from men projecting these imbalances on to them. Consequently, men are often allowed to dominate conversations and voice their opinions more strongly. This all contributes to women having difficulty with their own self-expression. Other ways in which women often struggle is with artistic expression, emotional self-expression or sexual expression. Whatever the reason for the oppression, women often suffer greatly from this problem, and this in turn contributes to the blocking of the middle Dan Tien. Every aspect of the human psyche is linked to an area of the energetic system, and the Heart centre really needs to express itself in order to be healthy. Perhaps here is the energetic basis for the undeniable healing effects of things such as art therapy.

As women become more accomplished at sound practice, we often see the results of this generating change with regard to their ability to self-express. Many women start becoming more confident when it comes to saying what they really mean or feel. Many start finding that they become more interested in artistic pursuits and overall this always brings great benefits to their level of wellbeing. Sadly, it has also been known for this positive growth to be difficult for their male partners, especially if they do not have an internal practice of their own. It was a real eye-opener for us to see just how many relationships seem to be based around male domination. As soon as the wife/girlfriend starts to reach a level in their training where self-expression becomes easier, problems start to develop at home as the threatened male partner does not like the change taking place. A balanced relationship should surely be based around both partners rejoicing in any personal evolution their partner has made.

THE ATTAINMENT OF INTERNAL SOUND

A strange phenomenon that seems to manifest out of prolonged practice of sound work is the development of the internal sounds. When you have experienced these internal sounds, it is a sign that your tone is as close to perfect as you are likely to get. You have successfully managed to resonate with the correct energy centre, and on top of that you have opened up one of the deep connections within the meridian system that joins the Dan Tien into the congenital rotations of the energy body.

An internal sound is a second sound which takes place on top of the noise you are making in your practice. This sound comes from somewhere deep inside the body and yet can clearly be heard. After a few times of experiencing these internal sounds, it is normal to realise that you are not 'hearing' the sound through your ears in the conventional manner, but rather your mind is directly interpreting the information contained in the energy moving within your body. These sounds cannot be missed; they are neither quiet nor subtle. They sound as though somebody has a flute and is playing one of the higher notes very loudly. The tone produced is generally constant and lasts as long as you are making the external sound.

With practice, you will find that each of the three Dan Tien has their own internal sound, although they each sound like different notes played on a flute. It is funny that nobody outside of you can hear them, because they are so loud that they drown out your own sounds!

Experience has shown us that practitioners generally experience these internal sounds for short periods of time as they practise. For most people, it tends to be over a few weeks if they are training regularly, and then the sounds begin to fade away as the body normalises the phenomenon. These periods then come and go if the practitioner is progressing well with their practice. Each time they appear for a practitioner, they bring with them great changes to their energetic and emotional nature, so they are a good milestone in your training. The other place they are often experienced is in meditation, particularly alchemical systems of meditation from the Daoist tradition. In the case of sounds heard in meditation, there tends to be a greater range of sounds due to the more subtle nature of the practice.

CONCLUSION OF SOUND PRACTICE

This chapter has outlined a basic exercise for regulating the breath as well as three simple sound exercises. As stated at the beginning of this chapter, there are other breathing exercises that can be used in Nei Gong, but we felt that women connect well with the methods outlined here, especially extending the breath outwards into sound practice. If a woman begins to work on these exercises regularly alongside her daily Qi Gong or Nei Gong training, she will find that it helps to establish a solid foundation in energetic awareness as well as with her health.

Chapter 4

THE MOON,
MENSTRUATION
AND MENOPAUSE

I t is clearly stated in classical Chinese medical literature that men are governed mainly by the quality of their Qi, whereas women should be concerned primarily with the quality of their Blood. This refers both to the Blood that moves around the body within the various vessels and capillaries and to menstrual Blood which is deemed to be a slightly different substance. One major facet of regulating the Blood is obviously to work with and understand the nature of the menstrual cycle and the impact this has on the energetic rhythms of a woman.

Any woman engaging in practice of the Daoist internal arts will find that she develops much faster if she is able to understand how her health is related to the nature of her menstruation. By working with and improving the quality of her monthly cycle, she can build a solid foundation from which to begin moving deeper into the Nei Gong process.

For a great many women, menstruation is a general nuisance which brings monthly cramping, discomfort and fatigue. Emotional upheaval is often expected, and few women understand how the act of menstruating can be a positive and cleansing experience. An internal arts practitioner needs to learn how to work with and harness the benefits of the menstrual cycle, rather than seeing it as an inconvenience. One of the worst things that a woman can do is actively seek to stop her menstrual cycle through the use of prescribed medication as many women do. This immediately causes the loss of the benefits of the menstrual cycle, which can lead to the development of energetic and emotional problems in later life.

In brief, the way to regulate the menstrual cycle is to bring it into harmony with the natural energetic rhythms of the external environment, in particular the moon. If this can be done, then the monthly cycle becomes a kind of regular detox for both the body and spirit. These monthly cleanses prepare the way for menopause, which is known in Daoism as the 'second spring', the dawn of a woman's spiritual maturity.

THE MOON

Human Beings and the Moon

The moon is continuously rotating around the Earth, causing a whole array of magnetic and energetic effects to take place over the course of a lunar month. These cycles take approximately 29.5 days to complete, the same length as a full cycle of menstruation. This direct correlation is no coincidence, and every ancient culture understood how the cyclical movement of energy within all living creatures was a direct result of the cycles taking place in the external environment. The human body is only a microcosmic reflection of the larger macrocosm in which we live, and this is why the easiest and most efficient way to improve your overall health is to bring yourself into harmony with the fluctuating energies that exist all around you. Unfortunately, in an age when artificial lifestyles have largely separated us from the environment, this is becoming increasingly difficult.

For women, many of the greatest health benefits can be had by learning how to reconnect with the energy of the moon, the astrological body long associated with feminine power.

The moon shifts through various stages according to human perception from the planet Earth. These stages are based around the four key points of Tai Yin, Shao Yang, Tai Yang and Shao Yin. Between these four points, the moon has a sliding gradient of Yin and Yang energy. This concept is shown in Figure 4.1. Note that on this diagram the inner ring of moon images shows how the sun's light is actually shining upon the planet. The outer ring shows how the moon is then viewed from standing upon the Earth's surface. This diagram is drawn showing the moon phases for a person living in the Northern hemisphere.

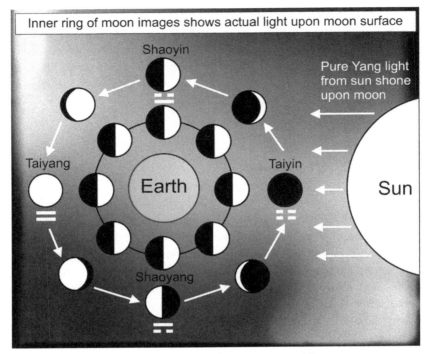

FIGURE 4.1: THE FOUR STAGES OF THE MOON

The various stages of the moon exert a different balance of Yin and Yang energy upon the planet, which in turn influences human life. The dark moon is the time when the position of the moon and the sun means that no light is shone upon the moon's surface as far as people standing on the Earth can see. This is the most Yin time of the lunar month. As the positions of the three bodies begin to shift, some of the sun's light upon the moon becomes visible from the Earth and so we have the emergence of Yang energy, which then rises until we reach the most Yang period, the full moon. From here the shift from Yang to Yin begins as we move back towards the apparent darkness of the dark moon. The comparative Yin and Yang balances of the four main stages of the moon are shown in Figure 4.2. Classically these phases were known as Tai Yin, Shao Yang, Tai Yang and Shao Yin as indicated.

Moon Phases of Northern Hemisphere

Tai Yin	**Shao Yin**	**Tai Yang**	**Shao Yang**
Qi and Blood are at their most Yin. They sink in the body	*Qi and Blood begin to rise*	*Qi and Blood are at their most Yang. They are high in the head*	*Qi and Blood begin to sink*

Moon Phases of Southern Hemisphere

Tai Yin	**Shao Yin**	**Tai Yang**	**Shao Yang**
Qi and Blood are at their most Yin. They sink in the body	*Qi and Blood begin to rise*	*Qi and Blood are at their most Yang. They are high in the head*	*Qi and Blood begin to sink*

FIGURE 4.2: THE YIN AND YANG BALANCE OF THE MOON'S PHASES

The key way in which the moon's movements affect the human body is through the movement of both Blood and Shen. Blood is considered to be the more Yin counterpart of Qi, and Blood is also considered to be the physical root through which Shen flows through the rest of the human system. In the same way that the phases of the moon exert their influence upon the shifting tides of the oceans, Blood and Shen move through us in time with the moon's phases. When the dark moon is in the sky, our Blood and Shen are in a more Yin state, while around the time of the full moon our Blood and Shen become more active and enter into their most Yang period. It is because of the moon's pull upon the Shen that psychiatric illnesses tend to flare up in people around the full moon.

The Moon and the Thrusting Meridian

As discussed in Chapter 2, we have a deep and powerful energetic branch of the congenital meridian system running directly through the core of our body. This is the vertical channel of the Thrusting meridian, which has long been known to be of prime concern to practitioners of energy work and meditation. In Chinese medical literature, it is often also referred to as the 'sea of Blood' because the movement of energy within the Thrusting meridian directly controls the level of energy stored in our Blood as well as its tendency to want to flow either inward or outward and down. This is more apparent in women as the movement of the 'sea of Blood', along with the Uterus, controls the menstrual cycle. Figure 4.3 shows the movement of energy within the Thrusting meridian according to the movement of the dark and full moon.

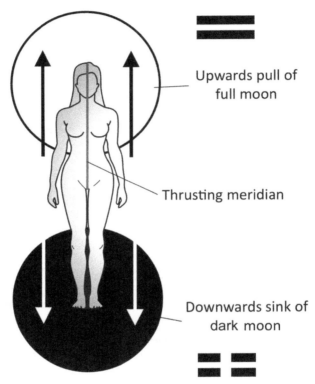

Upwards pull of full moon

Thrusting meridian

Downwards sink of dark moon

FIGURE 4.3: THE MOON AND THE THRUSTING MERIDIAN

At later stages in Nei Gong training it is possible for the Thrusting meridian to open up and connect with the external environment. This is a major part of the 'large water wheel' aspect of Nei Gong, which is considered a prerequisite for any internal arts practitioner who wishes to connect with the higher-frequency levels of awareness classically associated with the Heavenly realm. In this way we can say that the vertical branch of the Thrusting meridian serves as a kind of 'spiritual antenna' which leads us towards heightened states of awareness. These kinds of developmental stages are actually much easier for women to contact through their practice than men, as long as they can learn how to balance the energy of the Thrusting meridian; a large part of this is learning how to coordinate the body's menstrual cycles with the phases of the moon. This helps to regulate the movement of Blood, the physical transport of the Shen, which then invigorates the Thrusting meridian with information. The opening of this vertical energetic pathway takes place upon the night of the full moon.

The key reason this takes place is because the sun is sending Yang energy in the form of its light towards the moon's surface. As this light passes the Earth, it causes a rising of planetary Qi towards the moon. In this way Yin (the planet) is moving towards Yang (the full moon), creating a high potential for the growth and transformation of profound stillness. This concept is shown in Figure 4.4.

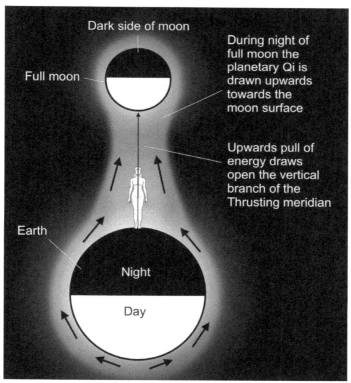

FIGURE 4.4: THE PLANETARY QI MOVING TOWARDS THE MOON

This concept also becomes useful for women at later stages in their training when they wish to begin opening up the vertical branch of the Thrusting meridian.

TIAN GUI – MENSTRUAL BLOOD

As discussed previously, the classical Chinese term for menstrual Blood is Tian Gui. This 'Heavenly Water' is seen as a different substance from the Blood that flows through the rest of the body. Figure 4.5 shows the Chinese characters for Tian Gui.

FIGURE 4.5: TIAN GUI

The term 'Tian' literally means Heaven, which denotes a connection between menstrual Blood and the movements of the Heavenly bodies, in particular the moon. It also denotes a spiritual connection that exists between the menstrual Blood and the Shen. 'Gui' is a term taken from a classical system of categorising the five elemental phases into Yin and Yang divisions. Gui is the Yin Water phase of this system which connects menstrual Blood to the Water elemental organ of the Kidneys, in particular its Yin substance of Jing. This shows us that menstrual Blood or Tian Gui is in part comprised of Jing, human essence. This Jing is converted into Tian Gui where it moves into the Uterus to be housed ready for menstruation.

THE MOON'S CYCLE

The Yang Phase

The moon's phase moves into Yang from the moment the first light begins to appear upon the surface of the moon. For roughly 14 days the moon moves towards being full. During this time Yin begins to fade away and Yang begins to increase. Figure 4.6 shows the increase of Yang over a 14-day period.

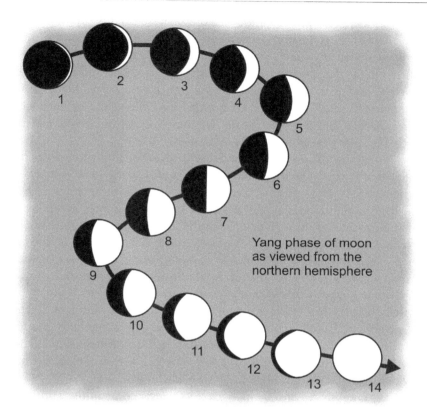

FIGURE 4.6: THE YANG PHASE OF THE MOON'S CYCLE

The movement of the moon towards being full exerts an upwards-pulling motion upon the body and in particular the vertical branch of the Thrusting meridian. Qi and Shen are caused to become increasingly more active and the Thrusting meridian is said to become increasingly 'full'. The upwards lift of the energy of the moon creates a pull on the energy of the Uterus, meaning that it is not a natural time for the Tian Gui to leave the body through menstruation. Ideally, in a perfectly balanced and healthy woman, this should be the period of time where a woman is most fertile and ovulating. In ancient times the druids saw the hare as a symbol of fertility because hares gathered together to mate under the light of the full moon. It is interesting to note, though, that in classical Chinese thought it was considered healthiest for a woman to be fertile and ovulating around the phase of the full moon. A child conceived around the phase of the full moon was seen as more likely to have a healthy abundance of Jing, Qi and Shen. On the flipside, parents with a history of psychiatric illness or hyper internal sensitivity were advised to avoid conception on the night of the full moon as there would be a chance that the child would be born with a hyperactive and unrooted Shen. For these parents, the night directly before or after the full moon was recommended.

During the full moon it was said that Qi and Blood fully nourished the muscles of the body, so on this day people should experience a high degree of vitality and strength. This increase takes place from the movement of the dark moon towards the full moon. As people grow more in tune with their body's cycles through practice of the internal arts, these fluctuations become increasingly apparent. The day before a full moon and on the full moon itself would be great times to run a marathon, but the dark moon would not be a good time; the run would be much harder indeed.

Women in particular should pay attention to these cycles if they wish to fully harness the benefit of the moon's effects. On the run-up to the full moon and on the full moon itself, they should engage in working strongly with their body in order to maximise their physical fitness. During the more Yin phase of the moon's cycle, regular exercise is still important but a woman should not push herself to the same level.

The Yang phases of the moon exert a strong pull upon the Thrusting meridian, which causes the Shen to become more active. This is shown in Figure 4.7.

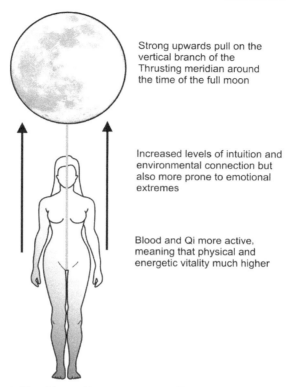

Strong upwards pull on the vertical branch of the Thrusting meridian around the time of the full moon

Increased levels of intuition and environmental connection but also more prone to emotional extremes

Blood and Qi more active, meaning that physical and energetic vitality much higher

FIGURE 4.7: THE YANG MOON AND THE THRUSTING MERIDIAN

When this happens, it means that a person's spirit is more capable of connecting outwards into the external environment. Innate intuition becomes more heightened, but, unfortunately, so do the imbalanced emotional aspects of the Shen, meaning that emotional extremes can be more prevalent around the full moon. It is important for a practitioner to understand this and learn how to work towards balancing their emotional state in order to avoid the moon's pull causing emotional upset. It is also quite normal for a person to have difficulty with calming the mind or getting to sleep due to the hyperactivity of Yang within the spirit.

The Yin Phase

The Yin phase of the moon's cycle takes place from the start of darkness appearing upon the full moon's face. Here there is an approximately 14-day decrease in Yang energy and an increase in Yin energy which peaks at the appearance of the dark moon. Figure 4.8 shows the Yin phase of the moon's cycle.

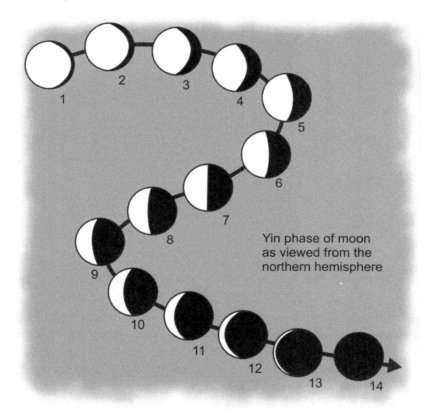

Yin phase of moon as viewed from the northern hemisphere

FIGURE 4.8: THE YIN PHASE OF THE MOON'S CYCLE

This waning of the moon's energy causes energy to take on a more subdued 'sinking' action. Those tuned in to their energetic state of being will find that they tend to have less energy and can even feel the sinking of their energy towards the Earth.

The descending, Yin action of the moon's energy causes the Thrusting meridian to react in the same way. This means that it is the most natural point in time for the Tian Gui to be released from the Uterus. Around the time of the dark moon, when the energy of the environment is at its most Yin, is the most beneficial time for a woman to menstruate. This is the time when the 'descending' action of menses matches the downwards effect of the moon.

The Yin action of the moon means that Qi and Blood are not invigorating the muscles to a very great degree and so people will naturally tend to have less vitality and lower levels of strength around the Yin phases of the moon. This should be a time of more peaceful activity, in particular for women who have managed to cause their menstrual cycle to move into sync with the phases of the moon. This is a time of internal cleansing and has long been considered the most beneficial time for women to engage in quiet contemplation. The attention of the Shen is naturally directed inwards and so women practitioners can draw great insights into the state of their own being if they learn how to harness the Yin state of this phase of the moon's cycle.

For women who have reached synchronisation between the moon's phases and their menstrual cycle, it is obviously not likely that they will conceive on the dark moon. The Daoists considered it potentially very harmful for a woman to engage in sexual activity during menses, and even women whose cycle was not in time with the moon's phases were advised against intercourse around the dark moon. A child conceived on a new moon was said to be likely to develop chronic illnesses early in life due to having a low amount of congenital essence.

MENSES AND EMOTIONAL CLEANSING

Emotional cleansing is an important aspect of menstruation which should be studied and understood by all female practitioners of the internal arts. Our emotions are simply forms of information that move through our energetic system. This information generates the experience of an emotion, as well as causing changes to the state of our energy body, which then has a continued effect upon our physical body. This is the mind–body energetic connection that is an important part of any Daoist study. Figure 4.9 summarises this concept.

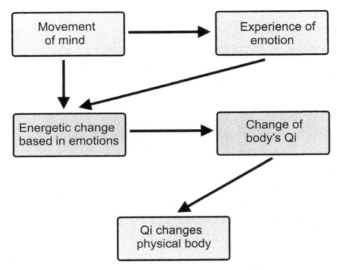

FIGURE 4.9: THE MIND–BODY EMOTIONAL CONNECTION

Our emotions are a product of the movement of mind as well as the interaction of the five spirits, aspects of Shen which interrelate over the course of our daily lives to generate conscious thought.

The Blood travels through the body via the arteries, capillaries and other blood vessels, driven by the Heart. In ancient Chinese medical thought, the Heart not only governs the Blood but also houses the core of our spirit and enables us to experience emotions. This means that all emotional information is processed by the organ of the Heart, where it then manifests within our mind, ready for us to experience the various shifts taking place in our consciousness. This is of particular importance for women to understand, as excessive emotional disturbances actually cause a woman to begin feeling drained due to the connection between the chest region and the Jing, which was discussed in Chapter 2.

The spirit that is housed within the Heart refracts into various parts corresponding to the five elemental energies of Fire, Earth, Metal, Water and Wood. These five elemental phases then exist within the Blood, which is a liquid crystalline structure. These elements are transported through the Blood out into the rest of the body. With this information is transported emotional debris, which then makes its way down into the Uterus where it combines with the acquired Jing of the Kidneys to form Tian Gui. What this means is that the emotional experiences a woman has had over the course of the previous month will result in pathogenic debris which is transported down through the body in the Blood to the Uterus. When she menstruates, she evacuates this emotional debris along with her menstrual Blood, which results in a cleansing of the body. If this can happen effectively, then the flushing of these unwanted emotional energies will help her to centre her mind and restrict the draining effect that these emotions would otherwise have been having upon the Jing stored in her chest. This is all summarised in Figure 4.10.

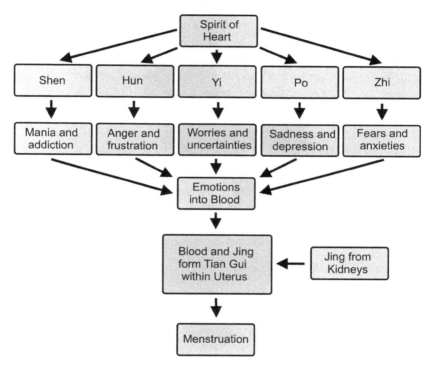

FIGURE 4.10: THE MOVEMENT OF EMOTIONAL DEBRIS
FROM THE HEART TO THE TIAN GUI

This is important due to the natural centripetal movement of female energy. The natural inclination for a woman's energy is to move from the outside of her auric field inwards towards her core, where it moves into the region of her Heart. It is here within the region of the Heart that the resultant collection point of this centripetally moving energy begins to be expressed through emotional movements. If a woman is unable to express her emotions healthily and thus vent them, she will likely begin to become drained by them. Part of the way in which a woman 'vents' these emotions is in the removal of the pathogenic emotional debris through her monthly cycle. Male energy naturally moves outwards in a centrifugal pattern. This means that men do not experience the same level of draining due to emotional patterns, but they do lose more energy through physical exertion as well as through other aspects of their psyche such as externally perceived desires, which can exert much more of a pull on the male consciousness.

It is this natural centripetal movement that needs to be understood and worked with effectively in order to ensure that a woman maximises the potential for her energetic health. This centripetal movement also becomes a female practitioner's biggest asset, because the inward movement of her energy makes spiritual elevation a more natural and fluid developmental process for her than for her male counterparts. Men often have to work to change the direction of their energetic flow in order to match women's if they wish to progress in an art such as Nei Gong.

THE FIVE-PHASE ELEMENTAL CLEANSE

Generally speaking, it is normal for a woman to menstruate for approximately four to five days of each monthly cycle. This timescale can vary slightly from person to person, but three to five days would be considered the norm. During this time the body will begin to expel emotional debris within the Tian Gui in the following sequence:

- Phase 1: The Water element – Kidneys and Zhi
- Phase 2: The Wood element – Liver and Hun
- Phase 3: The Fire element – Heart and Shen
- Phase 4: The Earth element – Spleen and Yi
- Phase 5: The Metal element – Lungs and Po

Each of these five phases is a time of letting go of different emotional information which corresponds to one of the major organ systems of the body as well as one of the five spirits. Each of these is discussed below. In the case of those women with a five-day menstrual bleed, these phases occur day to day, but in the case of women with a shorter period of bleeding, these phases can be much shorter. With observation, women will find that they will notice that the amount of blood shed may be slightly stronger during phases relating to emotions that are out of balance. There may also be shifts in the length of time that each phase takes during times of emotional difficulty. This is all quite normal and to be expected.

Western medical guidelines state that it would be considered normal and healthy to have a period of bleeding that lasts between two and seven days, but in Chinese medical thought these extremes would be seen as a sign of imbalance. Two days would indicate a deficiency of some kind, while seven days would be an excessive amount of time to be shedding emotional information. This length of time would be seen as a drain upon the person's spirit.

The Water Element Cleanse

During the first phase of menstruation a woman will begin to shed any emotional debris related to the emotions of fear, nervousness, anxieties or phobias. This has a powerful cleansing effect upon the Kidneys as well as the spirit of the Zhi. This is the spirit that gives us our strength of willpower as well as our connection to the higher will of Heaven, the Daoist equivalent of our destiny.

The Wood Element Cleanse

During the second phase of menstruation a woman will begin to shed emotional pathogenic debris resulting from any feelings of anger, resentment, frustration, inner loathing, jealousy or general stress. The release of these emotional factors helps to nourish the organ of the Liver as well as the spirit of the Hun, the ethereal aspect of the human soul that gives us our ability to dream and make plans. Through cleansing this element during the second phase of menstruation, a woman should find it easier to connect with these aspects of her consciousness.

The Fire Element Cleanse

During the third phase of menstruation a woman will begin to shed emotional debris related to feelings of excitation, mania, obsessiveness, lust, addiction or spiritual unrootedness. Shedding these pathogens has a healing effect upon the organ of the Heart as well as the Shen aspect of consciousness which is our connection to the divine. Cleansing the Fire element should begin to move a woman towards a state of inner contentment and enable her to connect with her higher spiritual self.

The Earth Element Cleanse

During the fourth phase of menstruation a woman will begin to shed emotional pathogenic debris resulting from feelings of worry, uncertainty, feelings of clinginess and family-related issues. Releasing these emotions has a strong nourishing effect upon the Spleen as well as the digestive system as a whole. It also helps to strengthen the Yi, which is the aspect of human consciousness that gives us our ability to mentally focus.

The Metal Element Cleanse

The fifth and final phase of menstruation is when a woman can begin to shed pathogenic factors relating to the emotions of sadness, grief, loss, depression and remorse. Shedding these pathogens helps to strengthen the organ of the Lungs as well as the spirit of the Po. This is the aspect of our consciousness that gives us a tangible understanding of the world in which we live. Any shock or emotional numbness a woman has been experiencing can begin to be cleared during the fifth phase of her menstruation.

SUMMARY OF THE MENSTRUAL CYCLE

So far we have looked at the nature of the Yin and Yang phases of the moon and how these affect the nature of a woman's menstrual cycle. These cycles and energetic movements ensure that a woman is able to cleanse emotional pathogenic debris over the course of her monthly menstruation. In the case of a balanced and environmentally connected woman, this should happen in time with the moon's movements. Below is a summary of the entire menstrual cycle that should take place over the course of a month once a woman has effectively regulated her internal cycles.

The menstrual cycle should begin after the dark moon has peaked and begun to transform into the new moon – the appearance of Yang within Yin. This is the period of movement from menstruation through to ovulation. In Western science, this is the period of time when oestrogen levels are increasing and women are moving towards being at their most fertile. The body is becoming more Yang, and there is more Qi and Blood in the system, making a woman feel strong and full of vitality. This process should take roughly 14 days but can vary between 12 and 16.

At the peak of the cycle, ovulation occurs, a process that can be clearly felt by women who are very in tune with their internal environment. At this stage it is normal for a woman's sex drive to increase for a short period. This is often around the time of the full moon, the most Yang period of the monthly cycle. It is a natural result of a woman being at her most fertile.

The second half of the cycle is the Yin phase of the monthly process. This is when many women begin to experience the negative symptoms that are commonly gathered under the heading of 'premenstrual symptoms'.

This usually begins to take place a few days after the peak of Yang with the full moon. These symptoms can include cramps, headaches, mood swings, swollen breasts and abdomen, food cravings and depression. These symptoms are a sign of the body attempting to regulate some kind of energetic imbalance, and practitioners will find that the symptoms gradually diminish in intensity once they manage to harmonise their cycles with that of the moon.

A couple of days prior to the beginning of menstruation, the ovaries cease to secrete hormones, which causes the lining of the uterus to break down and be shed along with the Tian Gui. This is the beginning of approximately three to five days of menstruation, which cleanses the body and the five elemental energies as discussed above. During this time the Tian Gui expelled should be even in amount and a healthy colour (bright red, not too dark and not too pale), with no clotting. Women will find that sometimes they will bleed more heavily on certain days of their menstrual cleanse; these days will correspond to a higher degree of emotions that need clearing from this particular elemental source.

Of course, this is an example of a balanced menstrual cycle, but many women do not follow this pattern each month. In many cases the menstrual cycle is not in sync with the phases of the moon, there is an irregular period of bleeding, including clots, and there are many uncomfortable symptoms associated with the time prior to and during menstruation. These are all signs of an internal imbalance within the body, issues that can be dealt with in a number of ways, including harmonising your cycle with the moon's movements.

MOON GAZING

The practice of moon gazing was a constant in many different ancient traditions. Although there may have been technical differences between them, each tradition based the practice upon the same principle. This is the principle that a woman's energy is largely dictated by the moon's cycles, and that if she can only reconnect with the energy of the moon, she will find that it naturally draws her back into harmony with nature's rhythms.

Moon gazing is a type of exercise that falls under the category of Shen Gong (神功). Qi Gong is the skill of learning to work with your body's Qi, whereas Shen Gong is the skill of working with your Shen. It is considered a more advanced practice than Qi Gong due to having to work with one of the most ethereal and highest vibrational frequencies within the body system. In Shen Gong exercises such as moon gazing, we learn how to use our Shen to connect with the surrounding environment. Through continued practice in this way we are able to give the energy system enough space to begin to harmonise itself with the frequency that surrounds us. This then begins to make adjustments to our inner cycles, adjustments that bring us closer to a natural state of being. The fact is that being able to accomplish any real level in Shen Gong exercises relies on having an energetic system that draws in from the environment towards the central space of the Heart. This means that male practitioners of the Daoist arts rarely have any success with Shen Gong exercises unless they have reached the more advanced stages of energetic development, whereby they have managed to adjust the natural inherent quality of male energy, which normally likes to move outwards. This is not the case for women who naturally find that they can connect with Shen Gong exercises quite easily.

In times past, when human beings lived outdoors for most of their lives, it was normal for the body to be in alignment with nature's cycles, but in modern times we are removed from the outside world. Natural light has been replaced with fluorescent electric bulbs, and the glaring light of the television set or computer is often the main light that people connect with before sleeping, instead of the moon. The nature of moonlight is that it carries a potent energetic charge, which is where the power of moon gazing comes from. If you have ever spent time living away from towns in the countryside, you may have already experienced the energetic differences between nights where the full moon is shining brightly and the stillness of dark moon nights. The nature of these energies is what we are trying to harness if we wish to bring ourselves into contact with the cycles of nature. Western science has found that the varying levels of light in the night sky have a direct effect upon a woman's hormonal levels, but the truth is that these fluctuations go much deeper, affecting every aspect of a woman's energetic and spiritual matrix.

The Practice

In order to begin moon gazing, a woman should go out into the night and look up into the sky every two to three nights for a month or more. If you wish to make it more effective, then engage in the practice every night for the duration of one or more lunar months; many women who have learned this method in our school find that it becomes a natural practice which feels so good that they adopt it for longer periods of time.

The best time to moon gaze is between the hours of 11pm and 1am, although these times can be inconvenient for a lot of people due to life commitments. In this case you should simply try to follow the practice once it is dark and the moon can be seen in the sky.

Stand outside in one of the three Qi Gong postures discussed in Chapter 5. The posture will depend upon your level of development. Now gently place your gaze and your awareness upwards on to the face of the moon. Try to keep your mind as still as possible while doing this and make sure there are no loud unnatural noises around you such as loud music, a television set or the sound of traffic going by.

After a few minutes of gazing at the moon you should then bring your mind back into the region of the chest and lightly rest your mind there while still looking at the moon. Stay in this state for around 20 minutes or so at first, although with practice you will find that your desire to stand with the moon causes your practice to extend into longer periods. After you have stood like this for a minimum of 20 minutes you should close down in the same manner as you would with any Qi Gong exercise and walk around loosening the joints for a few minutes.

When you are new to this practice, you will find that very little happens. It is the same with any new exercise; it can take time for your energy system to get used to what you are doing. Once you have practised for some time, though, you will find that a slight magnetic pull begins to take place between the moon and yourself. It will become strongest when you bring the mind back into the region of your chest. This pull can vary between a slight sensation of being magnetised by the moon through to being strong enough to pull you forward off your feet. If this happens, don't worry; it is a very normal reaction to the interaction between the moon's energy and your own. This reaction will subside after some time as the body normalises the magnetic connection and so enables the body to adjust enough to resist the reaction.

Stay with your practice until you get around to gazing at the full moon. This is when the full connection begins to take place. The result is that your perception of the moon will go through the four stages shown in Figure 4.11.

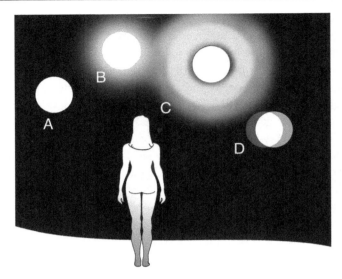

FIGURE 4.11: FULL MOON GAZING PHENOMENA

The four phases have been labelled A through to D and it is common to go through each of these stages in order, although this is not always the case. Each of the four stages of connecting with the moon is discussed below.

A. The first stage of looking at the moon yields little in the way of visual results. At this stage the white circle of the full moon does not alter in any obvious way. It is generally the case that in order to move through into the further stages of connection a woman must continue her practice through for a second cycle or more. Even without moving through to further experiences, a woman will still find that her menstrual cycle begins to shift through these practices.

B. The second stage of connecting with the full moon causes the moon to produce a halo of light which expands out around it for some distance. This halo of light is quite different from the usual white glow that generally surrounds the moon. This light is much brighter and almost feels as if it swallows up your perception so that only the moon and its surrounding halo are left in front of you. The light often pulses in time with your breath, becoming brighter as you exhale and fading as you breathe in. Some women have reported that the halo turns a deep purple for them, but this is not so common.

C. The third stage of connecting with the moon results in the halo of light beginning to separate out from the moon's border. It often still maintains its pulse but now spreads out like a ring of light which expands away from the moon itself. The size of the halo's expansion away from the moon varies from person to person, but in each case it is clear to see. Some women have said that they can hear a low humming noise coming from the moon when it reaches this stage.

D. The fourth and final stage of connecting with the moon comes with a very particular visual reaction. In this case the moon begins to look as if it is shaking from side to side. Like an image that is flickering in and out of focus, it can shake quite quickly and even begin to change with regard to how 'in focus' it is. Some women have also reported perceiving an alternate blurring and sharpening of the moon's edges. If you reach this level of connection, then your Blood and Shen are said to have begun fully resonating with the moon's influence. This should bring about strong nourishing effects for the body and the mind. A woman who reaches this level should experience a healthy shift in her menstrual cycle and any associated bodily symptoms that she generally has with regard to menstruation. This level of connection can sometimes bring about strong emotional releases, often in the form of tears, so do not worry if this takes place. In rare instances the connection to the full moon at this stage can cause a strong reaction in the pelvic region and some women have spontaneously reached orgasm through the moon's effect. Once again, this is nothing to be concerned about; the reaction is produced as a by-product of the moon's influence causing shifts within a woman's energetic makeup.

CHANGES TO MENSTRUAL CYCLE

There are various reasons why a female practitioner of Nei Gong should seek to regulate her menstrual cycle through practices such as moon gazing. These reasons are partly to do with nourishing health but also with establishing a solid foundation upon which to develop further through Nei Gong training. As you become more proficient, you should find that your menstrual cycle changes to match the moon, with menstruation taking place around the time of the new moon. Your bleed should become smooth, with no clots or discolouration. There should be a lessening of premenstrual symptoms and a settling of the mind, meaning that there should be no mood swings before your period begins.

If this can be achieved, then you will notice the following benefits:

• There should be an improvement in your levels of vitality. This is because of the relationship between the Uterus and Kidneys becoming more balanced.

- It is possible that many physical imbalances improve. In Chinese medical thought, the organ systems of the Liver and Spleen are also involved with the functioning of the Uterus. As your menstruation improves, it is normal for these associated organs to become nourished, which can lead to many changes to your wellbeing.

- There should be an overall improvement of your emotional wellbeing due to the Heart now efficiently expelling emotional pathogenic debris into the Blood, where it can be expelled each month from the body.

- Premenstrual symptoms, both physical and emotional, should subside.

- Due to the increase in efficiency of the Jing movement through the body that comes with regulating the menstrual cycle, it should be much easier to begin working through the foundation stages of Nei Gong training which involve awakening the lower Dan Tien. Of course, this stage can be worked on alongside regulation of the menstrual cycle, but if you have achieved a solid base in your connection to the moon, then lower Dan Tien work is much easier to progress on to and past.

- There will be a stronger flow of information along the length of the vertical branch of the Thrusting meridian when menstruation is regulated and a good level of connection to the moon has been achieved. This will assist a woman with developing a stronger connection to the external environment. This in turn will further develop her intuition when dealing with situations in life and those around her.

Even for a woman who does not wish to go further into any internal training, it can be useful for her to practise moon gazing simply for these benefits alone.

SLAYING THE RED DRAGON

The rather unsubtly named practice of 'slaying the red dragon' refers to a commonly practised internal method that aims to end the menstrual cycle. Women who have been through this practice literally end menstruation, meaning that they do not shed any blood at all each month. The logic behind this is that since women lose some of their essence each month through menstruation, stopping it will store this essence and so prolong their life. It will also help to establish a strong foundation for advanced alchemical practices. Although this logic is sound, it does come with various risks, not least being that menstruation has various cleansing benefits, as discussed above. As a practice, it is actually fairly simple, and with a few months of regular breath control and reversal of several internal flows, your menstrual cycle quickly ends. We have met many women who have practised this method, as it is quite common in the West as well as in China. A great number of these women actually had numerous health issues that resulted from this practice, and for this reason we strongly advise against it.

Slaying the red dragon is a practice that was originally reserved for those living full-time as nuns away from the rest of society. They would be practising under the strict guidance of an experienced teacher who was there to monitor every part of their practice. In addition to this, they did not have the responsibilities that many 'lay' practitioners of the Daoist arts do. Engaging in such a practice is much safer if you do not have the daily concerns of career, family, household and so on. Sexual activity was cut out for these women as well, since intercourse had a pulling effect upon the essence, which could disrupt the practice. If, however, you are one of the rare women who has undertaken this practice and been safe with it, then well done – there are always exceptions to the rule.

The major danger of this practice is to do with the Bao's function of storing Blood within the body. If there is a break in the natural cycle of developing and then shedding menstrual Blood, then there is a risk of stagnation occurring within the Blood itself. This will then stagnate the body's internal energy, which leads to various physical symptoms. The Shen is also rooted into the Blood, and so stagnation here will run the risk of disturbing a practitioner emotionally.

For the majority of female practitioners of the Daoist arts, we highly recommend regulating the menstrual cycle through healthy living, calming the mind and engaging in practices such as moon gazing.

MENOPAUSE

Women's energetic physiology can be divided up roughly into three key life stages. The first is pre-puberty when menstruation has not yet started, the second is post-puberty when menstruation has strongly activated the Blood's energetic cycles, and the third is the stage of entering the menopause.

Menopause is referred to as a woman's 'second spring' in Daoist literature. It is a stage in life when a woman enters a potential phase of spiritual growth resulting from the culmination of her previous years. For many women in the West, menopause is seen as something to be nervous of or even ashamed of. There is a great deal of completely illogical negativity around a woman's menopause. We have even heard of women saying that they feel worthless and less of a woman since they entered their menopause. On top of this, it often comes with various negative health symptoms, the most common being hot flushes. All of this added together means that the menopause is often seen by women as a negative phase in their life rather than the phase of potential growth it is supposed to be. In the West, we need to make a large shift in mindset and stop seeing menopause as something that must be treated almost as a disease, and instead see it as a natural phase of evolution.

Menopause is not something that just happens to a woman all of a sudden. It is a culmination of a process that begins at birth. Pre-puberty, post-puberty and menopause are one and the same thing; they are just three different stages on a continuum of development. Menopause was known as a 'second spring' for women because it was at this point that they were freed from many of the cycles of Jing and Tian Gui which obviously have a strong effect upon their vitality and mind states. The fluctuations of mood throughout the course of a month become more settled and so, providing a woman is experiencing a healthy menopausal shift, she will naturally find it easier to bring the mind inside. Although the cleansing of emotional debris during menstruation no longer takes place each month, a woman in her second spring should have a tendency towards a higher degree of mental stability. This is because the nature of her Heart-mind should be more settled.

According to classical Daoist thought, women operate to the numerological pattern of the number seven and so at the culmination of this number – seven multiplied by seven – we get the age of 49. This was said to be the age at which women should begin to recognise that they are entering the menopausal phase of their life. Chinese medical literature states that after menopause the Tian Gui is diminished, the Thrusting meridian and the Conception meridian no longer dominate a woman's energetic physiology, and she can no longer conceive. This age of 49 is only an approximate age, though; due to variations in women's health and lifestyle, this age can vary to a certain degree, with the majority of women actually entering the peak of the menopausal change in their early 50s. If a woman enters menopause very early, then this a sign of an internal imbalance which should be looked at, and it is wise to consult a skilled Chinese medical practitioner for guidance and treatment in this instance. In modern times a lot of women have entered menopause early because of having a hysterectomy. In this case it is also wise to go and receive Chinese medical treatment in the form of herbs or acupuncture as this can help greatly with any disruptions to the energy system that have taken place.

Menopausal Symptoms

The vast majority of women in the Western world will experience various negative symptoms associated with entering the menopause. These symptoms can last anywhere between a few months and several years. Common symptoms include hot flushes, headaches, insomnia, night sweating, fuzzy-headedness, tiredness, mood swings and backache. These symptoms are generated as a result of various organ imbalances. The chart shown in Figure 4.12 shows the various imbalances that can result from entering menopause.

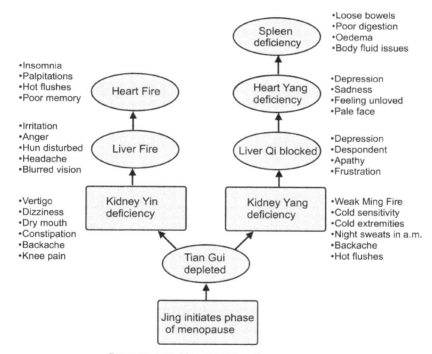

FIGURE 4.12: MENOPAUSAL IMBALANCES

We will now try to explore some of the reasons behind these imbalances and why they manifest within the body. Since this is not a Chinese medical textbook, however, we will try to keep discussion of the theory as accessible as possible. Those with an existing knowledge of Chinese medical theory should be able to explore these concepts in greater detail by looking into the many Chinese medicine textbooks that have been written on the subject.

At the base of the chart in Figure 4.12 we can see that a woman's Jing has reached the phase of its progression at which menopause has been entered into. This is a natural phase of a woman's development. Her Jing – the essence or 'blueprints' – has entered her into the next evolutionary stage of her development. This is the 'second spring', when her physiology will be moving towards becoming a platform for spiritual growth rather than reproduction. At this stage there is little transference of Jing taking place into the production of Tian Gui; the cycles of Jing now take place elsewhere in her body system. The result of this is that there is no more production of menstrual Blood and so her menstrual cycle ends. This does not mean that the woman is separated from the influence of the moon – she still circulates spiritual energy in time with its phases – but there is no more loss of menstrual Blood.

Commonly, practitioners of Chinese medicine will discuss a person developing a weakness in their Jing and then from here either the Yin or Yang aspects of the Kidneys being weakened. This is not quite correct according to Daoist Nei Gong theory, but since it is a common model which is easy to understand, we have drawn the diagram according to this theory.

The Kidneys and the Jing are closely related to each other, the Kidneys being the organ where the Jing is stored in its initial stages, as well as the organ system that is most commonly weakened if the Jing's developmental processes are imbalanced in some way. When Kidney Yang is discussed in Daoist terminology, it refers to the Kidney system's ability to generate warmth and active conversion of Jing, Qi and Shen within the body. This happens primarily as a result of the functioning of the Ming Fire, an expanding sphere of energetic information that we have sitting in the space between our Kidneys. This sphere of information speeds up the conversion of substances within the body and generates activity; it is for this reason that a person will often feel cold and weak when this Fire has become deficient. Kidney Yin is the Kidney's ability to store substances within the body, as well as the aspect of the Kidneys that keeps the Ming Fire's activities in check. If Yin is weak, then Yang moves into excess and so there will be too much hyperactivity, transformation and warmth within the body. The good health of the Kidney system exists when there is a perfect harmony between both Yin and Yang.

When Jing hits a phase of change such as entering menopause, any imbalances in a woman's wellbeing will generate negative symptoms. If she has been healthy up until this point in her life and the Kidneys are strong, there will be little in the way of menopausal symptoms. If, however, she has any weakness in either Yin or Yang, this weakness will begin to manifest within the body.

We will explore the two most common ways in which the imbalances of Jing will show up, first with symptoms pertaining to a Kidney Yin deficiency and second with symptoms of a Kidney Yang deficiency.

KIDNEY YIN DEFICIENCY

The storing and cooling aspect of the Kidneys comes under the heading of Yin. In alchemical literature, it is often known as Kidney Water – an energetic Water which controls the levels of Fire within the body. For this reason we can understand that if menopausal symptoms are based in Kidney Yin deficiency, then the result is that Yang is not held in check. Yang will become too excessive, or Water will not be controlling Fire, so there will be too much Fire in the body. An easy way to think of this is like a set of scales, as shown in Figure 4.13. When Yin is deficient, it can be thought of as going down. This raises Yang upwards; hence we get symptoms pertaining to Yang – excess and heat.

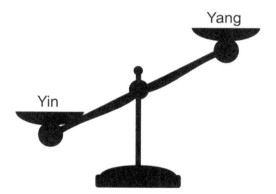

FIGURE 4.13: YIN DEFICIENCY SCALES

The key symptoms that can manifest from this deficiency of Yin are related to the Kidney system becoming weakened. In this case it is normal for the weakness to produce a weak back and knees. In addition, the extra energetic heat within the body can lead to a drying out of the bowels which can result in constipation. This same heat then leads to a chronically dry mouth, dizzy spells and, in some cases, vertigo.

If this deficiency of Yin starts to have an effect upon the Liver system, then it is said that the excess heat within this region of the body leads to the production of Liver Fire. This is a Chinese medical term which essentially shows that the Liver has become overly Yang; this causes it to produce a rising form of pathogenic energy which can lead to irritation and anger outbursts, headaches and blurred vision. There are other symptoms associated with this condition, but these are the key ways in which the Liver Fire affects a person's wellbeing during the menopause.

The deficiency of Yin will often lead to the Yang rising upwards past the Liver where it reaches the Heart organ system. As the Heart begins to generate Heart Fire, it is normal to experience bouts of insomnia, palpitations, hot flushes and a reduction in short-term memory.

KIDNEY YANG DEFICIENCY

The Kidney Yang aspect of the Ming Fire is important as it helps to generate the transformation of substances within the body, as well as providing warmth and movement. When Yang becomes deficient, we could almost think of it being like the fire going out in an old heating system. When this happens, it can lead a person to becoming overly sensitive to cold environments and having permanently cold hands and feet. It is also normal to develop night sweats, particularly around the early hours of the morning, from midnight until around 5am. There is likely to be backache and, strangely, hot flushes. Although hot flushes generally develop through Yin deficiency, there always seems to be a little heat rising upwards during any menopausal imbalances.

If this Yang deficiency starts to affect the Liver, then the lack of warming causes it to become stagnant. The Liver Qi will become blocked and so a person will become depressed, despondent and often show signs of being apathetic to their life. If this reaches a peak, then it can lead to feelings of inner frustration, which are difficult for a woman to express.

As the deficiency of Yang energy begins to reach the Heart, it can cause a lowering of a person's mood and a constant feeling of being unloved. This can lead to chronic feelings of being undesired or unsupported even by the most loving partner. It is not a feeling based in logic but rather the weakening of the Heart's function. It is also normal for a woman affected in this way to develop a pale complexion, although sometimes the cheeks can still be ruddy in colour.

In some cases the deficiency of Yang causes the Spleen to weaken. This then affects the digestive system, which will result in loose bowels and poor digestion. In Chinese medical thought, the Spleen system is also involved in the processing of internal body fluids, so problems can arise here, the most common being swelling and oedema.

The Second Spring

Once a woman has entered her 'second spring', she should find that she has a more settled mind. There should be less in the way of extreme emotional swings and it should be much simpler to enter into deep internal work such as meditation or advanced alchemical training. If a woman learns to trust herself, then her intuition should increase, along with her sensitivity to the energy around her. She should feel as though she is flowing through life events. Of course, this is dependent upon either going through a healthy menopausal transition or having been through it and come out at the other end. Because of the 'drying up' of the Tian Gui, there is less of a strong cycle of energy taking place with the cycles of the moon; this should cause the Shen to stabilise and the emotions to be less prone to fluctuations. The only real energetic shift that takes place within a woman during this phase of her life is an upwards lift through the vertical branch of her Thrusting meridian, a movement of information that should make it easier for her to connect with higher realms of comprehension. This should be the age at which a woman moves into her space of wisdom and has the potential to become a spiritual guide or teacher to others. Sadly, many women miss this opportunity because they do not recognise the inherent power involved in this stage of their lives.

During the 'second spring' of a woman's life she should apply the following principles if she is able:

- A woman should not work intensively during this phase of her life. The Kidney essence is not there to sustain constant mental and physical exertion. If possible, a woman should begin to cut back on her responsibilities and take it easy. Now is a time for a woman to focus upon her own internal cultivation more than anything else.

- A woman in this phase of her life should try to ensure she has some kind of still sitting practice. It does not matter what system – she should find one that suits her. There are many different meditation systems, ranging from observing the breath through to alchemical systems from the Daoist tradition. A woman in her 'second spring' will find that her ability to connect with her inner realm is much increased and she will benefit from leading the mind deeper into stillness.

- It is important for a woman to focus upon herself, not just on those around her. It is often the case that many women coming into our classes lead lives based almost entirely around other people. Whether these people are their husbands, their children or whoever, so many women rarely make time for themselves. During her 'second spring' a woman should ease back on her responsibilities for others if she is able. She should focus upon herself, her own cultivation and her own needs.

- The Heart centre will have the potential for great amounts of growth during this period of a woman's life and so it is vitally important that she find some kind of artistic outlet. The source of this outlet is unimportant, but it should be enough that a woman can learn to fully express herself with complete freedom.

- During a woman's 'second spring' she has the potential to enter into great spiritual change. In order to do this, she should only really surround herself with people who are beneficial to her growth – close friends and people who bring joy and meaning into her life.

- A woman in this phase of her life should be more naturally connected to her inner awareness, and so should trust her intuition. Her environmental connection should also be stronger, so she should spend more time in natural environments away from cities and urban living. There are great benefits to be had from connecting with the energy of nature, and this is much easier to do for a woman in her 'second spring'.

For women who have had an internal practice for some years, the transition through the menopause can often be fairly smooth. Due to the heightened self-awareness that generally comes with prolonged inner training, it is clear enough for these women to feel the shifts taking place inside of their inner environment. The result is a spontaneous transition into the 'second spring' accompanied by all of its innate spiritual strengths.

Many women come into an art such as Nei Gong either during the menopausal phase of their life or long after it has finished. For many, the menopause was or still is an uncomfortable process due to the accompanying negative symptoms. In this case it is wise to spend time working to restore some energy to your Kidneys in order to improve the situation. Soft, energetic exercises such as Qi Gong or Nei Gong are more than adequate to give your energy body a healthy source of nourishment, but a regular sitting meditation practice is also useful. Eat healthily and avoid overly greasy or sweet foods in order to help the body grow healthier. Women looking to ease menopausal symptoms should avoid drinking coffee and heavily restrict their alcohol intake; they should also avoid any unnecessary stress and not work too much. This is not a time for overexertion but internal development and self-nourishing.

Moon gazing is still a valid and important practice for women who are in the 'second spring' of their life. Although this practice will not serve to regulate the menstrual cycle, it will still connect a woman's energetic cycles into the governing force of the moon. Essence will still be stimulated, and movement along the vertical branch of the Thrusting meridian will still take place in time with the moon's phases. In fact, many of the strongest results we have had from women engaging with moon gazing have been from women who have been through the menopause.

IN CONCLUSION

This chapter has looked at the nature of the menstrual cycle, menopause, the connection of women to the moon and the practice of moon gazing. Female practitioners of Nei Gong should not underestimate the strength of these practices and their usefulness in building a foundation upon which to develop.

There is no need to become 100 per cent proficient in these practices before moving on to the basic exercises and trying to contact the lower Dan Tien. Practise these exercises alongside each other but understand that moving past the stage of working with the lower Dan Tien will take place much more quickly for those who have established a regular moon-gazing practice. Interestingly, this seems to be most important for those women who have spent their lives living in cities. The women we have taught who live in more rural areas, often working outside and close to nature, do not require such a great deal of work with the moon. It seems that the time they have spent outdoors has often been effective at keeping them connected to environmental cycles.

Chapter 5

LOTUS MOON QI GONG

In the previous chapters we have discussed the underlying theory of Nei Gong practice for women. Alongside this are the sound practices aimed at working with the three key Dan Tien and a method for connecting a woman to the cycles of the moon. In this chapter we will look at four moving Qi Gong exercises which are particularly useful for women to practise regularly. These exercises each serve to regulate a different aspect of a woman's wellbeing and as such, if practised regularly, will assist her in establishing a healthy foundation for further Nei Gong training. Collectively, these exercises are known as 'Lotus Moon Qi Gong' exercises and they consist of:

- Dark moon Qi Gong

- Three circles around the moon

- Rotating the moon

- The mysterious crucible Mudra

Each of these four exercises has specific effects upon a woman's energetic body. They are not generally practised by male Nei Gong practitioners with the exception of 'three circles around the moon', which is sometimes practised by men because of its effectiveness at improving the health and mobility of the spine and body.

DARK MOON QI GONG
This moving exercise assists in the regulation of the health of the Uterus. It causes the downward pull of the Uterus to increase around the phase of

the dark moon, which in turn assists in the emotional cleansing aspect of menstruation. It also assists in connecting women's energetic cycles into the Yin aspect of the moon, regardless of whether a woman is pre- or post-menopause. For this reason this exercise should only be practised for three days each month: the day before the dark moon, the day of the dark moon itself and finally the day after the dark moon. We have had women who practised this movement on other phases of the moon and it has actually caused an irregularity in their menstrual cycle. In many cases it brought on menstruation at the wrong time. When practising this exercise, it is most useful to train it at the correct time of the month and it is most effective if repeated for between half an hour and an hour in the evening when the moon is visible in the sky.

When preparing to practise this Qi Gong exercise, you should first stand for a few minutes in the Wuji posture, as shown in Figure 5.1. Full details of how to correctly stand in Wuji are discussed in Chapter 6.

FIGURE 5.1: PREPARING TO PRACTISE
THE DARK MOON QI GONG EXERCISE

Stand in this posture for a few minutes and simply breathe deeply. On each exhalation try to relax more and more, while at the same time allowing your mind to grow increasingly quiet. At this stage there is no need to focus on any particular region of the body; you are not using Wuji practice for any specific energetic process. By simply relaxing and breathing, you are giving the energy body time to grow more still prior to practising the movements of the exercise.

When you feel ready to begin the exercise, you should move through the sequence shown in Figure 5.2. This raising and sinking of the hands helps to establish a strong energetic connection between the Uterus and the Heart.

FIGURE 5.2: STARTING THE DARK MOON QI GONG

Begin by turning over the palms so that they face upwards towards the sky, as shown in image A. As you begin to inhale, you should slowly raise the palms up to the height of the Heart as depicted in image B. This movement should be long and slow so that you have time to fully inhale. As you begin to exhale, you should lower the hands back down towards the height of the Uterus, as shown in image C.

Throughout this movement you should gently move your awareness up and down within the body at the same height as your hands. Do not attempt to change anything that you feel taking place inside you; instead, you are simply 'listening' to your own body, with the movement of your hands guiding the placement of your awareness as it moves from the region of the Uterus up towards the Heart and then back down again.

The second part of the exercise is shown in the five images of Figure 5.3. This part of the exercise begins to draw the energy of the vertical branch of the Thrusting meridian downwards towards the Uterus. As it does this, it will begin to resonate with the ideal movement of Tian Gui within the body.

FIGURE 5.3: CONTINUING THE DARK MOON QI GONG EXERCISE

Beginning from the previous section of this exercise, turn the hands over, as shown in image A in Figure 5.3. They should rotate at the wrists until they face upwards and then you should begin to raise them, as shown in image B. This should all be carried out on a slow inhalation. Keep raising the hands upwards until they are above your head. At this stage begin to fold the elbows so that the hands move inwards on to your centreline where they move downwards in front of you, as shown in images C–E. The backs of the hands are nearly touching during this part of the exercise and the fingers are pointing down towards the ground.

You should be exhaling as the hands move downwards, and at the same time you should bring your awareness down through the core of your body at the same height as your hands. The dropping of the awareness in this manner will begin to have a sinking effect on the vertical branch of the Thrusting meridian.

The third and final part of this moving exercise is shown in Figure 5.4. In this section of the exercise we are attempting to dredge through the Uterus itself in order to ensure that there is no energetic stagnation which will otherwise interfere with the health of this region of the body.

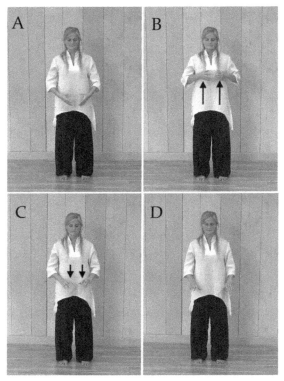

FIGURE 5.4: THE FINAL SECTION OF THE DARK MOON QI GONG EXERCISE

Continuing on from the last section, you should now begin to inhale as you spread the fingers and mentally connect them together into a kind of 'net' which you are going to use to dredge through the Uterus. In order to form this 'net', you should place your hands into the position shown in Figure 5.5 and then allow your intention to gently touch the energy of the fingers together as shown.

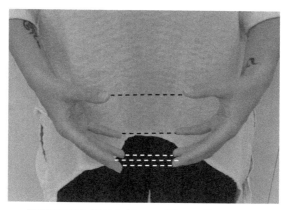

FIGURE 5.5: DARK MOON HAND POSITION

Then, while keeping your mind forming this connection, move the hands upwards, as shown in images A and B in Figure 5.4. As you exhale, bring the hands downwards again and then separate them back into the Wuji position, as shown in images C and D. This will complete one repetition of the sequence. Now repeat the movements for a period of 30–60 minutes.

At first you will feel little taking place within the body during this third section of the exercise, but with time you will start to feel how this hand shape starts to connect with the energy within the middle of the Uterus. You should start to become aware of a shifting sensation in the lower abdomen. Sometimes women have reported that the energy feels stuck and it is as if the 'net' is moving through resistance. If this happens, then try to mentally relax more and more until the resistance eases away. This will help to free up stagnation within the body.

As stated above, this exercise should be practised around the time of the dark moon, ideally in the evening, although the daytime is fine if your schedule does not allow otherwise. Add this exercise into your regular routine alongside whatever else you practise and you should find that it helps to regulate the health of the Uterus, assist with connection to the moon's cycles and, in the case of women who have not yet reached the age of menopause, help with regulating the menstrual cycle.

THREE CIRCLES AROUND THE MOON

The second woman-specific Qi Gong exercise is known as 'three circles around the moon' when taught in female Daoist sects. It is an exercise that can bring many benefits to female practitioners; in fact, it is so useful that many practitioners find this exercise alone powerful enough to maintain their energetic health completely. The widespread nature of Qi Gong practice means that this exercise is actually fairly well known, and now even men practise the exercise, although they will not derive the same level of benefit from the practice as women will. It is also commonly known by the name of 'swimming dragon Qi Gong', but in our school we have another exercise with this name so we tend to use 'three circles around the moon' in order to avoid confusion.

There are large lists of benefits that can be had from the practice of this moving Qi Gong exercise, so we have attempted to summarise the most important below:

- It generates more energetic activity within the body, which will in turn help to stimulate the more Yang functions of the organs. This is good for energy levels and general vitality.

- It helps the Heart and the Kidney energy to unite through the twisting of the Thrusting meridian. This serves to balance Yin and Yang within the body.

- The twisting and stretching of the torso assists with regulating digestive function as well as the health of the intestines. Many people carry blockages in this area of the body and so practising the 'three circles around the moon' exercise can help with many imbalances related to the bowels.

- The twisting of the upper body stretches open the Lungs and diaphragm, which will in turn help to bring more oxygen and energy into the body. Being able to breathe more deeply will help to quieten the mind and alleviate stress.

- The Kidneys are stimulated strongly through this exercise, which helps to balance the vitality of the Jing.

- The movements help to cleanse and warm the Uterus, especially as the hands move past the lower abdomen and when they rest on the Uterus region at the end of the exercise.

- The stretching of the spine helps to take care of all of the internal organs as each of them is connected both physically and energetically to the spinal column.

- In China, this exercise is often known as a 'weight loss' exercise as it famously causes fat and stored fluids within the body to begin disappearing. In fact, in one park we visited in northern China, there was a group of women practising this exercise under a large banner extolling the benefits of growing thin with 'three circles around the moon'.

There are many other benefits which develop with practice. As you go deeper into the exercise, you will discover increasingly subtle compressions and twists which bring change to the internal environment of the body.

There are no rules as to when this exercise should be practised; simply add it into your daily practice and work through the movements as many times as your schedule allows.

Begin the exercise by standing in the posture shown in Figure 5.6. Stand with your feet together and the hands resting on the lower abdomen.

FIGURE 5.6: PREPARING FOR THREE CIRCLES AROUND THE MOON

Placing the feet together like this begins to move the body's internal energy inwards towards the spine and the Thrusting meridian. The placement of the hands on the lower abdomen helps to warm the Qi of the Uterus.

Stand for a few minutes breathing deeply and relaxing the body. Allow the mind to settle and only begin the movements when it feels absolutely right to do so.

The first section of the exercise is shown in Figure 5.7. The hands come together into a 'prayer' position and begin to rise up towards the Heart region.

FIGURE 5.7: THE FIRST PART OF THREE CIRCLES AROUND THE MOON

From the starting posture shown in image A, you should raise the hands upwards where they press together, as shown in image B. The placement of the hands in this fashion closes off the palms, which helps the body's energy to begin warming up. The hands then continue upwards until they reach the height of the Heart. At this point you should begin your inhalation.

Figure 5.8 shows the continuation of the exercise into the second section.

FIGURE 5.8: CONTINUING THREE CIRCLES AROUND THE MOON

Stretch the arms up and away from you with the hands pressed together, as shown in images A–E. Your arms should stretch upwards to your left side. At the same time you should push your hips away from you to your right side. This will create a curved shape through the body as depicted in image C.

From this position, begin to bring the arms inwards until they are over the top of your head, as shown in image F. Your hips should move inwards as well until you are in the posture shown in Figure 5.9. This is the same position as in image F of Figure 5.8. It is shown here from a side view in order to highlight some postural details.

FIGURE 5.9: SIDE VIEW OF MIDWAY POSTURE

It is clear to see from this posture where the two-directional stretch of the body takes place during the exercise. Here, the top of the head is stretching upwards in the same direction as the hands, which are moving away from the body. At the same time, the pelvis is stretching downwards away from the head. This lengthens the spine throughout the more stretched parts of the movement. Ideally, you should try to maintain this stretch throughout the expanded parts of the sequence, although this is likely to be pretty difficult when you are first learning the movements.

From here, Figure 5.10 shows the next section of the exercise.

FIGURE 5.10: LOWERING THE HANDS IN
THREE CIRCLES AROUND THE MOON

From the previous posture, continue to inhale and slowly swing the hands down to your right side while pushing your hips out to the left, as shown in images A–C. Start with smaller hip movements and gradually build up to bigger circles, allowing the hips to loosen up with time. When you have lowered your hands to the height of your shoulders, you should begin to turn the hands over to face to the left, as shown in image D. From here, keeping the hands close to your neck, press the hands forward, as shown in images E and F. Throughout all of this you should maintain the hips being pushed out to your left. As depicted in image F, this section finishes when the hands are pressed together on your centreline at the height of your throat, with your fingers pointing towards your left side. This helps to ensure that a strong twist is placed upon your body.

Figure 5.11 continues with the movements. The five images show the passing of the hands over the midline of the body.

FIGURE 5.11: PASSING THE MIDLINE IN
THREE CIRCLES AROUND THE MOON

From the previous posture, continue to extend the hands out to your left side, as shown in images A and B. There is no need to fully extend the arms – they should simply pass the body. As you do this, push your hips out gently to your right. From here begin to exhale and lower the hands downwards in a swinging motion to the height of the base of your ribs. Images C–E show the lowering of the hands to this height and the movement as they pass by you to your right side. As the hands move past your body, you should return your hips to the middle and then push them out to the left as shown. In this way your hands and hips are moving in opposite directions.

Figure 5.12 shows the swinging of the hands down to the lowest position and then back up towards the middle height once more. Essentially, this is the lower of the three circles that are drawn in the air with your hands during this exercise.

FIGURE 5.12: THE LOWER CIRCLE

Continuing from the last movement, you should begin to lower your hands down and then swing them slowly across your body, passing the groin area over to the left side of your body once more. This movement is shown in images A–C. From image B, start a long inhalation. From here, continue the arc of the hands upwards back to the height of the lower ribs. When your hands reach this level, bring them across to your centreline. This movement is shown in images D–F. Throughout these movements continue to push your hips out in the opposite direction to the hands, as depicted. This ensures that the curved stretch on your body is maintained throughout the exercise.

Figure 5.13 shows the final curving movement of the exercise as you prepare the body for stretching upwards into the sky.

FIGURE 5.13: THE FINAL CURVE OF THREE CIRCLES AROUND THE MOON

Continue the last arcing movement of the hands upwards on your right side to the height of your throat, as shown in images A and B. Now turn the hands over and make an S-shaped movement with the hands, as shown in images C–E. Once again, swing your hips in the opposite direction to the hands. When your hands are to the left of your body, the hips are to the right and vice versa. This movement should bring the hands above your head on to your centreline, as shown in image F. Lightly stretch the hands upwards and the hips gently downwards. The inhalation continues all the way up until the arms are in the highest position.

The final section of this exercise is shown in Figure 5.14. It is the final stretching movement of the sequence.

FIGURE 5.14: COMPLETING THREE CIRCLES AROUND THE MOON

Continue to stretch the hands straight up above your head as high as you can. Open all of the joints of the body at this time so that you are trying to make your body as long as possible. Come up on to the toes briefly so that your heels are lifted off the ground. This is shown in image A. Once you have completed the stretch, you should begin to lower the hands down along your centreline until they reach the level of your lower abdomen, as shown in images B–E. As the arms start lowering downwards, begin to exhale. When you reach the completion of this movement, place the hands gently on to the lower abdomen, as shown in image E. Now stand and breathe deeply with a gentle focus upon the lower abdomen. This will help to nourish the health of the Uterus system. Feel the heat radiate from the hands into the lower abdomen and try to connect your hands with the lower Dan Tien. Stand for a few breaths and you will have completed one repetition of this exercise. When you feel ready, carry out this same sequence on the other side of the body and then repeat as many times as you wish. It can actually be difficult to follow the correct breathing pattern for many beginners. This is generally due to tightness in the torso or a weakness in the state of the Lungs themselves. In this case do not worry about breathing patterns; simply breathe naturally in a relaxed and smooth manner. With time and practice, you should find that your Lungs will begin to open up. At this stage you should find it easier to return to practising the correct sequence of breathing for each movement.

At first this exercise can seem very complex, but it is worth persevering with because of the great benefits it can bring. Practise daily until it becomes comfortable. Each time through the exercise, allow the body to relax and lengthen further, letting the top of the head lengthen up and the tip of the tailbone down. With each repetition, work towards making the circles larger and smoother.

ROTATING THE MOON

The third woman-specific exercise discussed in this chapter is designed to stimulate the Qi of the chest and breasts. Many health problems, ranging from painful swelling through to the development of masses, can manifest upon the breasts due to stagnation of energy in this region. 'Rotating the moon' works by connecting a woman's awareness into this region of the body and then 'stirring' it through rotational movements. This helps to break up stagnation and so maintain the health of the chest. It is an exercise that any woman can add into her daily routine; it does not have to be practised at any particular times of the day and there are no rules on how many repetitions you should perform. Simply spend around ten minutes or so carrying out the following movements. With practice, you will begin to clearly feel the movement of Qi in the chest region of the body and the breasts commonly start to feel very warm after the practice of this exercise.

In order to prepare for this exercise, stand as shown in Figure 5.15, with your arms in front of you and the hands lightly facing the breasts.

FIGURE 5.15: PREPARING FOR ROTATING THE MOON

Spend a short time in this position. The feet are shoulders' width apart and the hands are facing the chest. Breathe deeply and allow your awareness to hover in the space between your palms and your body. This will begin to develop an energetic connection between your hands and your breasts.

Then begin to rotate the hands outwards in front of your chest, as shown in Figure 5.16.

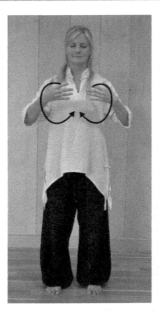

FIGURE 5.16: ROTATING THE HANDS OUTWARDS

Rotate the hands in the direction shown. Rotate them slowly and maintain your awareness in the space between your hands and chest. Breathe naturally and try to stay as relaxed as possible. With time, you will begin to feel how this movement causes the Qi within the breasts to be stirred. After a few rotations, change direction, as shown in Figure 5.17. Repeat this movement in the opposite direction.

Try to maintain the same number of rotations in both directions; other than that, there is no limit to how many times you may practise this exercise. If you wish to switch between rotating inwards and outwards several times, then this is fine. As long as your awareness remains in the space between your hands and your chest, you should attain the desired results.

FIGURE 5.17: ROTATING THE HANDS INWARDS

These three exercises are a useful addition to the daily routine of any female follower of the Dao. We advise that you become comfortable with these exercises at this stage and practise them until you are able to tangibly feel the effects that they have upon your energetic system. These should be considered the foundation exercises upon which the rest of the process outlined in this book is built. From the next chapter onwards, we are primarily concerned with the Nei Gong process.

THE MYSTERIOUS CRUCIBLE MUDRA

The fourth and final exercise in this chapter is the practice of the mysterious crucible Mudra. Although Mudra is a Sanskrit term, it has been adopted by the whole of the internal arts community to refer to a specific hand shape. This particular hand shape sets up an energetic connection to the Uterus, an organ referred to as the mysterious crucible in this exercise.

This exercise warms the Uterus through a specific visual exercise combined with the energetic properties of the hand shape held in the exercise. The benefits of this practice are that it helps to strengthen the Uterus as well as the entire abdominal region of the body. We have also had women use this practice daily over the course of a few months in order to help with infertility issues. In many cases female infertility is exacerbated by previous long-term use of oral contraceptives. In Chinese medical thought, oral contraceptives are Cold in nature, meaning that they cause the Qi of the Uterus to contract inwards. The result of this is that a woman's fertility is weakened. As this Mudra is practised, it helps the Qi within this region of the body to expand once more, dispersing the Cold stagnation that may have formed.

In order to begin this practice, stand in the posture shown in Figure 5.18. All of the principles outlined in Chapter 6 for the Wuji posture apply for this exercise apart from the fact that you hold your hands in the mysterious crucible Mudra.

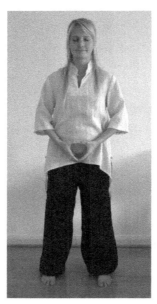

FIGURE 5.18: PRACTISING THE MYSTERIOUS CRUCIBLE EXERCISE

This position should be held for a few minutes. Simply relax as much as possible and breathe deeply to settle into the practice. Once you feel ready, drop your mind into the centre of the space between your hands and rest your awareness there. Ensure that you are correctly forming the Mudra, as shown in Figure 5.19. This Mudra is held directly in front of the lower abdomen at the height of the uterus.

FIGURE 5.19: THE MYSTERIOUS CRUCIBLE MUDRA

In this hand position, the 'pads' (area of the fingers where your fingerprints would be taken) of the fingers and thumb are touching. The only exception to this is that the tips of the middle fingers are touching. The middle finger relates to the organ of the Pericardium, the guardian of the Heart. It is also the finger through which we vent excess energetic heat from the body and so we seal this vent in order to develop expanding heat within the space between the hands. In order to help the development of heat within this space, we rest our mind between the palms and picture a flame burning, as shown in Figure 5.20.

FIGURE 5.20: PICTURING THE FLAME

Note that we are not generally a school that either advocates or uses visualisation or imagination to any large degree. The problem with this kind of work is that as soon as imagined images are added into the equation the acquired aspect of mind becomes overactive. This exercise is possibly the only exception to the rule in our system. We picture a flame here because fire is such a powerful archetypal symbol that it almost always generates the expansion of energy associated with the feeling of heat.

Continue to picture the image of the flame between your palms while holding this Mudra until your hands begin to warm up. It is often surprising just how warm the hands become after only a few minutes' practice. If you do not manage to develop warmth on your first attempt, do not worry; you should find that with a few times of practice you will develop the heat easily enough.

Once there is heat present, place your hands on to the lower abdomen, as shown in Figure 5.21. Rest the hands here and now observe what is taking place within your lower abdominal region. You should find that the feeling of heat moves inwards out of your hands into the centre of your lower abdomen where the uterus resides. This warmth will begin to break up Cold stagnation which will in turn benefit the Uterus. Remain with your hands in this position until the heat dies down. This should take between five and ten minutes.

FIGURE 5.21: CONCLUDING THE MYSTERIOUS CRUCIBLE PRACTICE

Chapter 6

STRUCTURING THE BODY FOR STANDING

When beginning any kind of internal practice from the Daoist tradition, we must begin to look at working with the physical body. It is our body through which we experience life and connect to the realm of physicality. If we ignore the physical body and attempt to move straight on to working with our energetic system, we will, at best, slow down our development and, at worst, cause a problem to develop. This is the same for all practices, from Nei Gong to Qi Gong and even Daoist meditation. Although meditation seems like a practice that would place importance solely on developing the mind, it also is based within the body, and so classical Daoism has a great deal of information on structuring the physical form during sitting practice.

In order to understand how to work with the physical body, we must first look at its current condition. Our aim is to try to make it as healthy as we possibly can within the limitations of what is possible for us due to physical injury or disability, for example. By making our physical body as healthy as we can, we are setting up the conditions for as healthy a flow of energy as possible. When engaging with a practice such as Nei Gong, you should view your physical body as your workshop and your energetic development as the work that takes place in it. If the workshop of your body is not of a high quality, then your work will be poor as well. For this reason we always make the same recommendation to beginners: take three or four months to really analyse what you can do to improve the health of your physical body alongside practising the exercises you are being taught in class. Do not fall into the trap of thinking that practising Qi Gong or Nei Gong alone will maintain your health. If you do not take care of other factors such as your diet, then you will not develop your health past a very low level. In fact, as you practise the internal arts, you are going to become more sensitive. This means that toxic food will now potentially be much worse for you due to an increased level of sensitivity to how food and lifestyle affect your body.

It is beyond the scope of this book to discuss everything a person can do to develop their physical health, but in brief here are some clear pointers which should be taken into consideration when building your physical foundation:

- First, look at your diet. Look closely at what you eat and drink on a regular basis, because food is basically your fuel. It is a great weakness of modern times that people have taken to seeing food as a form of entertainment, pleasure and self-gratification. While there is nothing wrong with enjoying the taste of a well-prepared meal, you should always keep in mind that food is essentially fuel for the body. The quality of the food that you consume will contribute both to your physical health and to the state of your energy body. Carry out some research into Chinese food theory and compare it with what you eat. Also look at the amount of food that you eat. In the West, far too many of us consume at least twice as much food as we need. Many people are surprised when they are shown what is a healthy amount of food to consume on a daily basis. An overly full digestive organ cannot function as efficiently as it should, and this will in turn affect the whole of your mind/body system.

- Look at your flexibility and the level of looseness in your joints. It is true that the more you practise Nei Gong, the softer your joints will become, but you still need to increase or maintain your flexibility through an effective stretching routine on a daily basis. There are many Qi Gong teachers who argue that any form of stretching is bad for you and you should not do it. In our experience, these same teachers are generally very stiff of body and therefore of mind. They also tend to age quickly as their Qi cannot flow smoothly and they injure themselves on a regular basis, as the lack of motion within their joints causes them problems. You do not need the hyperflexibility developed by many modern practitioners of Yoga, but you do need a certain mobility in the joints and an ability to lengthen the tissues without causing tension through contraction. We would advise finding a basic-level stretching routine if you don't already have one; attendance at a basic-level Yoga class or something similar will show you how to stretch your body efficiently.

- Often overlooked by internal arts practitioners is the concept of core strength. While you do not need a highly developed 'six pack' on your lower abdomen, it is wise to have a fairly good level of core stability. This helps to connect the whole of the physical body into one unified whole and gives an overall boost to your physical health. It also assists with the higher stages of training when a practitioner seeks to connect the vibrating force of the Dan Tien into the soft tissues of the body. If the core is not sufficiently developed, this force cannot be transferred out into the physical realm, which will slow down your developmental progress. Do some research and find a simple routine for core development that you can gradually use to improve your strength. This is of particular importance for women because a good level of core strength will maintain the health of the whole abdominal and pelvic region including the Uterus which sits within it.

Once these basic foundational aspects of your physical health have been taken into consideration, it is time to start looking at structuring your body through correct alignment. This is primarily studied through one of three basic postures which are known as Wuji (無極), Hundun (混沌) and Taiyi (太一). These three basic postures are the basic standing positions utilised in Nei Gong training. For women, they represent the key postures used when working with the lower, middle and upper Dan Tien. Wuji and Hundun are looked at in detail in this chapter. We have omitted any description of Taiyi because the posture is too advanced to cover in sufficient detail in this book. You should spend some time familiarising yourself with the principles from this chapter and ensuring that you can apply these principles to your body before engaging in any of the moving exercises in this book. The true skill of internal work comes not from the movements you learn but from the principles that are applied to them.

THE WUJI POSTURE

In the philosophy of Daoism, Wuji is the original gateway through which Dao manifested itself into the realm of existence. It is a non-state prior to the division of Yin and Yang and representative of many Daoist ideals such as Wu Wei (無爲) or 'non-governing'. Literally translated, Wuji means 'without projections', which refers to its key function of acting as a kind of blank canvas upon which the whole of reality is projected. This idea of Wuji being without any kind of projection placed upon it is reflected in the Wuji posture, which is the basic-level standing position when beginning a study of Nei Gong. This posture places a person into a neutral position where no major influence is put upon their energetic system; the centre of gravity is dropped down into the region of the lower Dan Tien and thus the initial stage of Nei Gong can begin: direct work towards the waking of the lower energy centre.

The Wuji posture is shown in Figure 6.1. This is the first posture that a female practitioner of Nei Gong should become comfortable with. This can take anywhere between a few weeks and a couple of years, depending upon factors such as prior experience and the condition of their physical body. It is also useful to have a skilled teacher assist you with this posture as there are quite a number of small details that are very difficult to pick up from a book alone.

FIGURE 6.1: THE WUJI POSTURE

The key factors of the Wuji posture are that the body is lined up in such a way that the weight from the top of the body is evenly distributed down towards the ground without it 'catching' on any of the joints. If you can correctly align your body in this way, you should essentially start to feel weightless. This is because no excess tension is required in the muscles; your structure alone is holding your weight. As the muscles grow increasingly relaxed, they begin to lengthen; habitual misalignments are corrected and after a while the body becomes softer. This is particularly important for when we wish to drop our centre of mass down into the lower abdominal region to coincide with the location of the lower Dan Tien.

Starting from the ground upwards, each of the key elements of the Wuji posture is discussed below.

The Feet in Wuji

The positioning of the feet is very important in any standing practice. The placement of the feet, along with which part of the foot is pressurised, will greatly change the energetic effects of each posture. If this is not understood or practised correctly, then many of the functions of each posture will be lacking.

When looking to understand the placement of our feet in Nei Gong practice, it is important to understand how the physical body controls our internal energy flow. If we view the physical body as a kind of vessel for our Qi, then whatever shape we place this 'vessel' into will have a direct effect upon how our energy moves. This then places great importance on entering into a very detailed study of the structure of our physical form during any internal exercise. Although development with energy work is not wholly dependent on a very exact physical alignment, without it progression will be slowed or even halted at some stage.

Figure 6.2 shows a practitioner with their feet at a distance wider than shoulders' width apart.

FIGURE 6.2: FEET WIDER THAN SHOULDERS' WIDTH APART

This placement of the feet causes our internal energy to move outwards away from the core of our body. This is commonly used in more martially orientated forms of standing Qi Gong, including the 'horse stance' used in many martial arts styles. The movement of energy outwards causes a practitioner's Qi to nourish the tendons and muscles of the body, which are much nearer to the surface of the body than the deeper meridian pathways commonly utilised in Nei Gong practice. For this reason we rarely, if ever, use this placement of the feet in Nei Gong standing practice. We have included this foot placement here to show a common error for many beginners in the internal arts. If we wish to consolidate our energy and gain control of it in Nei Gong training, then this posture will be inadequate. Because we are directing our energy outwards without any contraction of the muscles to trap the Qi, we will essentially begin to disperse our internal energy, which will obviously slow down our progress.

Figure 6.3 shows the placement of the feet at shoulders' width apart. This is the correct positioning of the feet for the Wuji posture.

FIGURE 6.3: FEET AT SHOULDERS' WIDTH APART

When the feet are at shoulders' width apart, there is little or no directional force placed upon the flow of our internal energy. This is why we adopt this foot placement for foundation-level postures such as Wuji and many moving forms of Qi Gong. If we place no directional force upon the flow of Qi with our feet, then it can flow naturally. In order to place the feet at shoulders' width apart, you should visualise your shoulders as two spheres. The centre of each of these spheres sits directly above the centreline of each foot, as shown in Figure 6.3.

Figure 6.4 shows the third option for the feet in Nei Gong practice, which is placing the feet closer than shoulders' width apart. At this point they are essentially aligned with the hips.

FIGURE 6.4: FEET AT CLOSER THAN SHOULDERS' WIDTH APART

If the feet are closer together than the shoulders, then you will begin to exert an inwards-moving directional force upon the body's internal energy. Your Qi will move from the extremities deeper towards the core areas of the meridian system. The Hundun posture places the feet at the width of the hips as shown in Figure 6.4 in order to begin directing energy inwards.

The next stage in working with the feet is learning how to pressurise the correct part of the foot in each posture to access the correct part of our body system. Figure 6.5 shows the three areas of the foot that are commonly utilised in Daoist Nei Gong practice.

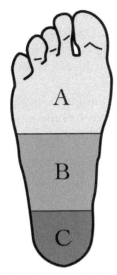

FIGURE 6.5: THE THREE AREAS OF THE FEET

The region of the foot marked A is the front of the foot. This region of the foot serves to open up the tissues that activate the origin of the Kidney meridian. This in turn causes energy to enter the body and rise upwards through the energy body.

The area marked B is the middle of the foot. When a person directs their weight towards this region of the foot, they cause the soft tissues of the body to lengthen and activate. This serves to relax the body and regulate internal energy flow which is neither added to nor depleted when this region of the foot is emphasised.

The heel is marked as region C. When weight is directed towards this area of the foot, it activates the skeletal system and relaxes the tissues which actually become somewhat 'slack'. Qi is depleted through long periods of standing on this region of the foot and consequently it is rarely utilised for any length of time in Nei Gong training.

In the Wuji posture we place our weight over the front area of the foot so that the meridian point known as Yong Quan (涌泉) (KI 1) or 'bubbling spring' is stimulated. You will know when you have correctly directed your weight to the correct part of the foot as the metatarsal bones of your feet will spread open. This will begin to widen the soft tissues of the foot, creating more space for energy to flow into the body. It is normal for the foot to ache when you first start placing your weight here, and some students have even experienced a burning sensation as the fascia around the metatarsal bones begins to open up. This is nothing to worry about and should pass in a short space of time as your body begins to adjust to standing in this way. When the Yong Quan meridian point fully opens, it will result in a strange sensation of bubbles moving underneath your foot. It is as if you were standing on one of the holes through which air is pumped in a Jacuzzi. This is usually a temporary experience and a clear sign of your connection to the Qi of the planet opening.

By placing our weight on to the foot in this way during Wuji standing practice, we help to bring energy from the planet into our body, as well as taking more weight off our lower back.

The Knees in Wuji

When standing in any posture, it is important we learn how to protect the knees from injury. If we stand incorrectly for any length of time, then we will direct our body mass down to the knee joints and so begin to strain them; over time, pain will begin to appear and then injury. Despite the Daoist arts being primarily known as health practices, many people damage their knees through incorrect training and alignments.

The first thing to ensure is that your knees do not project out beyond the line of your toes. If they do, then your body mass will begin to collect on the underside of the kneecap and pain will quickly begin to manifest.

Second, your knees must not collapse in or be forced out. If the knees collapse inwards, then you will begin to feel pain on the inside of your knees. This is because the alignment of your legs is directing your body mass down unevenly through the knee joint to an area of weakness. This problem is shown in Figure 6.6. Note that in this diagram we have exaggerated a bad alignment of the knees so that it is clear to see. When students align their knees in this manner, they are generally doing it to a lesser degree but the results are the same.

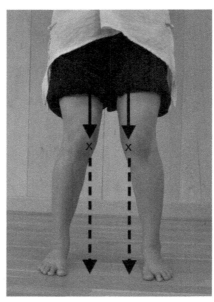

FIGURE 6.6: INCORRECT ALIGNMENT THROUGH COLLAPSING THE KNEE

Many times beginner students of the internal arts are told to align their knees correctly in order to avoid this issue. Although this is important, it is difficult to align the knees properly if they have a tendency to collapse inwards. This is because it will require a certain degree of muscular 'holding' to keep the knee in the correctly aligned position. As soon as you relax or 'zone out', which is common in Nei Gong, you will find that your knees move back into the wrong alignment. In Figure 6.6 each solid arrow shows the pathway that your weight is taking through the legs as it is dropped down towards the floor. Each dotted line shows the direction that this mass will take as it draws a line straight down towards the ground. Because of this common misalignment in the knees, the force of your weight will be directed towards the inside of the knee, the area marked with an X. This is where pain will begin to manifest and, with time, injury.

It is wiser to look for the source of the problem. In many cases it is the alignment of the feet and ankles that is causing the knees to drop inwards, generally through a collapse of one or both of the arches. You should aim to align the feet correctly with a focus upon the arches rather than the knees. If this is the issue, then standing in front of a mirror each day and observing your alignments, as shown in Figure 6.7, will help you to build the correct stabilising muscles to alleviate the issue.

FIGURE 6.7: USING A MIRROR TO CHECK ANKLE ALIGNMENT

If you stand like this, focusing upon the ankle for 10–20 minutes per day, then over a few weeks you should find that your alignments improve and this will take the strain off your knees.

Another possibility for why your knees may be collapsing inwards is tightness in the hips. If the hip joints are holding too much tension, they will force the tops of the legs inwards. This will collapse the knees. In our experience, the vast majority of people have problems with this region of the body, but luckily it is easy to fix. Every day, simply relax into the position shown in Figure 6.8 for around ten minutes at a time.

FIGURE 6.8: STRETCHING THE HIPS

Do not force yourself towards the floor but rather just relax into the exercise. Try to relax and let your muscles switch off so that the weight of your hips is carrying out the stretch for you. If you practise this stretch daily, then in a short space of time the tightness on the inside of your hips will have eased off, meaning that your knees will begin to align themselves more correctly.

Once you have aligned your knees, you should understand how bent they need to be. Often, beginners in arts such as Qi Gong are told simply to bend their knees a little, with no further guidance. In actual fact, the knees should be bent enough that the centre of gravity is dropped down from the chest region into the lower abdomen; to be specific, it is at the height of the lower Dan Tien. This means adjusting your centre of gravity, as shown in Figure 6.9.

FIGURE 6.9: LOWERING THE CENTRE OF GRAVITY

When you are learning to hold the Wuji posture, it is wise to bend the knees enough so that you feel your centre of gravity drop downwards. Part of the skill in Nei Gong training is learning how to refine your centre of gravity until it can be rested exactly upon the lower Dan Tien itself.

The Kua in Wuji

Moving up from the knees, we reach the region of the body that the Chinese know as the Kua (胯). It is difficult to fully translate the meaning of this word as it refers to the physical area of the inguinal crease, but also to the energetic pathways of the meridian system flowing through this region. In essence, you do not need to worry too much about an exact definition; simply think of the Kua as the region of the hips shown in Figure 6.10.

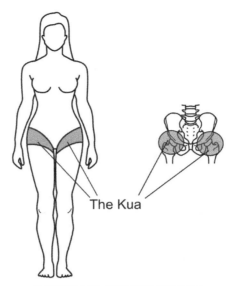

The Kua

FIGURE 6.10: THE KUA REGION

The Kua is an important area of the body which should be studied by anybody engaging in Daoist body work. It is an area often ignored by many practitioners. In the early stages of working with the Kua, we must learn how to change the way in which our body functions so that force is directed to this area. In beginners there is often tightness and a general lack of function within the Kua region; Daoists refer to this state as the Kua 'being asleep'.

The Kua does not function as a hinge joint or as a simple ball-and-socket joint as in the case of the hips. Instead, it is both of these but also a sling of connective tissue which, when awakened, serves to support the entire structure of the body. If we look at the way in which a toddler walks, squats and moves around, it is easy to see that their Kua is awake; there is a kind of semi-spherical way in which the whole of their lower body operates. If we compare this with the linear manner in which an adult controls their lower limbs, it is clear to see the difference.

The Kua is structured around the pelvis, which forms a shape much like the 'keystone' on top of a stone arch. By sitting in the correct position, the pelvis helps to distribute our mass down through the centre of the long bones of the legs so that no tension appears within the hips. If we have habitually been misaligning the pelvis (pretty much every adult we have ever taught!), then our mass will have been travelling down to the hips, which results in increasing levels of tightness; with time, this serves to put the Kua 'to sleep'.

To align the pelvis correctly, you should ensure that when you move up and down with your body, you fold at the hip joints and not the lower spine. This will mean that you can adjust your height without pushing out your butt or tucking in your hips, as shown in Figure 6.11. If either of these two misalignments occurs, then your mass will not be distributed down through the 'keystone' of the pelvis and so tightness will develop.

FIGURE 6.11: PELVIC MISALIGNMENTS

Once you have aligned the pelvis correctly and practised the Wuji posture for some weeks, the Kua will begin to 'wake up'. This happens because your new posture is enabling your mass to travel through you to the floor. In addition, the muscles around the Kua region can begin to relax and then they open up in a kind of 'unfurling' manner. When this happens, all weight and pressure of any kind vanishes from the lower body and legs. It is as though your lower body and joints have become completely weightless. In some cases it can actually feel as if your joints have spaces between them, as if air is passing through you. For many people, this is the first time they have ever felt their lower body fully relax since they were young children and it can be a very distinct and satisfying feeling. The level of buoyancy developed in the hips from the Kua waking up is also a sensible skill to take through into old age when hip injuries become commonplace.

It is worth noting here that no body work can be carried out through a practice such as Nei Gong without there being a corresponding effect upon the energy within that region. This will take place because of relaxation of the muscles which have been holding habitual tension, usually for a very long time. In Daoist thought, physical tension is a result of energetic stagnation. On top of this, much physical tension develops as a form of protection from the emotional damage that you have experienced in the past. As you have these negative emotional experiences, the energy body stores the memory as a form of vibrational wave which then goes on to change the quality of your overall energy body. In an attempt to isolate this emotional energy and prevent it from spreading, the body builds a protective layer of tension around it. This has the advantage of stopping you from re-experiencing the emotional energy in a repeating loop, but the negative aspect of the body's defence mechanism is that it traps the energy inside and prevents it from escaping. As you learn to relax, you give the body space to let go of these pent-up emotional energies. Surface muscle relaxation does little more than calm the mind, but deep muscular relaxation, such as happens when the Kua opens up, can release a great deal of these pathogenic energies.

For women, the area around the Kua is a large storehouse for negative energy related to sexual fears and guilt. In a society that surrounds women with negative media imagery based on their sexuality, it is no wonder that guilt and fear regarding female sexuality is likely to be a factor. As the Kua relaxes and opens up, do not worry if these feelings start temporarily rising to the surface of your awareness. It is normal to cry or feel upset as they leave the body, but this will pass; simply allow it to happen and do not focus on it. If this happens, then relax afterwards, walk around and shake out your limbs for a couple of minutes.

Spinal Alignment in Wuji

Often the most difficult alignment for beginners to get right is the positioning of the spine during the Wuji standing posture. This is because the alignment of the spine will actually result in a very slight forward incline of the body. The vertical alignment for Wuji is shown in Figure 6.12. This alignment is based around the spine, rather than the torso.

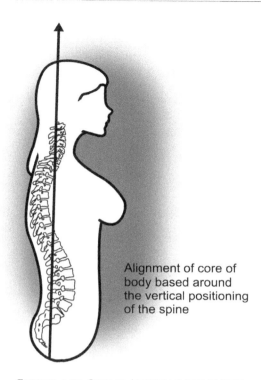

Alignment of core of
body based around
the vertical positioning
of the spine

FIGURE 6.12: SPINAL ALIGNMENT IN WUJI

The reasoning behind aligning the spine rather than the torso is that your spinal column actually sits at the back of your body, and your ribcage, torso and breasts project outwards from the spine. During Nei Gong practice it is the spine that we wish to have with a strong vertical alignment, not the torso. As you can see in Figure 6.12, the spine actually sits towards the rear of the body and beginners will almost always wish to align the centre of their torso rather than the centre of their spine.

To align the spine, stretch the top of your head gently upwards and open up the spine by relaxing the muscles of your back as much as you can. Then ease your body forward ever so slightly from the Kua region so that the weight comes off your lower back. This will then direct your body mass forward over the correct area of your feet. If you were to drop a plumb line down from the region of your chest to the floor, you would see that your body mass is now resting over the centre of your Yong Quan (KI 1) meridian points rather than your heels, which is how many practitioners incorrectly stand. The correct alignment is shown in Figure 6.13.

FIGURE 6.13: THE CORRECT ALIGNMENT FOR WUJI

By taking the weight slightly forward, as shown in Figure 6.13, you will direct your mass downwards to the area of your feet, which helps to bring in energy from the planet. In addition, you will enable your lower back to relax. The space between each of the vertebrae of the lumbar spine will increase; this is important for later stages of the practice when we begin to move energy through the Du meridian which runs along the centre of the back.

As you bring the weight forward, ensure you do so from the Kua and not by bending the spine. If the spine bends forward, then you will collapse the abdominal region, which will lead to stagnation in this region. This will prevent you from awakening the lower Dan Tien and slow down the process of refining the Blood.

The Shoulders, Arms and Hands in Wuji

In order to align the shoulders, do not round the chest. This practice can be particularly detrimental to women and is certainly not needed. It is true that for men it can help to lead Qi down from the chest into the lower abdomen, as well as send energy back towards the Du meridian, but women do not need this. Women's energy will naturally flow to the correct place on its own, and collapsing the chest actually runs the risk of stagnating the Heart energy. It also causes the breasts to slacken downwards, which will in turn result in a sinking of essence away from the chest. Instead, simply relax the shoulders into a neutral position.

The arms should be lightly stretched out so that armpits and elbow regions feel 'open', as shown in Figure 6.14. Do not close off any of the joints in the arms, but at the same time do not hyperextend the joints either; both of these errors will lead to stagnation.

The position of the hands and fingers is especially important as they control the level of elastic connection through the whole body. If the hands are allowed to collapse, then the entire body's connective integrity becomes compromised; and if they are stretched out with an excess of tension, then the whole body becomes tight.

FIGURE 6.14: SHOULDERS, ARMS AND HANDS

The exact height of the hand placement is something that different teachers disagree upon, and we were given many conflicting ideas when we were being taught. The reason for the height of the hands is that they direct the emphasis of energetic movement on a vertical plane. For this reason it is classically taught that the hands should be at the height of the lower Dan Tien during Wuji so that energy is directed down towards this region of the body. This is fine in theory, but in practical application we find that many Westerners have arms that are too long for this alignment to apply. If they place their hands at the height of the lower Dan Tien, they are actually quite bunched up. For this reason we teach that women place their hands at the height of the lower Dan Tien or below. Extend out the arms until they are open and comfortable.

The Face in Wuji

It is always funny to see how many practitioners of Qi Gong and Nei Gong attain the perfect Wuji posture after many hours of practice but still stand with their faces screwed up! If the face is held in tension, then you cannot relax any of the body. Relax your face as much as possible and then gently bring the start of a smile to your face. This will help to connect the head into the body.

PRACTISING WUJI

Once you have become comfortable with these principles, you will have learned how to stand in Wuji. The complete final posture of Wuji is shown in Figure 6.15. Here a group of students are practising Wuji together in order to facilitate the awakening of the lower Dan Tien.

FIGURE 6.15: THE COMPLETE WUJI POSTURE

Once you have become proficient at standing in Wuji, you should practise standing in this way for short periods of time until it becomes a natural position for you to stand in. Hold the posture and relax into it as much as you can. If you know the 'Sung breathing' method, then practise it in the Wuji position; otherwise, simply breathe deeply with your eyes gently closed and tune in to the body. By giving your body gentle attention, you give it space to begin to change and adapt into this posture.

To give you an idea of how long it can take to become used to Wuji standing, we have had students who became comfortable with it after a number of weeks of regular practice, while others have taken a couple of years. Everybody is different, so don't worry if it takes some time; it is a surprisingly complex standing posture. You should continue with your practice until you can fully relax into the position and the Kua awakens. It is always easier under the guidance of a teacher who uses this method, so if you have anybody in your area who can help, this will speed up the process.

THE HUNDUN POSTURE

The second of the three main postures for women to learn for Nei Gong training is the Hundun standing posture. This posture is designed to bring the focal point of energy up towards the Heart centre, and as such is the next step in your practice beyond the Wuji standing practice. Male practitioners of Nei Gong can use Hundun as well, but it is nowhere near as useful or as important for them. Female Nei Gong practitioners, on the other hand, will find the Hundun posture the mainstay of their standing work once they move beyond the foundation stages of their training. In this section we will look at two variants of the Hundun posture. There is no hard and fast rule as to which is the best to use; we tend to see an even split of women who feel more comfortable with one or the other.

Hundun is a philosophical term referring to the original state of the cosmos prior to the formation of life. It is often translated as meaning 'chaos', but this, in our opinion, is a little misleading as it implies no sort of order whatsoever. Rather, Hundun refers to an original state just prior to the formation of life and reality when the potential for existence is just about to spill over into a frenzy of creative energy.

Alignments for the Hundun Posture

Many of the basic bodily alignments for Hundun and Wuji are the same, and so here we will focus on those alignments that are slightly different. Essentially, these differences are the placement of the feet, the location of the body's mass and the positioning of the hands.

The adjustment of the alignments in the Hundun posture is designed to help a practitioner gently direct their energy inwards and up towards the region of the middle Dan Tien. This in turn takes a practitioner up into the intermediate stages of practice where they begin to work directly with the conversion of the acquired nature. Traditionally, it was said that women should reach this stage of their training much faster than men, and in our teaching we have generally seen this to be the case.

The Hundun standing posture should have a slightly narrower stance than Wuji, with the feet pulled in to the width of the hips, as shown in Figure 6.16. This is to help direct internal energy inwards towards the centre of the body.

FIGURE 6.16: FOOT PLACEMENT IN HUNDUN

If you picture your hips as two spheres, then the centre of these spheres should be placed directly above the centreline of your feet. This will ensure that the feet are neither too far apart nor too close together. For those used to standing in Wuji, this can feel a little awkward, although women always find it a more natural stance than men.

The area of the feet where the weight is directed is also changed. Now you should bring your weight back so that it is evenly spread across your feet. It should feel as though the centres of your feet are spreading open. Ensure that your weight does not go back too far with an emphasis on the heels, though, as this will cause your Qi to sink and collapse your structure. By taking the weight into the arches, you enable the soft tissues of the body to stretch open. This will help the riverbeds of the Jing Jin lines – the pathways of connective tissue and fascia through which the meridians travel – to open up.

As you take your weight back to this region of the feet, you should still slightly incline the body so that the spine remains vertically aligned. This will involve manipulation of the folding of the Kua.

You now need to bring your centre of gravity upwards into the region of the middle Dan Tien, which sits in the middle of the chest at the height of your heart. To do this you should decrease the bend in your knees until you feel your centre of gravity rise up to the correct location. The result will be that your knees are only very slightly bent, a lot less than in Wuji. This will direct the emphasis of your energy body upwards into the middle Dan Tien to generate an awakening reaction there.

The final adjustment to the posture is the movement of the hands to in front of the chest. They should be placed in either position A or B as shown in Figure 6.17. As stated above, either hand position is fine to use; it depends which feels the most natural for you. Try them both and see which feels most comfortable. Once you have selected one of these hand positions, this is your posture, and you should not keep switching between them.

FIGURE 6.17: HUNDUN HAND POSITIONS

In hand position A, the palms are facing upwards at the height of the heart. They are held a couple of inches out from the body and the elbows are allowed to relax. Do not extend the elbows out to the sides of your

194   Daoist Nei Gong for Women

body with any force, as this will encourage your Qi to move outwards away from the middle Dan Tien.

In hand position B, the middle fingers are allowed to lightly touch the centre of your chest in the region of a meridian point known as Shan Zhong (膻中) (CV 17). In this position the hands are allowed to fully relax. The tip of the middle finger corresponds to the Pericardium meridian which you are joining with the entry point to the Heart. If you are a woman with larger breasts, you may find this position less comfortable, so hand position A will likely be a better choice for you.

If you have built a genuine foundation in the early stages of Nei Gong using the Wuji posture, it will be fairly easy to settle into Hundun. It is less demanding on the body and more simple to relax into. Hundun should be less 'physical' than Wuji with regard to the level of effort involved; it is a posture aiming to lift a practitioner beyond body work into direct contact with their energy and spirit.

USING THE POSTURES

When moving between Wuji and Hundun, it is important to understand when each posture should be used. Essentially, a sincere practitioner of Nei Gong will most likely be using Wuji exclusively for the first couple of years at least. Experience has shown us that three years of regular training with the work at a Wuji level seems to be enough for the majority of women to move on to Hundun. If their practice has not been daily, then this timescale is obviously increased somewhat. Table 6.1 shows the differences between the Wuji and Hundun postures.

TABLE 6.1: COMPARISON OF WUJI AND HUNDUN POSTURES

	Wuji	Hundun
Feet placement	Shoulder width	Hip width
Area of feet	Front of foot	Whole of foot
Centre of mass	Lower Dan Tien	Middle Dan Tien
Hand position	By hips	By chest (two variations)
Qi movement	Neutral	Inwards
Awakens	Lower Dan Tien	Heart centre
Cultivates	Blood and Jing	Qi

Chapters 7 and 8 outline the initial stages of awakening the energy body and working with the Heart centre. To simplify the timing of their usage, Wuji is used almost exclusively to awaken the energy body as discussed in Chapter 7, and Hundun is used for Chapter 8 when working at a higher level. The correct posture will be indicated for each exercise.

Chapter 7

THE SMALL
WATER WHEELS

O
ne of the most important aspects of Nei Gong training is the circulation of energy along the various pathways of the 'small water wheel'. The most famous of these circulations is undoubtedly the 'small Heavenly orbit', the cycle of Qi that takes place up the middle of a person's back through the Governing meridian and then down the centre of their front through the Conception meridian. This is the first of several rotations of energy that we need to establish in order to move deeper into Daoist internal work. Much has been written about the first of these rotations but, once again, most of this has been from the viewpoint of a male practitioner. Women engaged in Nei Gong training have a couple of unique considerations when they engage in this practice.

There are various methods of activating the circulations of Qi in Nei Gong practice. Some of these methods use the mind and some use moving Qi Gong exercises, but in this book we are going to look at the practice of awakening the lower Dan Tien in order to utilise it as a driving force for the orbits. This practice is the same whatever your gender, because in the early stages our first challenge is connecting with the lower Dan Tien and gaining a conscious link between its movements and our mind.

LOCATING THE LOWER DAN TIEN

Almost every system of internal work from the Daoist tradition will at some point discuss the importance of the lower Dan Tien. It is generally the starting point for all other energy practices and is considered the first aspect of the energy body that a person should learn to work with. This sounds easy enough in theory – placing the awareness on the lower Dan Tien – but in fact it is generally more challenging than that.

A great number of practitioners fall down in the earliest stages of their development because they either don't know how to locate the lower Dan Tien or they work with it in the wrong manner. If you miss the lower Dan Tien with your mind, then this will obviously slow the practice down, and if you focus on it incorrectly, it can lead to the development of internal stagnation.

The exact location of the lower Dan Tien will vary slightly from person to person. This is due partly to body shape and also to people's energetic nature. In textbooks it is normally discussed as being a few inches below the navel, when actually it is a little more complex than that to locate the Dan Tien. In order to locate it, a practitioner can go through various stages.

We first use two key meridian points as reference points to locate the lower Dan Tien. These points are Qi Hai (氣海) (CV 6) and Hui Yin (會陰) (CV 1). Qi Hai sits in the front midline of the body, two fingers' width below the lower border of the umbilicus. Hui Yin sits on the base of the body between the opening of the anus and the edge of the genitalia. Figure 7.1 shows how these two points can be used as a cross-reference for locating the lower Dan Tien.

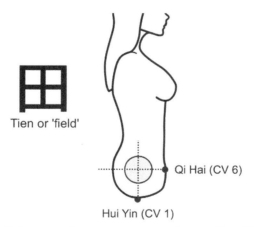

FIGURE 7.1: LOCATION OF THE LOWER DAN TIEN

Alongside the diagram is the Chinese character for Tien, as in Dan Tien. Looking at the character, we can see a way to cross-reference these two points in order to locate the lower Dan Tien. Maybe that is not really an aspect of the meaning behind the character, but it is an easy way for us to remember this concept!

The point at which these two lines cross each other gives the rough location for the centre point of the lower Dan Tien. From here we then need to move our awareness around a little until we find the exact location.

When attempting to understand how far back in the body the lower Dan Tien is located, remember that it sits directly upon the line of the vertical branch of the Thrusting meridian. This meridian travels like an upright bar through the core of the body. This is what places the lower Dan Tien directly above the Hui Yin meridian point. The majority of Qi Gong practitioners we have met actually place their mind too far forward within the body and so miss the Dan Tien by quite some distance. The awareness is a curious thing, as it likes to have certain locations to grab on to. If you ever try to put your awareness into a single point within a large space, you will see what we mean. Those of you with enough internal sensitivity to know where your awareness actually is will find that it quickly seeks to attach itself to a physical object within that space if there is one. If you want an easy experiment, just extend your index finger and then try to focus on the air a centimetre or two from its tip. What you will most likely find is that your awareness is dying to shift across on to the tip of the finger, and only an intense level of concentration will keep it where it is. If your mind wanders for just a second, your awareness will be on the fingertip. Locating the lower Dan Tien can be similar because within the space of the lower abdomen you basically have two points that the mind will be able to attach itself to. The first is the true lower Dan Tien and the second is the false Dan Tien. These two points are shown in Figure 7.2. The false Dan Tien corresponds with the Qi Hai meridian point.

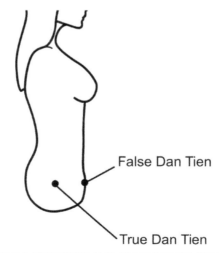

FIGURE 7.2: THE TRUE AND FALSE LOWER DAN TIEN

The true location of the lower Dan Tien is what we seek. If we are able to find it, then our awareness will have a 'tangible' spot to attach itself to. If we cannot find this exact point, then it will almost always have a tendency to attach itself instead to the false Dan Tien point which sits on the front of the lower abdomen.

When new students come into our school, we generally ask them to place their mind where they think their lower Dan Tien is located. We then ask them to contract the muscles around the region of the perineum a few times. From this muscular contraction they can find the Hui Yin meridian point. If they then trace a line up within the core of the body from this point, it gives them the line of depth upon which the lower Dan Tien resides. In nearly every case students are surprised to find that they have had their focus too far forward; their mind has instead been resting on the surface of the lower abdomen in the location of the false Dan Tien. The Daoists long recognised the mind's tendency to travel to this point and so it was known as an early hurdle to a person's practice.

If a practitioner focuses on the false Dan Tien for any length of time, they will find that they start to develop energetic stagnation within the region of the lower abdomen. This will generally lead to physical swelling and weight gain in this region of the body. This is because your awareness is leading Qi to a point in the body from which it cannot be circulated away. Although the meridian point will initially stimulate an increase in vitality (the point is used for this in acupuncture), it will, over time, slow down your development. For women, focusing incorrectly upon this point for any length of time will run the risk of developing Blood stagnation within the Uterus, an issue that can cause painful cramps, a worsening of premenstrual symptoms and a great number of unhealthy conditions around their monthly bleed.

Once you have used the height of Qi Hai and Hui Yin to locate the approximate location of the centre of the lower Dan Tien, you need to then move your awareness lightly up and down along the pathway of the vertical branch of the Thrusting meridian. Move your awareness gently up and down along the length of the line shown in Figure 7.3. Move slowly in order to give your mind a chance to translate any sensations that take place during this practice.

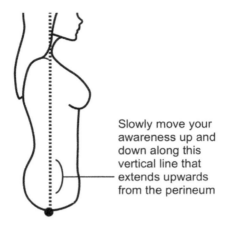

Slowly move your awareness up and down along this vertical line that extends upwards from the perineum

FIGURE 7.3: THE LINE OF THE LOWER DAN TIEN

You should only have to trace your awareness up and down along the portion of this vertical branch shown in Figure 7.3. The most that your lower Dan Tien location should deviate from the height of Qi Hai is an inch or so.

Stick with this practice until you experience one of two different sensations. There does not seem to be any pattern as to why certain people experience one of these over the other, but it does not matter as both are positive signs of success. The first sensation is one of heat and the second is of a pulling feeling as though a deep muscle is gently contracting. As your mind runs over this point, you will find that there is a point that is hot and sometimes, if you are very healthy, slightly bubbling, like boiling water. The second experience when your awareness touches the correct point is of a gentle tightening of something inside the abdomen. It is an unusual feeling because there is no literal muscle there to tighten, but the feeling is nonetheless quite distinct. Either of these will only come when your mind passes over the exact right point. Do not worry if this takes some time, though; learning to feel the lower Dan Tien is not necessarily a fast process.

At first this practice can be a little tricky, but persevere and take some time to explore the region of your lower abdomen in this manner. Keep trying regularly until you successfully find the point of the centre of the lower Dan Tien. Once you have found it a few times, it starts to become easier to do. Your mind learns that this a point it can grab on to, and before long you will be able to simply drop your awareness down on to this point straight away with no risk of it moving forwards on to the false Dan Tien. It should not take you too long; as a rough guide, most people seem to manage it within a few weeks of trying each day.

AWAKENING THE LOWER DAN TIEN

Now that you have successfully located the lower Dan Tien, it is time to start looking at the practice of waking it up. This is accomplished through combining the location of the lower Dan Tien with your breath, your intention and your centre of mass. There is quite a skill involved in accomplishing this. It is much easier to do with the assistance of a skilled instructor, but if you move step by step and do not hurry past any stages, then it should be achievable by anybody. It should be noted that as soon as you start to wake up the lower Dan Tien, you will immediately start to generate change with regard to the quality and circulation of your Blood and Jing. In order to make sure you do this effectively, you should take the following guidelines into consideration:

• An internal arts practitioner should be aiming to eat healthily anyway, but certainly before trying to wake up the lower Dan Tien you want a good solid couple of weeks with a healthy diet. If you are not usually a healthy eater, then it is vitally important that you change this for the period building up to direct work with the Dan Tien. Try to cut out sugar and spices from your diet, along with any processed food and carbonated, sugary drinks. It is not necessary to be a vegetarian but it is wise to restrict your meat consumption at this time. In our opinion, the majority of adults who are not vegetarian should only really eat meat in two or three meals per week anyway. This is the absolute maximum amount of meat a healthy internal arts practitioner needs.

• Of course, there is a clear link between Jing and a person's sex drive. For this reason men are advised to stay away from sexual activity for a period of time prior to working with the lower Dan Tien or attempting to wake it up. This is actually not so much of an issue for women as they do not lose anywhere near as much of their essence through sexual activity and orgasm as men do. Despite this, it is still wise to avoid sexual activity of any kind for a couple of days prior to starting to wake up the lower Dan Tien. This is to ensure that the energy within the lower abdominal region is as stable as possible before any rotations begin.

- Do not engage in this practice if you are feeling very low in energy or unwell in any way. This is because the initial process can be quite demanding. If you are unwell, then there is a chance your condition could temporarily worsen. Either wait until you are better or seek out Chinese medical treatment in order to get ready for this practice.

- Do not practise this exercise when under the influence of drugs or alcohol of any kind. It is wise to avoid any alcohol for the whole period of time you are working on the lower Dan Tien, and no internal arts practitioner should ever smoke or combine these exercises with drugs, especially hallucinogens of any kind.

- If possible, do not practise around mobile phones or any devices that are attached to the internet. You are trying to attach your mind to an internal vibration. Your awareness will find this more difficult if there are a lot of other vibrations moving through the area. These devices also serve to scatter a person's energy and we are trying to consolidate it through the practice.

- No internal work of this kind should ever be practised when pregnant. While pregnant, a woman is going through a great deal of spontaneous energetic transformation due to the development of a new life taking place inside her. There should be no disruption to this process through working with the lower Dan Tien.

- This practice can develop a lot of internal heat in the early stages of the training due to an increased movement of Qi and Jing. Please be cautious if you have any weakness of the heart or high blood pressure, as this heat can tax the heart. If you are unsure of this, please consult a Chinese medical practitioner for assistance or train under a qualified teacher who can advise you on your development.

Once these guidelines for the practice have been taken into consideration, it is time to start looking at the awakening of the lower Dan Tien. The first thing we need to do is learn how to consolidate the various required elements into the lower Dan Tien region. These key elements are shown in Figure 7.4. They are each discussed in detail below.

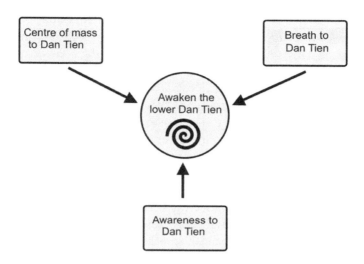

FIGURE 7.4: THE THREE ELEMENTS OF LOWER DAN TIEN AWAKENING

If one or more of these elements is not effectively connected to the location of the lower Dan Tien, then the chances of you managing to wake it up are greatly lessened.

Centre of Mass to Lower Dan Tien

The Wuji posture (discussed in Chapter 6) is the easiest position to use in order to get your centre of mass to the correct location. This is largely because one of the key functions of this posture is to enable you to work with the lower Dan Tien in the foundation stages of Nei Gong practice.

Before starting to use the Wuji posture as a practice to bring your centre of mass down to the lower Dan Tien region, you will first need an internal point of reference. For this reason you should persevere with the previous exercises of searching for sensation around the lower Dan Tien region of the lower abdomen until you are successful. Once you have managed to locate this point, you will know exactly where your body mass has to be focused towards.

If you have practised the Wuji posture from the previous chapter to a point where it has become comfortable, then your next task is to continue with the refinement of its alignment principles. Stand in Wuji for a short time and use your awareness to tune in to and locate your physical centre of mass. It is a key realisation of anybody who has trained in the internal arts for any length of time that your centre of mass is actually a relatively 'fluid' thing which can be moved around your body according to how you structure it. It seems that with a fairly high level of skill it can even be transmitted through the soft tissues of the body according to intention. For our purposes in Wuji training, we don't need to reach this level, though; we simply need to bring our centre of gravity down from the chest into the lower abdomen and then adjust our posture so that our mass is directed downwards to the location of the lower Dan Tien. The pressure of your mass going to the lower Dan Tien is then released down through the legs into the Yong Quan (K 1) meridian points as previously discussed. Once you have explored this concept and brought your centre of mass to the correct place, you will have folded your knees and Kua to the correct degree. There is never any need to go lower than this in any of the standing practices of Nei Gong. You will find that you don't really need to go very low in your stance. In order to give you the right idea of the height of the stance, Figure 7.5 shows one of our students standing with their Wuji posture at the correct height for working with the lower Dan Tien.

FIGURE 7.5: WUJI WITH CENTRE OF MASS IN LOWER DAN TIEN

The arrows on the image show the direction of force within the body generated by the positioning of the body in this manner.

Awareness on Lower Dan Tien Region

The second 'ingredient' involved in the awakening of the lower Dan Tien is the effective placement of your awareness upon this same point that you have by now located. The awareness should be placed as exactly as you can on to the point to which you are directing your body mass through the Wuji posture. The skill in achieving this is twofold: first, the strength of the awareness needs to be at a correct level; second, it needs to be constant with no lapses in your focus. For many practitioners, this is very difficult; no matter how challenging any physical exercises become, nothing is as difficult as getting to grips with getting your acquired mind under control.

One of the greatest risks to your internal health when engaging with a practice such as Nei Gong or Qi Gong is misunderstanding the required strength of your awareness. The more force you put behind your level of focus, the more energy you will lead to a region of the body and thus the more risk there is of stagnation occurring. Many practitioners we have met over the years have walked a very dangerous path, using incredibly strong focused attention in everything they do. Although some had come very far in their practice, most of them had paid some kind of a price with regard to their physical or mental health. We cannot stress enough to new students that the ideal level of awareness is that of a 'casual observer' to the process taking place, all the while keeping your mind resting on a specific point within the body. The mind never has to generate or force anything in your practice; it simply remains calm and observes or, as the classical Chinese teachings say, 'listens' to the process. By learning how to regulate the strength of your awareness in this manner, you will create a definite enough point to draw energy to the correct location but nowhere near strong enough to cause it to stagnate. It is better to have your awareness too weak, which will result in it wandering. At least a wandering mind will not cause you any danger; it will simply slow down your development.

Once you have practised enough to regulate the strength of your awareness, you should bring it to the point of the lower Dan Tien in your Wuji standing practice and rest it there.

Leading the Breath to the Lower Dan Tien

The final ingredient for awakening the lower Dan Tien is actually quite simple to achieve, although it relies on your awareness already being in the right place. As previously discussed in Chapter 3, as we breathe, we cause an expansion and contraction of the energy within the auric field. In addition, our breath leads Qi through various regions of the energy body. By placing our awareness on to the region of the lower Dan Tien, we cause a certain amount of the energy shifted by our breathing to travel down towards the lower Dan Tien. As the classical saying goes, where the awareness goes, energy follows. This energy begins to take the form of an internal wave which is led downwards to generate a reaction with the lower Dan Tien on each exhalation.

It is much like gently blowing on the dying embers of a fire in order to get the heat to grow once more. The 'fire' you are trying to ignite within your body is the energy required to awaken the lower Dan Tien.

Once you have successfully brought these three aspects together, your practice at this stage should consist of Wuji practice with a continuous effort to refine them. Once they all work together in an efficient whole, then the lower Dan Tien will begin to stir.

HOW LONG TO CONTINUE WITH THIS PRACTICE

Possibly the most important question for any internal practitioner to ask is how long they should continue with any practice. Once the correct principles have been learned, timing becomes a major issue. In order to answer this question, we can divide practices into two main categories:

1. The first category of practice has no defined aim or set limit to the amount of growth it can bring. Many Qi Gong exercises, meditation forms or martial arts practices fall into this category. These practices are a lifelong study which sincere practitioners should only stop doing when they are on their deathbed. The skill with this kind of practice is to understand where it is supposed to be leading you and so in turn ensure that it keeps leading you down a continuous path of development. Many practitioners fall down in these kinds of practice simply because they lose sight of a developmental process and so allow their practice to become stagnant. Once it does not lead to growth, it does not help along the 'path' and it has become a useless practice.

2. The second category of practice leads to a very set place. These practices have a very specific goal, a set amount of time they should be practised and a limit to how far they can take you. It is normal to practise them until you have reached whatever the aim of the practice is and then to leave them and move on. It is worth noting here, however, that these practices should be left but then returned to on occasion. It is always an important part of internal

training to occasionally return to the beginning. In these cases it ensures that you maintain the strength of the foundation upon which everything else is built.

Awakening the lower Dan Tien is an aspect of Nei Gong training that falls into the second category. It is a practice that has a definite conclusion, but it should then be returned to every now and then to ensure that you have consolidated your foundations.

When the lower Dan Tien begins to wake up, it generally produces the following result:

- First, you will begin to generate a reaction within the Jing of the lower abdomen, back and hips. As stated previously, Jing is simply a form of vibrational energy which carries with it a source of information. As it begins to react to the awakening of the lower Dan Tien, your mind will translate the information of the lower Dan Tien into something that it can tangibly understand. In the vast majority of cases this will manifest as waves of heat around the lower abdominal region or even a feeling of warm flowing fluid which travels around the body, including down through the legs. This heat is rarely subtle. If you experience a slight increase in body temperature which you could possibly explain away as autosuggestion or your imagination, then ignore it. The heat that comes with the movement of Jing is very clear to feel. It is normal for students in Wuji to be standing in sweat-drenched clothes, small puddles forming under their feet. Thankfully, this rather unpleasant stage only lasts for a very short time as your body learns how to normalise the experience. When this happens, it becomes a much more bearable warm, glowing sensation. It is generally only shocked-looking newcomers to the practice who end up being completely wet!

- Beyond this stage the lower Dan Tien then starts to generate more life and movement within the energy body. This sends more information through the meridian system, which in turn stimulates movement within the physical body. A student who has reached this stage will generally begin to shake or vibrate at a very high rate. At first these vibrations will be localised to within the legs, but after some time it is normal for these vibrations to then move through the rest of the body, through the arms and out to the hands. They are nothing to worry about and simply a sign of increased energetic movement through the body. As they take place, they cause a great deal of energetic repatterning to take place, changes that have a positive effect upon your health. These shakes should come and go in short bursts.

As with the experience of heat, once the body has normalised the experience, they will quieten down and become more subtle, and you will be left with a gentle feeling of vibration through the body which is practically invisible to any onlooker.

• Once the Dan Tien starts to become consolidated to a point of waking up, it will begin to make sudden jerks within your lower abdomen. These jerks come quickly and can take you by surprise. Don't panic when they begin to manifest, as they can sometimes be quite strong. They generally come quite a few minutes apart in your practice, with no observable pattern as to when they appear; as far as we can ascertain, they are not linked to either your mindset or your breathing. They are a clear sign of developmental progress when working towards awakening the lower Dan Tien, though. As these jerks go off within the lower Dan Tien, they motivate the physical body to follow. Do not be surprised if the sudden twist of the lower Dan Tien causes you to turn around abruptly to either side. We have even had many students who were thrown off their feet by the movement of the lower Dan Tien. The lower Dan Tien is the energy centre of movement, activity and action. It is the driving force for energy and life. As it wakes up, we are simply accessing these aspects of its nature and so we experience these various reactions.

Once you have started to experience these reactions, the lower Dan Tien is successfully awakened enough for you to move on to working with the 'small water wheels' of Qi, which are important for your Nei Gong practice. As a rough timescale, we have had some students achieve this after only a few weeks and yet others take around a year. It is individual from person to person. The secret is continuous refinement of the principles and regular daily practice.

THE FIRST SMALL WATER WHEEL

In order to initiate the rotation of energy within the first orbit of the congenital energy system, we need to learn how to consciously rotate the lower Dan Tien. This practice is not actually so difficult, providing that you have built a strong enough base in the previous practices in this book. Through rotation of the energy along the Governing and Conception meridians we establish the basis for Yin and Yang to begin stabilising within the energy body. The driving force for this rotation is the actualising potential of the lower Dan Tien.

The correct direction for the initial rotation of the lower Dan Tien is shown in Figure 7.6. This is the same direction of rotation for both genders. It is only beyond this stage that female followers of the Dao are required to establish further rotations.

FIGURE 7.6: THE INITIAL ROTATION DIRECTION

In Daoist Nei Gong practices, the rotation of this initial 'small water wheel' is actually differentiated into two aspects: the inner orbit of the rotation and the outer orbit. The outer orbit is the complete circulation of energy through the Governing and Conception meridians, while the inner orbit is a helpful 'beginner-level' orbit which serves to establish the correct directional force. When we first begin to rotate the lower Dan Tien, it is the inner orbit that we are trying to achieve.

In order to do this, place your mind on to the point that you have already ascertained is the central focal point for the lower Dan Tien. Use your Wuji stance to drop the body mass down to the correct place and stand like this for a few minutes simply relaxing and breathing. Ignore any sudden jerks the lower Dan Tien may make, although you should have progressed past that stage by the time you get on to controlled Dan Tien rotations.

After a few minutes you should simply begin to rotate the lower Dan Tien forward, as shown in Figure 7.6. Use your awareness to establish a smooth rotation of the lower Dan Tien in this direction. The vast majority of beginner students find it easiest to carry out this rotation in time with their breathing, although it is not vitally important that this is the case.

In order to understand exactly what Dan Tien rotation is, we should clarify one thing: we are not discussing a physical rotation of any muscles or joints within the region of the pelvis or lower abdomen, nor are we talking about using your imagination to picture a rotating ball in your gut. Instead, we are referring to setting up a forward rotational direction with your awareness within the lower abdomen and then being patient! After some time the lower Dan Tien will begin to rotate and you will experience a full rotation of this energy centre. It is a clear sensation of something turning over deep within your lower abdomen in time with your awareness. This turning has strangely been compared to a 'fish turning over in the guts'. It is a very strange sensation at first, but after some time it becomes normal like anything else.

As the Dan Tien rotational practice becomes easier, you will find that the connective tissues within the lower abdomen begin to follow its movement. Once again, we wish to underline that you do not make any movements with the body yourself; you simply stand in Wuji. As the Dan Tien turns, it will begin to strengthen the connection between the energetic and physical bodies, and this is what starts to generate tangible movement within the lower abdomen.

There are various bodily reactions that often take place when the lower Dan Tien starts to make a full rotation. These are quite normal, very common and nothing to be concerned about.

- As the lower Dan Tien starts to rotate, it is normal for the body to enter into a period of energetic and physical purging. A combination of poor diet and negative emotional debris has left many people's bodies full of stagnant toxins. As the Dan Tien wakes up and begins to move energy through the body, it will aim to naturally reverse this state and the result can be feelings of nausea or even vomiting. These should only last a day or two at the most and seem to occur in about a quarter of the students we teach, far more often in male students. In every case, after the temporary sickness has ended, students state that they feel much better for it.

- The second 'purging' body reaction that may manifest is a kind of colon cleansing which gives a new practitioner loose bowels for up to a week. The material that comes out during these spontaneous colon cleanses is not just faecal matter but also the same strange toxic leftovers that a person will experience leaving the body when completing prolonged fasting and enemas. As with the previously mentioned nausea, this only ever seems to happen once at the beginning of a Nei Gong student's training and always seems to improve their health. This reaction is much more common than the nausea and affects roughly half of those starting to rotate the lower Dan Tien.

- If the rotation of the lower Dan Tien causes an increase in heaviness of the flow during menstruation, then stop and wait until you have moved past this part of your monthly cycle before continuing practice. The extra heat generated by the beginning stages of rotating the lower Dan Tien can sometimes increase the expulsion of menstrual Blood by the Uterus.

If any of these reactions take place, don't worry – it is quite normal. You are entering into some of the stronger aspects of internal work and so bodily reactions like this are common. They should only last for a short space of time. If they last any longer, then please go and see an experienced Chinese medical practitioner and they should be able to assist you.

THE INNER ORBIT

Once the lower Dan Tien begins to make full rotations, it will generally start to awaken the inner orbit of the 'small water wheel' of its own accord. This is a rotation of energy along the pathway shown in Figure 7.7. This rotation moves through the lower back, along the underneath of the diaphragm and then down the front of the abdomen where it reconnects with the Dan Tien once more.

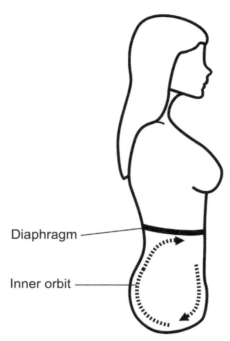

Diaphragm

Inner orbit

FIGURE 7.7: THE INNER ORBIT

This small rotation of energy is a direct result of the turning of the lower Dan Tien. It helps to establish the power for the remainder of the first 'small water wheel' and to open the lower back up enough for the first stages of movement along the line of the Governing meridian to take place.

The opening of the lower back is an important part of the process as it ensures that no blockages appear in the early stages of the circulation. It has long been recognised that although moving energy can stagnate anywhere along the line of the 'small water wheel', it is far more likely to occur at certain points along the two meridians involved. These points of potential stagnation are classically named the 'clipping passes' and they are shown in Figure 7.8. Effectively moving deeper into Nei Gong requires freeing up any blockages in these particular areas of the body.

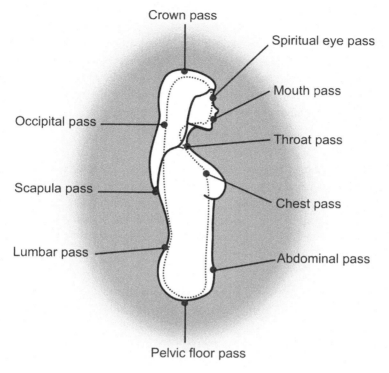

Crown pass

Spiritual eye pass

Mouth pass

Occipital pass

Throat pass

Scapula pass

Chest pass

Lumbar pass

Abdominal pass

Pelvic floor pass

FIGURE 7.8: THE CLIPPING PASSES

In the majority of classical Daoist texts, these points are given esoteric names. These names would only have been relevant to people 'in the know' in these traditions and in this way they could keep their training secret. In modern times there is a great deal more openness around energetic training and so consequently these esoteric names are generally replaced by the names of meridian points which are more commonly understood. We actually find the meridian point names to be a little misleading, as the energy does not always stagnate in such an exact location. Its blockage can deviate from the meridian point location by up to a few inches sometimes. For this reason we have simply named each clipping pass after the body region it sits within. For each of these points we have outlined the risks of energy stagnating to a large degree within this area of the body.

Pelvic Floor Pass

If the practice of the 'small water wheel' causes energy to stagnate strongly within this region, then it can lead to a dramatic drop in vitality. A practitioner will find that they quickly become very Qi-deficient, which generally results in a pale face, dizziness, weak breathing and becoming very easily tired. They can also be prone to experiencing great pain in the region of the groin as the energy becomes trapped.

Lumbar Pass

If energy becomes trapped within the lumbar clipping pass, then it is normal for energy to begin forcing its way into the lower back where it causes pain and weakness. This pain then often radiates down the backs of the legs, causing tingling sensations, numbness and weakness of the legs. It is a serious energetic condition which is not so easy to treat.

Scapula Pass

If energy gets caught in the region of the scapula, then there is almost always sharp stabbing pain in this region of the spine. Functional control of the arms and hands can be affected and it is common to experience tingling and numbness in the fingers.

Occipital Pass

This is one of the more dangerous clipping passes to become blocked. If energy cannot pass through this region of the neck, then it can lead to increased levels of aggression and anxiety. In extreme, prolonged cases it can lead to the development of mental illness. In classical teachings, it was said that a person was likely to begin talking crazily to themselves and hear the voices of the dead.

Crown Pass

If the crown pass is blocked and energy builds up here, then migraine-type headaches will develop as well as stabbing pain localised to the top of the head. It is a very intense pain which generally only clears after the blockage is removed.

Spiritual Eye Pass

In the centre of the forehead, between the eyebrows, is a common potential clipping pass of the 'small water wheel'. If energy becomes trapped here, then it is normal to experience frontal headaches, pressure behind the eyes, sinus problems, insomnia and flickering lights in front of your vision. In extreme cases it can also lead to depression and psychiatric imbalance.

Mouth Pass

If energy becomes trapped here, then a practitioner can develop pain and aching sensations in the mouth and face. The early stages of this blockage often show up through spontaneous itching sensations on the face as soon as you begin your training, but after some time this blockage can become more serious.

Throat Pass

This is a very dangerous clipping pass point if it becomes trapped. Blockages here can lead to a whole-body stagnating of energy as well as a restricted feeling in a person's breathing. In chronic cases it can also prevent a person from being able to express themselves and can even lead to irregularities such as a stutter.

Chest Pass

At the centre of the chest sits a large clipping pass which is largely controlled by the health of your emotions. If this point becomes blocked, then it can lead to either a hyperactivity of your emotional state or a lowering of your mood towards chronic depression. It can also affect the level of Jing in the breasts, causing it to disperse. The first sign of this is that along with an uncomfortable tenderness in your breasts they can also begin to decrease in firmness.

Abdominal Pass

If the energy within the 'small water wheel' becomes blocked here, then it is generally the digestive system that becomes affected, as well as the Uterus. Various menstrual issues can arise and they will normally be accompanied by distending pain which originates in this region of the body.

DEALING WITH THESE ISSUES

We decided to include the issues associated with clipping pass blockages in this book because we are contacted by so many people who have experienced them. It is only when you start to reach out and talk to the wider internal arts community that you realise just how many practitioners have suffered problems from their practice. The truth is that while some practices are safer than others, all internal energetic training will involve at least some degree of risk. This is why training under a skilled instructor is the wisest option. In spite of this, we have made the decision that people reading this are adults and probably already engaged in the energetic arts in some manner, and so we hope they are aware of the risks they may be taking. With this in mind, we are trying to present as much information as we can, as we feel it is better to be well informed than to have half the information before you begin your practice.

To keep it simple, if any of the above negative symptoms begin to manifest out of your practice of the 'small water wheel', then you need to step back from the training immediately. If this is the case, then you are simply not ready to move on to this kind of work. Instead, you should seek out assistance from either a skilled teacher or a Chinese medical practitioner who can help you with the blockage. In many cases you simply need to turn to a more gentle Qi Gong practice for a while until the blockage is freed up or spend more time on the foundation practices prior to engaging in the 'small water wheel'.

THE LOGIC OF THE INNER ORBIT

There are various ways of working with the initial circulation of the 'small water wheel' of Qi. Some schools favour externalised movements and others use guided intention. With this second method, the primary mechanism is the rotation of the lower Dan Tien. The logic behind using the lower Dan Tien as a driving force is that a practitioner never actually has to have any interaction between their own energetic pathways and their mind. Almost all of the potential issues that can arise, such as those discussed above, are due to the strength and quality of a practitioner's focus not being correct. If a person is to use their mind to lead energy around the circulation of the Governing and Conception meridians, then at some point they have to rest their awareness on each of the clipping passes in turn; if they mistakenly use an overly strong intention (which is quite likely if you have a direct goal of leading Qi somewhere), then there is the potential for energy blocking at one of the passes. If this continues for too long, then serious issues may appear. If you are familiar with the technique of Sung breathing, then feel free to use this technique on any of the clipping passes in order to help free them up. Sung breathing is gentle and will cause no problems, providing you are skilled with the method.

As the inner orbit begins to open up, there are several clear signs that will likely manifest within your body. The first and clearest of these is that as the energy moves through the lower back it will begin to increase the size of the spaces between your lumbar vertebrae. The expansion of these spaces is the body's way of ensuring that there is enough of a physical opening for the energy being directed from the lower Dan Tien to pass through. There is no discomfort when this happens; in fact, it often feels pretty good for anybody who has been suffering with a stiff back up until this point. The clear sign that this is happening, though, is that as the lower back opens up it generates more length around the spine, and this has the added effect of causing the practitioner to spontaneously start bending forwards, often so much so that they are thrown to their hands and knees. Figure 7.9 shows a practitioner who is experiencing exactly this process.

'FIGURE 7.9: OPENING THE LUMBAR SPINE

Do not panic when this happens; it is a very common sign of progress which a large number of our students go through. It is a temporary stage that usually lasts a few weeks during your daily practice – at the most a couple of months – if you are practising regularly. When the rear aspect of the inner orbit has opened up, this reaction will stop, as there is now enough space in the lower spine for the energy to pass through. This is a sign that the lumbar clipping pass has successfully been cleared.

After this there is generally a period of calm in people's training, apart from perhaps a little vibration as the inner orbit starts to complete itself. When it is done, you will be left with the feeling of a clear rotation taking place in the space below your diaphragm, as shown in Figure 7.7 above. For some people, there is a small degree of muscular undulation that spontaneously takes place in the lower abdomen for a while, but this does not seem to be a very common reaction.

THE COMPLETION OF THE SMALL WATER WHEEL

The inner orbit serves to establish the base upon which the rest of the Governing meridian opens up. This should happen of its own accord when you reach this stage. By now your Dan Tien should be so active that it is no longer necessary to rotate it forward. Instead, you should just bring together the three 'ingredients' of your awareness, your centre of mass and your breath in order to enable the rotation of your energy system to happen of its own accord.

The curious thing about reactions in Nei Gong training is that they seem to come in stops and starts. Your training will generally move through peaks of Yang activity followed by more gentle periods of Yin quietude. It is during these quiet periods that the body begins to integrate everything that has been happening, so that your training becomes a part of you. One teacher put it well by saying that you do not really ever integrate your training into your life, but rather your training integrates you into it. It is at these times that you should trust what you are doing and continue onwards. A great many people we have known have a powerful experience through internal arts training which changes their complete view on life, and then they enter into a period of relative stillness. Disappointed that the entire process is not as exciting as before, they quit their practice. It is a real shame when this happens, because if they had just continued onwards, they would have moved through more of these peaks and troughs.

After the inner orbit has been achieved, there is normally one of these quiet periods until, when it is ready, the rest of the spine will begin to open up as the energy starts to flow through the Governing meridian. Once again, you are likely to be tipped forward as the spaces between the vertebrae become larger. This time, though, there is a clear feeling of expansion taking place along the length of your entire back. At this stage, as people are often pushed forwards on to their hands and knees, they will find it more natural to stay on the floor for some time as they can often feel the spine continuing to open under the influence of the energy as it continues to move through the Governing meridian. If this happens, then simply remain on the floor for some time and give your energy body enough space for this to happen unimpeded. For many people, this can be a very pleasant sensation − one that they do not wish to end too quickly.

A particular type of Qi begins to move into this orbit once the spine has successfully been opened up. This Qi brings with it the direct experience of expansion. It is a curious feeling, as if somebody has expanded the meridians with a bicycle pump! Some students say that this energy brings with it a feeling of warmth, while others state that they can clearly feel something like air or liquid moving around the orbit of the 'small water wheel'. Experiences will be individual from person to person, depending upon how your own mind translates the information contained within the energy moving through your meridian system. At this stage, when the circulation has completed, up the back of the body and down the front, all bending-forward reactions will end and standing will become relatively quiet once more. When you reach this stage, you will have completed the first orbit of the 'small water wheels'.

THE REVERSE ORBIT OR THE WIND PATH

The energy flowing within the Governing and Conception meridians also has the ability to flow in the opposite direction. In this case the Qi moving from the lower abdomen flows upwards along the line of the Conception meridian, over the head and then down the centre of the back. This flow is known either as the 'reversed small water wheel' or sometimes the 'wind path', although this second name tends to be more accurately applied to alchemy training rather than Nei Gong.

The reverse cycle of energy through this orbit is a very important aspect of training for female practitioners. Although men will also on occasion find that their own energy flows in this direction as well, it is not such an important part of their training. Men will find that it is generally a brief experience and then it is over for them. They should never attempt to make this circulation happen through any kind of directed willpower.

Women will find that this orbit begins to take place of its own accord, and they should simply allow it to happen. It will be far more regular for women than it is for men, and will happen more and more the deeper they go into their Nei Gong practice. Sometimes it will even happen for women long before the 'regular' direction of the first 'small water wheel' has opened, but generally it will start to manifest a little later in their practice. In the practice of Daoist alchemical meditation, women actually learn how to utilise this cycle in time with the phases of the moon, but in a practice such as Nei Gong we do not worry. Nei Gong is not as advanced as alchemy; we are not working on such a deep level and so there is no need for the connection of this cycle to the outer environment. In Nei Gong we are working primarily with energy at this stage in our training and so it is better to give the body the space it requires to repattern itself as it sees fit.

The key role of the reverse flow of energy in this orbit is to extract Jing from the Tian Gui stored around the Uterus. This Jing is then raised upwards through the Conception meridian towards the chest, where it is stored. This has the benefit of ensuring that women have a healthy amount of acquired Jing stored around the Heart centre so that they can establish a solid foundation in the intermediate stages of their training. Figure 7.10 shows the pathway of this flow of energy as well as the movements of Jing that take place.

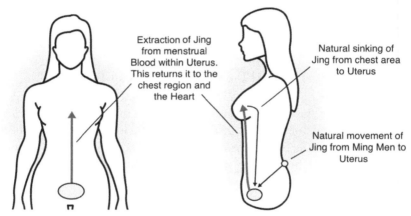

FIGURE 7.10: THE REVERSE FLOW OF THE SMALL WATER WHEEL

As shown in the diagram, the general direction of flow of Jing within a woman's body is from the region of Ming Men towards the Uterus where it becomes menstrual Blood. There is also a natural sinking motion that takes place as Jing from the region of the chest sinks downwards towards the Uterus. The reverse cycle of energy within the 'small water wheel' causes some of this Jing to be raised upwards away from the Uterus towards the chest where it moves into the region of the breasts to be stored.

As this cycle begins to open up, there is a clear feeling of upwards movement which begins low down in the abdomen before rising upwards into the chest region. Women will have the distinct sensation of their chest expanding outwards and sometimes you will even find that your body physically begins to stretch around the ribcage and behind the breasts. As the Jing moves along this line, it is also normal to experience sensations of heat moving upwards towards the chest and this can leave a woman with a feeling of warm energy expanding across the chest and breasts. If Jing moves into the nipples, do not be surprised if they become somewhat swollen. This is a normal reaction to the energetic movement taking place within your body.

This raising of Jing upwards into the region of the breasts is important for female followers of the Daoist arts as it helps to strengthen what is one of the biggest weaknesses for women with regard to energy work. Although men struggle with the stabilisation of Jing around the region of the lower Dan Tien, women do not; instead, they struggle with the hurdle of the middle Dan Tien. Because of the close connection between the Heart centre, the emotions and the Jing within the chest region, any extreme emotional swing will actually cause depletion of a woman's vital essence. Although acute emotional experiences are quite normal, chronic states of emotional imbalance are the biggest drain on a woman's health. On top of that, if a woman wishes to open up connections to higher states of awareness, then the emotions want to be relatively centred, and this is much easier to achieve with a healthy supply of Jing within the chest and breasts.

According to Daoist thought, women are born with a certain degree of Jing within the region of their chest; as they age, it naturally sinks downwards towards the Uterus to contribute to the formation of menstrual Blood. In addition, it converts into breast milk during lactation as this is a vital source of acquired essence for a mother's newborn child. As the Jing within this region of the body becomes depleted, a woman will find that her breasts naturally begin to loosen and 'sag' downwards. If, however, this Jing can be moved through the reverse cycle upwards into the chest region, then much of this will be avoided. A clear sign of this working is that a woman should find that her breasts begin to tighten and some women even find that they begin to shrink to a certain degree. Although, of course, this physical effect upon the breasts is not something we are aiming for, it is a clear sign of progress.

As the reverse flow begins to extract Jing from the menstrual Blood, it is normal for a woman's menstrual flow to lighten to a certain degree. Although there should never be a complete ending of a woman's period, it is fine for it to become a little lighter. This is simply because there is not as much Jing present to generate the material basis for the creation of Blood itself.

The key factor to keep in mind with regard to this direction of flow within the first 'small water wheel' is that women will find that it happens of its own accord. You should find that sometimes it takes place for a small portion of your practice and other times it will be for the whole practice session. On the other hand, there may be weeks on end where it does not manifest. Do not worry about any of this, and do not look for patterns; the body will know what is best. Continue with your training, and if the reverse flow starts to take place, then simply leave it to happen. Do not worry about any particular method at this time, and don't rotate the lower Dan Tien; simply observe what is taking place and give the energy the space it needs to move in the most efficient manner.

THE GIRDLING MERIDIAN CIRCULATION

As with the previously discussed orbit, rotation around the pathway of the Girdling meridian will activate of its own accord. When this happens, you should once again just observe and allow it to happen. This is normally a relatively brief aspect of the process. You should not experience this anywhere near as often as the reverse cycle of the first 'small water wheel'.

When the Girdling meridian opens up, there is often a clear feeling of the lower Dan Tien rotating on a clear horizontal axis. Women will find that they naturally have a tendency towards one direction over the other while the Dan Tien is turning; this is fine – there is no need to worry about the two directions evening each other out. Figure 7.11 shows the two possible directions that you may experience the lower Dan Tien rotating.

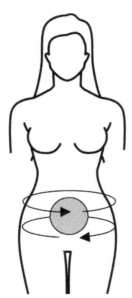

FIGURE 7.11: HORIZONTAL DAN TIEN ROTATION

After some time that same expanding feeling will move into the pathway of the Girdling meridian. At this stage you will find that energy almost 'sluices' around the Girdling meridian in both directions. It is a very fluid and free-feeling meridian. In many cases women's energy is quite 'slack' around the lower abdomen. This is generally due to issues around menstruation and the health of the Uterus. When the Girdling meridian begins to develop a healthy circulation, women often report that they feel as if this area has become more 'bound up', as if it has become wrapped up by something unseen. This has a healthy effect upon the Uterus and the digestive system.

The Girdling meridian also pertains to the energetic aspects of a person's balance and the feeling of being 'centred' in themselves. If a person's Girdling meridian is deficient in any way, then it is normal for them to suffer from minor traits such as a poor sense of direction, but also more severe imbalances such as feelings of not being in their own body at certain times. This may be a difficult state to understand for somebody who has never experienced it, but it affects a surprising number of people. All of these issues should begin to be rectified as the Girdling meridian rotates healthily.

The Uterus and the Heart have a close connection to each other. Although this relationship is often mentioned in Chinese medicine, it is rarely taken into account in women's energetic practices. The connection between these two organs serves to generate a healthy relationship between a woman's spirit and her unborn child when it is developing in the womb. The emotional bond that develops between mother and child is a powerful force, which relies on the energetic connection between these two organ systems. Figure 7.12 shows the connection between the Heart, the Uterus and the Girdling meridian.

As the Heart sends information down to the Uterus, it generates powerful shifts in the energetic field of the Uterus system. During the child's development this serves to build a bond between mother and child as well as imprinting certain family emotional traits into the next generation. It is for this reason that a pregnant woman should spend so much time regulating her emotional and spiritual health prior to giving birth. Any great stresses during different stages of the pregnancy will cause a shift in the spirit of the Heart, which will in turn start to adjust the child's developmental processes.

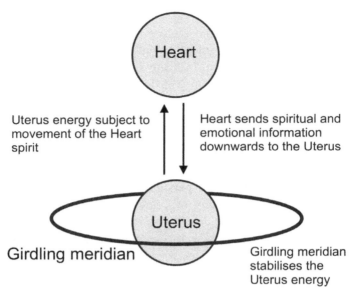

FIGURE 7.12: HEART, UTERUS AND GIRDLING MERIDIAN

Unfortunately, the nature of the Heart's spirit can also cause the Uterus and its function with regard to both fertility and menstruation to be affected while a woman is not pregnant. Here is the link between a woman's emotional state and the quality of her menstrual cycle. Part of the role of the Girdling meridian is to stabilise the Uterus Qi against any great imbalances that may otherwise result from the Heart spirit's movements. It is for this reason that awakening the orbit of the Girdling meridian is important for women in the early stages of their Nei Gong practice.

THE SIDE BRANCHES OF THE THRUSTING MERIDIAN SYSTEM

The next circulation that opens up usually takes a little longer than the previous rotations. Once again, it tends to happen of its own accord and happens long after you have stopped needing to work on lower Dan Tien rotation. It will come as a by-product of your standing in Wuji and working systematically through the various rotations that develop prior to this stage in your development. The side branches of the Thrusting meridian pass through the left and right sides of the torso, connecting strongly to the Liver and Spleen systems as well as the breasts and nipples.

When the side branches begin to open, you will become aware of a series of fluid changes taking place within the middle of your torso. Many people have reported sensations of warm fluid rushing quickly through the body, while others say it feels more like slow, sloshing movements. It is quite difficult to feel exactly which direction the side branches are flowing due to their depth within the body, but this is essentially not that important. As these channels open, there are clear signs that can be seen and felt on the outside of the body. A person will find that they can open and close all of the joints of the body very easily. The easiest to experience is the opening and closing of the ribs, which comes very easily to somebody who has successfully awakened the side branches of the Thrusting meridian.

After some time at this stage you will find that your body becomes highly fluid in its motions, and yet it is strongly connected to its centre. It is a tricky stage for beginners to reach in their Nei Gong training, but an important one in connecting the energy body to the physical body when it moves.

CIRCULATION OF QI INTO THE LIMBS

Many practitioners of Qi Gong refer to the flow of Qi through the lengths of the arms and legs as the 'large water wheel' or sometimes the 'macrocosmic orbit'. In this system of practice, we simply see them as further extensions of the 'small water wheels'. For us, the 'large water wheel' is an extension of the energy out of the body into the surrounding environment, the 'macrocosm'. That is not to say that other teachers are incorrect – it is just a different use of terminology, nothing more.

After all of the orbits have been opened up within the body, there will be a flow of Qi that extends right through the arms and legs out towards the hands and feet. This comes with a feeling of expansion all the way through the joints of the body including the shoulders, elbows, wrists, hips, knees and ankles. This is a very pleasant stage which makes your arms and legs feel incredibly light and free. The expansion feels as though you have been 'inflated' right through to the tips of your fingers and toes. It is common for the arms to even float upwards of their own accord without you realising. We often see the surprised faces of students as they realise they are standing with their arms high in the air during Wuji practice.

It can take longer for the legs and hips to open up than the arms –
sometimes several months longer. This is largely because we are standing
with our weight in our legs for most of our daily lives, whereas our arms
are relatively weight-free.

When a person has reached the stage of circulating energy down
through the arms and legs, it is normal for them to look as if they move
very fluidly when they perform their Qi Gong exercises. Their arms and
legs can even take on a slightly 'boneless' look to them, and yet when
you touch them, they still contain a great deal of strength. This strength
is based on an emptiness within the joints and a healthy flow of Qi rather
than physical strength; it is the internal power that is often felt in the
touch of high-level internal martial artists.

THE REJUVENATING EFFECTS OF
THE SMALL WATER WHEELS

As the energy begins to circulate through the various orbits of the 'small
water wheels', you should experience the sensations discussed above.
In addition, there are several key signs to look for in order to ascertain
whether you are progressing in the right direction or not. Although
these are not really phenomena we are aiming to achieve, they are useful
signposts along the road of our journey.

- It is normal for the face to become a little smoother than it was before
  as the movement of energy begins to nourish the skin. In some people,
  it can actually look as if their face is slightly moist, but in the majority
  it simply begins to smooth out many of their wrinkles. This is partly
  why so many internal arts practitioners look fairly youthful even when
  they are well into old age.

- A practitioner who has reached this stage will naturally develop very
  sharp and slightly piercing eyes. The movement of energy upwards
  in the body helps to bring a person's spirit into their gaze. This was
  a common way for teachers to check the relative skill level of their
  students.

- The skin on a practitioner's body often becomes quite loose and
  rubbery. As Qi permeates the layers of the skin and fascia begins to
  unbind, the skin stops being so 'bound up'. This is a particular quality
  to a Nei Gong practitioner's skin which is easy to detect if you touch
  them.

- Some practitioners find that their grey hair begins to change back to its original colour. Although the entire head of hair may not change, patches of hair may begin to grow back coloured once more. This has long been an issue of pride among many teachers in China and so many of them hide their grey hair by using hair dye. During a class outdoors, it can be quite a shock when the rain causes their hair dye to begin running down their face!

- A person with all of the orbits opened up should be very relaxed and fluid in their movements. Flexibility is not about how far you can stretch your limbs but rather to do with how fluidly your joints move and rotate within whatever range of flexibility you have. It is always very impressive to meet a skilled Nei Gong practitioner who is in their later years, as they maintain a great softness in their body movements. An internal arts practitioner with large amounts of stiffness in their body has likely never fully achieved the various rotations of the 'small water wheels'.

- Women should find that their breasts become somewhat more firm and may even begin to shrink a little. This is the result of the tightening of the Jing around the chest region. They may also find that they develop slightly more swollen nipples than they had previously.

In order to ascertain exactly where you are in your training, it is wise to use these signs, as well as the guidance of an experienced teacher. In a practice such as Nei Gong, there is always a great deal of confusion involved in what a person should be doing next and where they are exactly in the process. In modern times it has become all too common for teachers to simply state that the whole process is 'purely internal' and that there are no outside signs of progress. This is simply not true. Look for bodily changes in order to see where you are. Nothing can change within either the consciousness or energetic bodies without there being clear observable results within the physical body.

Chapter 8

HEART-CENTRED PRACTICE

It is here, at the intermediate stages of Nei Gong training, that women really start to move into a very unique aspect of the training. The work carried out by women with the middle Dan Tien is very important to them; it is a stage of development far more pivotal for women than it is for men. In order to progress to this level of inner development, it is wise to have ensured that you have already attained a healthy level of rotation within the orbits of the 'small water wheels', as discussed in Chapter 7. If you progress to this stage too early, then there will be a limit to the levels that you can reach, as well as a higher chance of generating imbalance as the 'recycling' function of the 'small water wheels' is not in place. The 'small water wheels' serve, in part, to make sure that any excesses you accidentally generate within the upper regions of the energy body are drawn back downwards towards your lower Dan Tien region where they can safely be retransformed or discharged through the legs.

If you are sure that you are ready to move on, then it is time to switch from the basic practice of the Wuji stance towards the more advanced Hundun posture; either of the two variants of this position are fine. This stance raises your centre of mass upwards towards the middle Dan Tien, which will assist you with progressing on to work with the more refined aspects of the energy body.

It should be noted here that you would normally expect male Nei Gong practitioners to begin working with opening the vertical branch of the Thrusting meridian once they have attained the various rotations within the congenital energy body. Men can empower this aspect of the process using the foundation they have built within the lower Dan Tien, although, to be honest, hardly any ever manage to do this because they first have to change the aspect of their acquired mind related to their base desires. If men open this channel prior to dealing with this aspect of their acquired mind, it will instead fuel the acquired mind with raw energy. The by-product of this is that they begin to distort their nature more and more. These characters then generally go on to become larger-than-life caricatures of themselves in the Daoist community. All of the desires for money, power, sex, fame and recognition overtake them and they become lost on the path. Their journey is essentially over.

Women generally work in a slightly different manner to their male counterparts and so change the focus of their study to opening up the Heart centre. When this has been achieved, a very natural and spontaneous opening of the vertical branch of the Thrusting meridian normally takes place for them. The process of opening this channel for women relies very little on the strength of their lower Dan Tien; this energy centre is basically responsible for initiating the 'small water wheels' in women's Nei Gong and little else. Women only really need to return to the lower Dan Tien when they begin a study of more advanced practices such as Nei Dan meditation. The biggest challenge for women with regard to timing is that if they progress on to the middle Dan Tien work too early, they run the risk of fuelling the surface layers of the acquired mind. This causes their emotional state to become greatly imbalanced, an issue that can result in emotional swings and heightened feelings of stress. If you move on to work with the middle Dan Tien and find that your emotions begin to run out of control, then consider stepping back to the foundation stages of Nei Gong training.

WHAT IS THE MIDDLE DAN TIEN?

As discussed in Chapter 2, the middle Dan Tien is also known as the Heart centre due to the close relationship that exists between these two aspects of the human body. It is the energy centre that roots the consciousness body into the realm of human existence and the key location where Qi is transformed within the body into Shen. This ethereal source of energetic information then travels onwards to generate development in the intellect and other cognitive aspects of the human mind. The Daoist view of human consciousness is that it essentially exists in a state of fragmentation. This division of spirit into several parts is much of the reason for human beings not existing in a state that naturally leads them towards spiritual elevation. Existence of consciousness itself leads to a refraction of our awareness into several aspects, and only through reversing this process can we find the unified original state of human seed consciousness – that which can lead us towards direct contact with Dao.

The interesting problem with human consciousness is that it generates various energetic fluctuations that we know as emotions, which then go on to form the seeds for mental activities that we call thoughts. These fluctuating movements of mind then cause a 'leakage' of energy from the middle Dan Tien, which weakens our ability to either connect with or empower true human consciousness. It is for this reason that so many Eastern traditions discuss the importance of settling the mind. Once settled, our thoughts can be stilled, emotions can be regulated and thus we can connect to higher states of conscious evolution.

THE FIVE SPIRITS – A MODEL OF FRACTURED CONSCIOUSNESS

The model of the five spirits is a universal model that is used heavily in Daoist alchemy, Nei Gong and even Chinese medicine. It is a model that shows how the human mind interacts with the external universe, and how emotions are generated from the distorted activities of these five spirits. In the Daoist model of human development, life began with seed consciousness, a spark of spiritual life which provided the blueprints for the development of the energy body and then finally physical existence. During this developmental process of creation, true human spirit was refracted into the five spirits shown in Figure 8.1.

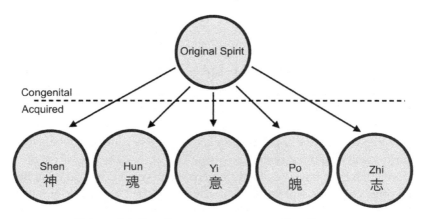

FIGURE 8.1: THE REFRACTION OF THE FIVE SPIRITS

True human spirit is the congenital state of human consciousness prior to it moving into the acquired state of mind. Once the acquired mind is created, then the five spirits begin to manifest within each of us. The spirits are briefly discussed below.

Shen

Shen can be a confusing term because sometimes it is used to refer to one of the five spirits, as in this case, and it can also be used as a general term for the highest-frequency manifestation of the three internal treasures, the other two being Jing and Qi. To be honest, if you are new to the Daoist arts, then this is always a challenge; you find after some time, though, that you become used to the contexts in which these terms are being discussed and so there is less confusion.

With regard to the Shen of the five spirits, it is this aspect of human spirit that connects us to the divine information of Dao. A person's concept of the spiritual aspects of life is dependent upon the strength of their Shen. If the Shen is weak, then they will be ruled by their intellect rather than the deeper aspects of human consciousness.

Shen is also very important for human connection because it is the aspect of human consciousness that enables us to develop compassion, love and the ability to care for others.

Hun

The Hun is the Yang aspect of the human soul; it is the element of human consciousness that continues to exist after our death through the act of transmigration. During human life it is in charge of our ability to dream and generate plans. If the Hun becomes constrained for whatever reason, then it can lead to great feelings of inner frustration. Almost all emotional feelings of being 'trapped' by some aspect of your life are to do with constraint of the Hun.

The Hun is also interesting because it is the key aspect of human consciousness that is said to become active at night when you dream. If a person is far from being able to contact their innate wisdom, then the Hun presents confused imagery during the night in the form of abstract dreams. However, if a person is able to reach a sufficiently high state, the Hun can serve as a messenger from the Dao and therefore skills such as prophetic dreaming will begin to unfold in a person.

Yi

The Yi is our awareness, our focus and the general term used for our cognitive faculties. The strength of the Yi depends in part on the health of our digestive system and the acquired Qi, but also on the balance of the other four spirits. It takes the information delivered to it from the other four spirits and processes this information into concrete thought patterns.

If the Yi is weak, then a person will find it difficult to think properly. Mental focus and the ability to concentrate on anything for long periods of time can be compromised.

Po

The Po is the Yin aspect of the human soul and as such is paired with the Hun. These two work together to connect us to our outer world. The Hun connects us with the entity of Heaven, while the Po connects us to the more tangible aspects of life, usually referred to as being a philosophical manifestation of Earth.

The Po gives us our ability to tangibly 'feel' things, both physically and emotionally. If the Po is weakened or disturbed in some way, then a person will often become quite emotionally 'numb' to the events taking place around them. They can protect themselves emotionally by building up layers of emotional 'shielding', which can make them appear cold to those they meet.

Zhi

The Zhi is our willpower, our ability to see things through. Without a healthy Zhi, we will never take the dream-like plans of the Hun or the mental processes of the Yi and turn them into actions that we complete. Many people lack a healthy Zhi because of its connection to the Jing and the fact that the Zhi is rooted in the physical organ of the Kidneys. This is why the majority of people never really manage to commit to any kind of inner path. They generally find that they do not have the Zhi to see the training through.

On another level, the Zhi is also connected to the grand scheme of life, which is closely related to what we in the West would know as our destiny. This is perhaps not a totally accurate term to apply, though, as destiny implies that every person has a high-minded goal that is inherently part of their life. The Daoist concept of this is known as a person's Ming, and the only guaranteed aspect of a person's Ming is that they are going to be born, travel through life and then die. How smoothly they manage to do this will be due, in part, to how closely they are following the path of their Ming. This is in turn dependent upon the strength of their Zhi. A person with strong Zhi will find that they naturally seem to follow their Ming, while those with a weak level of Zhi will often find that they simply have no idea what direction they are supposed to take in their life.

This has been a brief overview of the functions of the five spirits. It is enough for practitioners of Nei Gong to understand in order to move on to working with the middle Dan Tien, but it is far from the whole story. A full discussion of the nature of human consciousness would require several volumes in their own right. If you would like more detailed information, please refer to Damo Mitchell's *White Moon on the Mountain Peak: The Alchemical Firing Process of Nei Dan.*

EMOTIONS OR VIRTUES

Arguably more important for Nei Gong training is understanding the manner in which the five spirits express themselves within the acquired mind. If the five spirits sit at the core of our being, responsible for the processing of our interactions with reality, it is the information that comes out of these interactions that begins to change the nature of our being. The manner in which the five spirits can be expressed generally falls into two main categories: they express themselves either through emotions or through virtues. Table 8.1 shows a summary of the emotions and virtues that come from each of the five spirits.

TABLE 8.1: THE SPIRITS, THE EMOTIONS AND THE VIRTUES

Spirit	Emotion	Virtue
Shen	Excitation	Contentment
Hun	Anger	Patience/understanding
Yi	Worry	Empathy/compassion
Po	Sadness	Bravery/conviction
Zhi	Fear	Wisdom/clarity

When looking at the Daoist model of the emotions, it can initially appear too simple. As a model of the human mind, it appears to come nowhere near close to discussing all of the various emotional traits that a person can have. This is because the five key emotions are just broad headings, beneath which should be placed all the other emotions that a person can experience during the course of their life. As an experiment, I (Roni) once sat down and listed as many emotions or emotionally based character traits as I could think of and then I put them under the obvious headings of the five key emotions listed here. In fact, it was very easy to do, and so the Daoists perhaps did indeed manage to successfully identify the key characteristic traits of human consciousness.

Alongside these key emotional headings are the five virtues, or De (德) in Chinese. The virtues are stated to be the congenital manifestations of their corresponding emotions. This is to say that if the five spirits are operating in a balanced manner, they will produce the virtues instead of the emotions. Each of these is explored individually.

Excitation to Contentment

The spirit of the Shen resides within the Heart. It is the spiritual manifestation of the element of Fire. Excitation and manic outbursts are the most extreme ways in which this spirit will express itself when it is in a state of excess. During these times the Shen is at a high and often completely out of control. This would be considered to be like the flames of the Fire burning high. Like a burning flame, it cannot burn so brightly for ever, and so this state of heightened emotional activity must come to an end. The high turns into a low and so we experience the opposite of excitation, a low time where the more Yin emotions come to the surface.

Also contained within the range of the Shen's emotional 'bandwidth' are the emotions of joy, happiness, pleasure, love, connection and even lust. All a natural part of human life, it is the Heart and its spirit of the Shen that produce the emotions upon which so many place great importance. Of course, there is nothing wrong with these emotions in themselves; ultimately, it is their transience that is more of an issue. Joy cannot be permanent by its nature, pleasure cannot be such for too long without ceasing to be pleasurable, lust is often easily sated and even love all too often fades away. This is the nature of emotions; they are fleeting experiences which we only register because of their comparison with their opposites. We require the entire range of emotions to register even one of them, and so no matter how much we seek to remain within the positive emotional highs of the Shen and the Heart, we will undoubtedly also be subject to the movement of the other spirits as well. Excessive, prolonged states of excitation cause the Qi of the Heart to flicker and 'burn'. If this becomes a constant pattern, then it will cause the Qi of the Heart to become deficient.

The virtuous expression of the Shen is an experience of contentment. This is a more constant feeling of satisfaction with the situation you find yourself in. Unlike the flickering flames of the emotions of the Shen, contentment is more stable. This satisfaction begins to stir the Heart towards more extreme manifestations of connection and so this satisfaction pulls you into a more powerful relationship with your life. This is especially important for many women to move towards, as society has so often conditioned them to seek out love in their life. Countless times we hear from women students how the most important thing in their life when they were younger was finding the 'right man' to settle down with and marry. Of course, there is nothing wrong with being in love or being married, but it should be based on a stable loving connection between two people rather than a fleeting experience of heightened love and lust, as these will fade very quickly. Many people are subject to huge feelings of disappointment and hurt which touches them deep within their Shen once the initial magic of their relationship has faded away, to be replaced with more negative emotional aspects. It is an interesting facet of the spirit of the Heart that it also likes to connect with other people and so often fears being alone. For this reason many people will remain with a partner they don't like very much rather than be on their own.

Anger to Patience and Understanding

The spirit of the Hun is rooted in the Liver. It is the spiritual manifestation of the element of Wood. Wood energy flows out of the Hun and through the body with a driving force that generates the potential for growth and energy. When directed into something positive, Wood energy can generate huge amounts of creative power. It is often the spiritual basis upon which a great number of ethical and political movements have been based. Wood energy gives us the power to stand up for rights and what we believe in. This potential for taking action is important for human existence, but unfortunately it also has the opposite characteristic of being responsible for all of the destructive aspects of human nature. In its most extreme or undirected manifestation, Wood energy produces outbursts of anger and rage along with feelings of jealousy, placing importance upon status, a need for power and a number of other negative personality traits. Although quick to flare up, often these feelings leave a stain upon the acquired nature that makes them easy to return to time and time again.

If Wood energy is not able to flow freely, it often has the opposite effect of moving inwards and becoming trapped inside a person. The result is a feeling of inner frustration which can cause a person to become angry at themselves. In the case of interactions with people who make you feel angry, if you cannot express this anger, it often contributes to these feelings of frustration which can be very self-destructive. Often the only way this energy can be expressed is through manipulative or passive-aggressive behaviour patterns.

When the spirit of the Hun is able to express itself in a virtuous state, it produces the quality of patience. Patience in this case is largely concerned with your ability to deal with others. It is the patience to interact with the rest of your life without allowing it to lead to anger or frustration. The other virtue often listed as being related to the Hun is understanding. A great deal of conflict in the world is related to people's inability to relate to or understand each other. Confusion due to distorted information passing between two people has been the root of many conflicts throughout history. As the Hun starts to express itself in a virtuous manner, it increases a person's ability to apply understanding to life's situations.

Worry to Empathy and Compassion

The spirit of the Yi is rooted in the Spleen. It is the spiritual manifestation of the element of Earth. Classically connected to the emotion of worry as well as chronic overthinking, the spirit of the Yi is often overly concerned with possible future outcomes and perceived problems. In an increasingly fast-paced world which is set up to draw people's awareness out of themselves towards external concerns, the Yi is often existing in a state of constant tension. For many people, a practice such as meditation would be the most positive activity they could introduce into their lives. Even if the lofty aims of enlightenment of immortality are stripped out of the practice, sitting with the awareness gently inside the body would help to calm the Yi.

On top of this, the Yi is intimately connected to the rest of the five spirits, meaning that its health is a reflection of the whole spectrum of human emotions. Any emotional disturbances are going to throw a person's Yi into a state of overthinking. This has the effect of draining a person's acquired Qi, which will then affect the rest of a person's health.

An interesting facet that appears within people with an imbalance in their Yi is their need either to receive support from others or to be overly sensitive to the idea of sympathy. Character traits such as neediness will appear in somebody with an imbalance in the Yi. The need for extreme amounts of sympathy from those in their life goes hand in hand with an oversensitivity to perceived insults from others. The Yi can also lead a person to being overly smothering when dealing with close family or friends. If none of these needs are met, then the Yi can feel undernourished and a deep sense of loneliness can set in.

The virtuous expression of the Yi is empathy and compassion towards all beings. These are virtues based in healthy levels of connection and awareness of the needs and inner nature of those around them. Possibly the most important of the virtues with regard to dealing with others, the Yi constructs compassion from the combined spiritual information of the other virtues.

Sadness to Bravery and Conviction

The spirit of the Po resides in the Lungs. It is the spiritual manifestation of the element of Metal. The emotions resulting from the movement of the Po are almost heavy in nature. When they move into a state of extreme imbalance, they can cause a person to feel as if they have a tight ball constricting their insides. These are the emotions of sadness, grief, an awareness of loss or depression. These emotions are heavy and binding. A person who has suffered for a long time with them will generally start to develop a very closed-up posture in their body. The chest will close up as if the Heart itself is attempting to hide itself away from the world. This is particularly unhealthy for women, as it will have a detrimental effect upon the Jing stored within the chest region as well as the strength of the middle Dan Tien. In extreme cases of emotional hurt derived from the spirit of the Po, the Metal elemental energy will actually begin to separate a person from the outside world. This results in feelings of emotional numbness or symptoms of shock. Rather unfairly, to the outside world this can appear as if this person is emotionally cold or aloof, when in actual fact their Po is simply seeking to protect them from any more emotional damage.

The virtuous expression of the Po spirit is classically listed as bravery, although in modern times perhaps conviction is a more appropriate term. Like the finely forged blade of a steel sword, the virtues that develop from within the heart of the spirit of Metal serve to enable a person to cut through any feelings of sadness and grief, as well as many perceived problems in life. The virtue of courage is important for those walking the internal path of Daoism as there are always many challenges put in a person's way. Daoism long recognised this, which is why such importance is placed on this character trait in Daoist discussions of virtuous behaviour.

Fear to Wisdom and Clarity

The Zhi is the spirit that resides in the Kidneys. It is the spiritual manifestation of the element of Water and responsible for the emotions of fear and anxiety. In extreme cases this spirit will manifest through feelings of chronic perceived threats, a psychological trait that is practically crippling as it prevents a person from seeing any life event in an undistorted manner.

Fear is often a subtle emotion which, like water seeping through the cracks in a rock face, permeates into a person's being. Although these small pockets of fear-based energy may go unnoticed for a while, they begin to increase in amount until they are the basis for almost all of a person's thought processes. Just as the Kidneys are seen as the foundation of a person's health in Chinese thought, so the emotion of fear is often seen as the foundation of all emotional imbalances.

In its virtuous state, the spirit of the Zhi has the potential to manifest in pure wisdom – the ability to see the nature of the world and its underlying phenomena with a high degree of clarity. The conversion of Zhi is often considered the most difficult of the spirits to convert into its higher state, which is why the virtue of wisdom was so highly prized in the Eastern traditions.

Emotions as the Glue of the Acquired Mind

What this all means is that the process of working with the middle Dan Tien is the first stage in learning to convert the emotions into the virtues. Since the middle Dan Tien and its associated organ, the Heart, are the portal through which all emotional movements are experienced, it is here that the real inner transformation takes place.

The emotions are produced in reaction to external events during the course of our daily lives, as well as through the actions of our mind. These then distort our perception of the world and build up layers around our consciousness, as depicted in Figure 8.2.

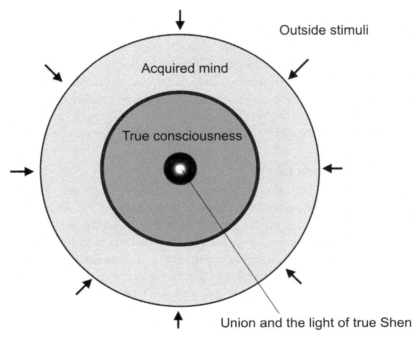

FIGURE 8.2: THE HUMAN MIND

It is perhaps easiest to think of the emotions as the 'glue' that binds the layers of the acquired mind on to the outside of our true consciousness. Because of this, the majority of people never fully experience true consciousness or the potential for spiritual elevation that it contains. Self-identification generally lies with the acquired mind and all of the biases and conditioned thinking from which it is made. It is when working with the middle Dan Tien that we first experience the breakdown of the acquired mind. As this happens, the 'glue' of the emotions begins to be released and so we experience varying degrees of emotional release and shifts during our practice.

At the heart of the mind lies the potential for unification of the five spirits, which will result in perception of the white light of true Shen. This is a sign of healthy progress into the more advanced stages of Daoist inner work, and the point at which the virtues begin to become a part of our nature.

WORKING WITH THE MIDDLE DAN TIEN

When women reach the stage of working with the middle Dan Tien, they should change their practice so that it is based around the Hundun stance, as discussed in Chapter 6. It is generally the case that women who have been regularly training in Nei Gong will intuitively find themselves moving towards this posture after a few years of practice anyway. It becomes a natural posture for the body to enter into after the various 'small water wheels' have been opened and a healthy foundation has been built within the region of the lower Dan Tien.

When women begin to practise this posture, there is generally little work that they have to do to initiate the process. Just through observing the very nature of the energetic circulation taking place within their body, the stance begins to open up the next phase in their development and thus change begins to take place of its own accord. All women should do is continue with their training, and when entering into sessions of practising standing postures, they should adopt the Hundun stance. Try to ensure that all of its alignment principles are correct and then place your awareness gently on to the meridian point named Shan Zhong (膻中) (CV 17). This point is shown in Figure 8.3. It sits within the centre of the chest at the height of the heart.

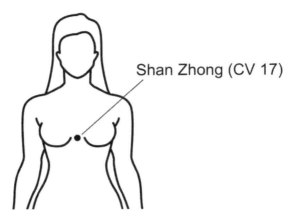

Shan Zhong (CV 17)

FIGURE 8.3: THE SHAN ZHONG MERIDIAN POINT

Note that at this stage in the training we do not wish to place our awareness directly on to the middle Dan Tien itself. In actual fact, male practitioners can place their awareness here, but the middle Dan Tien in women has a different quality to it. For women, it is important to set up the awareness in such a manner that energetic expansion from the middle Dan Tien is encouraged. There is also the danger of allowing the mind to interact directly with the middle Dan Tien itself. If the focus is even a little too strong, then you will run the risk of sending your emotions into a hyperactive state. The Shan Zhong meridian point is the exit point for the middle Dan Tien, and so gently placing your awareness here will cause the energy of the Heart centre to expand outwards from the core.

Once the mind has been placed here, then simply observe what takes place and your body will begin to move through the next stages in the internal process of Nei Gong. If, after some time, you do not progress as expected, then the chances are you will need to return to the foundation practices for some time instead.

The first phenomenon that women should experience at this stage is that the Heart centre begins to expand outwards away from your body, as shown in Figure 8.4. This is a clear stage of development which can tangibly be felt.

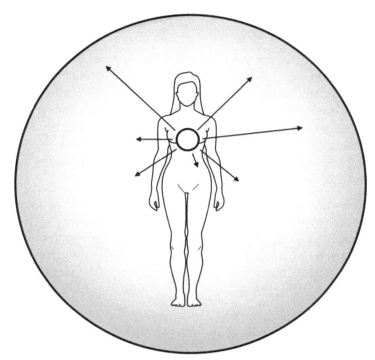

FIGURE 8.4: EXPANSION OF THE MIDDLE DAN TIEN

As the energy from the middle Dan Tien begins to move outwards, it is common for women to go through the following stages in their practice:

- First, the middle Dan Tien starts to pull open the chest region. It is common for women in the Hundun posture to find that they are stretching open their chests automatically. This stretching power comes from within the body and is happening completely of its own accord. In some cases women throw open their chest with such power that they almost bend their spine backwards. Although this would appear to break many of the alignment principles of Nei Gong, it is a positive stage. The energy body is doing this of its own volition in order to establish a healthy connection with the outside environment.

- From here, once the chest has opened up, it is generally the case that the Shan Zhong meridian point begins to open up. This usually comes with a warm feeling that spreads across the chest region as well as the breasts. Those with a high degree of internal sensitivity will find that the meridian point itself is vibrating at a high frequency. With some practice, it is even possible to feel the clear line of energetic movement taking place from the middle Dan Tien outwards towards the surface of the body at this point.

• As the energy of the middle Dan Tien grows stronger, it will begin to expand the auric field, which will grow into a large bubble around you. This is the information from the Heart centre beginning to change the emotional information contained in the energy surrounding you. It is at this stage that the emotional stagnation within the body begins to shed itself, resulting in brief flashes of emotional release. Women will begin to cry, shout or laugh for short periods of time as the acquired layers of the mind begin to break down.

• As women move deeper into connection with their own spirit, they are left with a feeling that the entire body is opening up from the inside. The joints can feel gently pulled open through the body. It is clear to feel that this pulling motion is coming from the region of the chest. The epicentre of the stretch is coming from the middle Dan Tien.

As the layers of the acquired mind begin to transform, it is completely normal for emotional releases to be present. These are nothing to worry about. As information contained within emotional energy moves out of us, it triggers a reaction. If these releases continue for any length of time or they are too strong, simply relax, practise some deep breathing and walk around briskly for ten minutes or so. If you feel that each time you practise you are entering into emotional releases that you don't feel ready to have, then you should return to the previous levels of Nei Gong training. The more solid your foundation, the smoother the later stages in training will be. While it is good to cleanse the body of negative emotional information, there is also no need to suffer during your practice! We have had some students who really seem to want to drive their way through their emotions. Their practice becomes a form of self-flagellation, which is really not healthy. The body should only really release emotional energies when it is ready to do so. If it is forced, then you run the risk of over-stressing the energy body, which can be damaging. Instead, keep working on more basic practices and wait until the time is right to go deeper into your art.

THE LIGHT OF TRUE SHEN

If the energy of the middle Dan Tien is allowed to expand outwards to a large enough degree, it will begin to give women access to the innate stillness that exists at the centre of their consciousness. During periods of standing, if you go deep enough into work with the middle Dan Tien, it is possible to touch upon a state of unification of the five spirits. As this happens, a brilliant white light can appear in front of your mind's eye. This white light is the mind translating the information contained within true Shen, the state of human consciousness prior to its refraction into the five spirits. This light starts as a small point of light, which is often compared to the full moon on a clear night. From here it generally expands to engulf your entire vision. There is no mistaking this light for anything else. It is not subtle; it is as though somebody has shone a high-powered torch beam right into your eyes.

When this light appears, it is a positive sign of progress, a sign that conversion is taking place within the deeper parts of your being. While experiencing the light, it is normal for women to find that their minds have become incredibly still. The incessant chatter of the acquired mind grows still and this is what enables a brief glimpse into a state of true congenital being.

There is nothing to be done when this light appears in front of your vision. It is simply a sign of progress like any other. It should be enjoyed but not focused upon or strived for in your practice. It will come and go; some people will experience it once and then never see it again for years on end. The state of human consciousness is complex. It is beyond our understanding, and so its rhythms and manifestations will often be a mystery to us in our practice. During Nei Gong practice, this light often manifests, but we can do nothing with it as Nei Gong is not a deep enough training method to stabilise it into anything useful for us. Those who progress on to the stage of working with the white light of true consciousness require the more advanced alchemical training of Nei Dan. It is only through sitting practice of this sort that a person will ever be able to access the deeper parts of Daoist training. Nei Gong is simply a bridge that can lead us there.

THE OPENING OF THE THRUSTING MERIDIAN

There are several benefits to women of opening up the middle Dan Tien. First, they require this practice to nourish their health; this is accomplished because of the connection of the chest region of the body to a woman's Jing. The second benefit is that they begin to enter into the process of shedding emotional pathogens as well as the layers of the acquired mind. The third benefit is to do with the Nei Gong process itself, as it unlocks the major blockage that prevents a woman from opening up the vertical branch of the Thrusting meridian.

The process of opening up the vertical branch of the Thrusting meridian is shown in Figure 8.5.

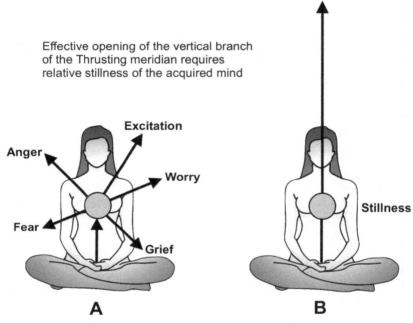

FIGURE 8.5: OPENING THE VERTICAL BRANCH
OF THE THRUSTING MERIDIAN

Generally, this has to be accomplished while in a sitting posture as shown in the diagram. Since this practice is not specifically meditation but rather a form of energy work, the exact sitting posture is not that important. As long as the spine is upright and the practitioner is seated near to the floor with her legs crossed, any meditation pose will suffice. It is fine to prop the hips up with a small cushion in order to ensure that your legs don't go numb after sitting for some time.

When you begin this practice, it is wise to place your hands into your lap in the position shown in Figure 8.6. This is a hand shape known as the Taiji Mudra in Daoism.

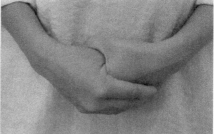

FIGURE 8.6: THE TAIJI MUDRA

Place the thumb of one hand in the centre of the opposite palm and then lightly close your fingers so that both hands are gently clasped together as shown in Figure 8.6. In many schools of internal arts, it is stated that there is a difference between the way in which men and women should use Mudras. This is true for more advanced practices such as meditation, but for an exercise such as this it really does not matter. Simply make this posture with either the left or right hand being the one that clasps the other's thumb. Go with whichever hand feels the most natural to you. The fact is that when the vertical branch of the Thrusting meridian opens up, you will not be able to hold this hand shape anyway; this is discussed below.

The obvious question here is: When should a woman progress from the Hundun posture into this seated exercise? It would be nice if it was easy to answer this question, but it is not possible to give such structured guidelines at this stage in a woman's internal development. What generally takes place is that a woman will be practising the Hundun posture. This will normally be the case for the first several months of her reaching this stage. After this time she will begin to find that she is naturally drawn downwards towards the floor by a combination of the planet's energy and her own intuition. When this happens, she should simply follow her instincts and progress into the sitting practice. The challenge here is actually recognising when this is the case. Many students cannot feel the difference between the correct time to move on and a desire to sit down because their legs are tired from standing! Our guidance on this is that if it happens after only a few weeks of reaching the Hundun stage, then you should ask yourself if it is really time to progress. You should also try resisting the urge to go to the floor on the first few occasions. If it is the right time for you and your energy body wants to move on, then you will find the instinct to sit down overpowering. You will find it very difficult to resist what it wants to do, because your energy body knows the correct time to move on in your practice.

It is interesting to note that male practitioners of Nei Gong often have to engage in a specific practice to open up the vertical branch of the Thrusting meridian while female practitioners do not. Men are working primarily with the driving force of the lower Dan Tien and as such are spiritually a manifestation of the will of this energy centre. Once they reach the stage of working with the Thrusting meridian, they should engage in seated exercise and it can take them quite some time to accomplish this task. Women, on the other hand, are connected to the middle Dan Tien, which is more concerned with spontaneous creativity than will and effort. This means that once they have successfully opened up their Heart centre, they will generally move naturally into the further stages of training. The vertical branch of the Thrusting meridian is one of those stages that should open up automatically for them after some time, and on our courses we have had women reach this stage at the strangest of moments, during completely unrelated internal exercises! The fact is that no practice in Nei Gong is very difficult as long as you ensure the foundation has been built in the prior stages of your training. It is the preparation that really dictates how well you do in your practice.

As the vertical branch of the Thrusting meridian begins to open up, you will become aware of a deep internal vibration moving from the base of your body right up to the crown of the head. As shown in Figure 8.5, this line must move through the region of the middle Dan Tien. In order to develop past this region of the body, there has to be a relative degree of stillness in a practitioner's mind. If much energy is being lost through the emotional activities of the mind, then the energy of the Thrusting meridian will become dispersed. If, however, the mind is still, then the energy will continue unimpeded through the body.

ADDICTION TO INTERNAL SENSATION

There is a pitfall at this stage in the training into which many practitioners of Nei Gong may fall. This is an addiction to the sensations that accompany the opening of the vertical branch of the Thrusting meridian. As this channel opens, there is an increase in vibrational information which spreads throughout the whole of the energy body. This is the internal vibration that Nei Gong practitioners seek because it generates a powerful connection between the mind and body; it is a level of internal integration that can only be achieved by working at this deep stage with the congenital energy body. This information generally brings with it waves of euphoria or bliss.

In many cases it can bring with it very sexual sensations which can feel somewhat akin to whole-body orgasms. These sensations come in waves during this stage in the practice and it is important that a practitioner does not become mentally attached to them.

It is a fact of how humans function on an energetic level that where the mind goes, energy follows. What this means with regard to our practice is that if we allow the mind to attach itself too closely to any experiences, then it will begin to fuel these experiences. Energy will be led there and so these experiences will become stabilised within the realm of our attention. When we reach a stage such as this whole-body euphoria, which develops out of the Thrusting meridian, we should simply try to sit back and observe what is taking place within us. If our mind begins to subconsciously place too much importance on the sensations, then we will actually become stuck there. It will be a long time before we ever manage to progress past this stage – in fact, some people never will.

It is interesting to note that many of the sensations that can arise from training in the internal arts are often related to sexual experiences. As soon as a person's Jing begins to stir, then it is normal for there to be an increase in sex drive, and many of the movements of energy that take place are similar to sensations only experienced before or during orgasm. It is these sensations that trap so many practitioners in their base desires and are the reason many contemporary schools of Qi Gong seem to be focused heavily on sexual practices – practices that may be good for your health and relationship but will never assist in the conversion of your spiritual state.

THE DIVISION OF THE TWO POLES

If you manage to remain mentally centred during the development of the internal vibration, then you will not be drawn into addiction to the sensations that arise. In this case the vertical branch of the Thrusting meridian will continue to extend upwards until it reaches the crown of the head. At this stage the two poles of Yin and Yang will begin to divide within your energy system. When this happens, you will feel as though your head is being raised upwards into the sky and your hips are being drawn downwards towards the planet. A spontaneous physical stretch often begins to manifest within your body and it is normal to shake quite violently for a few weeks in your practice. Do not worry; just continue with your training and you will swiftly progress past this stage.

It is wise when entering into this aspect of Nei Gong training to take yourself away from your normal life for a short while so that there are no distractions for you. Some of the changes you will go through during this practice are best done with no outside concerns getting in the way. You will also find that by this stage, in order for this process to take place, you will have to be sitting for an hour and a half to two hours at a time. If all of the 'small water wheels' have opened up, then your legs will not go numb, so sitting for a couple of hours will not be difficult. You will also find that this is no chore; rather, you will want to sit for this length of time for several sessions each day. This is a sign of the consciousness body knowing how you should progress in your development. If you are not at this stage with your sitting practice, then you may need to return to the previous stages in the Nei Gong process.

THE SPIRITUAL ANTENNA

Though obviously not a classical name, the vertical branch of the Thrusting meridian is most easily understood as a kind of 'spiritual antenna' which has the potential to connect a person into increasingly high states of awareness. As it extends upwards through a high-level practitioner's crown, it serves to bring information back down from the realm of pure consciousness into the energy body. This is a very advanced stage which generally takes a minimum of several years of daily, dedicated practice to reach. On the whole, women seem to reach this stage much faster than men, who require almost twice the amount of practice from what we have seen. This is most likely due to the challenge of the lower Dan Tien for men, as well as women's natural centripetal movement of energy which assists in the vertical raising of information along the Thrusting meridian.

As women reach this stage in their practice, they begin to externally manifest one of the most fascinating and beautiful reactions that can come out of Nei Gong training. Down through the vertical branch of the Thrusting meridian comes a torrent of spiritual information which begins to make major shifts in the nature of women's energy body. This then begins to transform their nature on a large scale. It is a deep and powerful stage in a woman's Nei Gong journey.

As this information moves through them, women begin to make complex Mudras and spiralling, dance-like movements which are in equal parts complex and graceful. Many of these movements are reminiscent of the dances we have seen women performing throughout India and the Far East. Figure 8.7 shows a female student spontaneously producing some of these effects in her practice. Sadly, a still image does nothing to capture the beauty of these reactions.

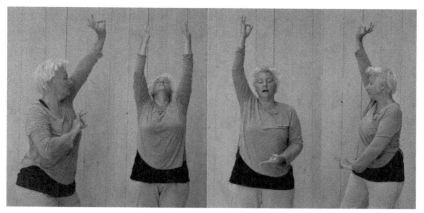

FIGURE 8.7: STUDENT REACTING TO SPIRITUAL INFORMATION

The majority of women at this stage in their training are pulled to their feet completely against their will. They enter into these movements often in the middle of an advanced class of Nei Gong even if the rest of the class is quietly sitting or practising standing exercises. The movements are always spiralling in nature; each twist reflects a movement of energy within the congenital meridians. The Mudras produced each carry with them an individual piece of spiritual information which begins to filter into the practitioner's consciousness. Often the women entering into this state also begin to sing or make sounds spontaneously. These sounds each serve to repattern different energetic frequencies within the body. In many cases these spontaneously produced sounds take the form of pleasant-sounding chanting.

Throughout all of this spontaneous spiritual activity, female practitioners enter into a mental state of deep inner peace and stillness. There is generally a large smile across their face as they go through the movements, movements they can almost never recreate on purpose afterwards. At this stage it is normal to feel the sounds and activity originating from deep within the region of the Heart. These movements often feel as if they spread out through the meridians of the body – like a surge of fluid running along their length. This has the feel of purifying the energy body and is a powerful stage in the practice.

This stage generally lasts for a few months but, again, if a person wishes to move on with their practice, then they should not attach themselves to the experiences. Attachment of the mind to these reactions will prevent the practitioner from ever progressing further into Nei Gong.

SPIRITUAL SKILLS

It is never a good idea to write extensively on the abilities that can come out of this kind of internal practice. Many Daoist lineages placed great importance upon neither demonstrating internal skills nor attaching significance to them. Many of these skills were kept secret in order to prevent people from striving for them in their training. In recent years we have come across students of the Daoist arts who are actively striving to achieve almost superhuman skills through the study of a practice such as Nei Gong. The nature of Ming is that it serves some kind of strange justice and so these people obsessed with developing such skills rarely have any success.

That being said, it is not abnormal, or that rare, for students who reach the stage of opening the vertical branch of the Thrusting meridian to start manifesting various internal skills. These skills range from the ability to consciously transmit mental information, heightened mental sensitivity and intuition through to spontaneous hands-on healing skill and countless other abilities. This is all just a reaction to the connection of consciousness to higher frequencies of spiritual information. As already stated, these abilities should neither be sought after nor focused upon. They are healthy signs of development and nothing more; simply continue with your training.

THE LARGE WATER WHEEL

One of the highest-level skills that can be obtained through Nei Gong is the development of the 'large water wheel' of Qi. This is the circulation of information that can take place out of the body, as shown in Figure 8.8. This circulation extends out of the vertical branch of the Thrusting meridian and then rotates through the external environment back into your body. The exact size of this rotation will vary from person to person, depending upon the strength of their spirit.

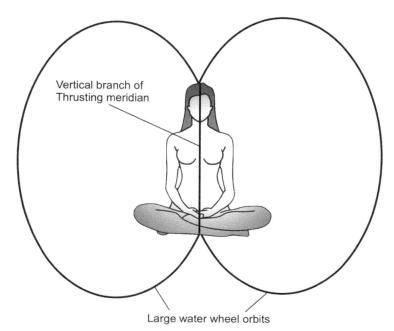

Vertical branch of
Thrusting meridian

Large water wheel orbits

FIGURE 8.8: THE LARGE WATER WHEEL

Generally, a practitioner who reaches this stage will have progressed on to the practice of Nei Dan, but on occasion some practitioners will have accomplished the 'large water wheel' without the need for alchemical sitting practice. Those practitioners are almost always women. This is because female energy naturally moves into the vertical branch of the Thrusting meridian when it is open, while men will have to reverse the natural outwards flow of their Qi before this can happen. This can only really be accomplished through prolonged sitting practice in order to change the nature of their natural consciousness.

When the 'large water wheel' opens, it enables a person to exchange information with their environment to a very high degree. There is a natural increase in sensitivity as well as a development of body awareness that is beyond what is possible without internal training. A person at this stage will know intuitively what is good for them to eat or drink. An awareness of the nature of environmental energetic fluxes is developed and you will generally find that they border on becoming 'psychic' with regard to their understanding of a situation or event. On top of this, the natural high-vibration energy that they circulate through the 'large water wheel' will begin to generate change around them. Practitioners who have opened up the 'large water wheel' will find that they naturally begin to draw people to them. This is the stage of becoming life's natural spiritual teachers. Any words or teachings given by somebody at this stage in their internal development will have strong influences on those around them. This is the stage at which internal cultivation is required in order to stop the acquired mind over-attaching to the role of teacher that has naturally grown out of the practice. There is a fine line to be walked for teachers of this level, as it is all too easy for a group of internal practitioners to transform into a religion or cult – a situation that is good for nobody involved.

INTERNAL SKILL IS NOT ENLIGHTENMENT

This chapter has explored many of the intermediate and more advanced stages of Nei Gong training for women. It is easy to see how the foundation stages are based in regulation of Jing and Blood as well as the circulation of Qi through the 'small water wheels'. Beyond this, the practice is based upon working with the middle Dan Tien, the cultivation of spirit and the circulation of energy outwards into the external environment. Beyond this, the concluding chapter of this book will briefly outline the highest of Daoist practices, Nei Dan.

By moving through this process, a person will undoubtedly experience a series of inner evolutions. This is the nature of intense Daoist inner practices. These changes can often be challenging because they can affect every aspect of a person's life. The people in your life can find this difficult to observe, despite the fact that these changes are always a positive development for the Nei Gong practitioner. What we have witnessed is that often this process is quite difficult for a lot of women who come into Nei Gong training. This is generally due to the husbands and partners of these women. A constant development we see with women who practise Nei Gong for any length of time is that first they improve their health and then they begin to increase in confidence. There is often a glowing sense of self-assuredness that comes out of these women. Sadly, it is this that so often causes difficulty with regard to their daily life. Many husbands and partners seem to struggle with their wife or girlfriend becoming more confident. This is an issue that is rarely discussed in internal arts literature, but it is certainly an aspect of the training that women should be aware of before engaging with the practice.

As these changes take place, women find that they become more aware of their own inner being, the layers of the acquired mind begin to fall away and they change their emotional standpoint from which they observe life. This is when students gain glimpses of their innate virtues, although those virtues will never be the whole of a person's spiritual makeup unless they become fully realised beings – the immortals of Daoist legend.

It is worth remembering that no matter how positive these changes are, how internally strong a person becomes and what internal abilities develop out of their practice, none of this is an indication of 'enlightenment'. This is not really a term used in the Daoist tradition, but it has become commonplace in the alternative community. Although nobody can really agree on a definitive explanation of what enlightenment is, most agree that it is a state of high spiritual cultivation which few manage to attain. It is important to conclude this section of the book by reminding people that none of the signs or developments listed in this chapter relies on a person being enlightened, a Buddha, an immortal or even a saint. They are skills that can be developed by anybody prepared to put in the practice.

CONCLUSION

This book has been exploring the stages of development that are generally experienced by students entering into a regular and diligent practice of Nei Gong training. As with any internal system, of course, a person may have multiple goals when engaging with the training. Nei Gong is often practised from a medical point of view, and in this case the teachings are far more influenced by Chinese medical theory. Many people come into Nei Gong from the point of view of martial arts, and here they are attempting to build large amounts of internal power. The personal interest of both authors of this book is in the alchemical teachings of the Daoists, and for this reason our Nei Gong training is to serve as a platform for spiritual cultivation. Along the way, this type of Nei Gong practice also forces a person to deal with and transform the state of their consciousness. The human mind sits at the root of a large proportion of disease, and so we can say that Nei Gong for spiritual cultivation also works to improve a person's health, even if this takes place as a by-product of everything else we are doing. When writing about Nei Gong, it is our belief that if the spiritual growth aspects of the art are emphasised, then it is fairly simple for somebody with the right knowledge to apply this information to their own field of interest.

Of course, alongside the various stages discussed in this book there are also countless other internal experiences to be had along the way. No person's process is going to be exactly the same as anybody else's. The nature of the energy body is that it is complex and unique to each of us. On top of that, the state of our consciousness is at such a level of intricacy that no teacher can ever fully predict how the Nei Gong process will unfold for a person. In writing this book, we wished first to discuss the process from the point of view of female practitioners of the Daoist arts; this was of key importance to us. We felt that women in Daoism are not currently able to access the same amount of information as men if they ever wish to move beyond the most basic Qi Gong training. Second, we wished to give an overview of the entire process so that female practitioners may gain a 'bird's eye' view of how Daoist practices may unfold for them. In the future, it may be the case that we write in more detail about specific areas of female internal practice, but for now we decided that a general overview of the practice was wisest.

The partner book to this is Damo Mitchell's book *Daoist Nei Gong: The Philosophical Art of Change*, which looks at the Nei Gong process in a similar manner but with less of an emphasis upon women-specific training. Although it perhaps leans more towards approaching the training from a male perspective, there is still a great deal of useful information that will apply to women as well. When writing *Daoist Nei Gong for Women*, we wished to give a parallel view of the process from a woman's point of view but avoid repeating too much information, which is why it is wise to use both books together.

SPONTANEOUS ENERGETIC MOVEMENT

One important aspect of the internal arts that has not been discussed extensively in this book is the phenomenon of spontaneous energetic movement. Part of the reason is that the book was written in a sequential manner and it is difficult to state exactly where spontaneous energetic movement would fit into this process. It can be present in some people right from the initial stages of Qi Gong training, while for others it does not begin to manifest until the lower Dan Tien wakes up. Many teachers of the internal arts actually demonise spontaneous energetic reactions of any kind, when in actual fact they were classically a large part of many transformational practices.

For those who do not understand what these reactions are, they are a response to an increased flow of internal energy through the meridian system. As this energy flows, it carries with it information that then manifests itself within the physical body. The body reacts by shaking, folding, vibrating, running or any one of countless spontaneous movements which happen without the conscious control of the practitioner. As these reactions take place, they work their way through various layers of a person's being, shedding unwanted information and repatterning a person's energetic matrix. The downside of these reactions is that they cause the energy system to go into a very Yang state, which can be too extreme for some people. They also stress the nervous system a great deal, meaning that problems can potentially arise from these movements if they are allowed to take place over a prolonged period of time.

The fact is that there are great benefits to be had from engaging with spontaneous energetic reactions if they are trained and used properly. To simply bring them on in your practice and then indulge in them is incorrect; they should be channelled effectively through the body so that the benefits can be drawn but the reactions not allowed to move into an overly Yang phase. There are many groups in both the East and the West that use these reactions to varying degrees. In some cases the reactions are used effectively, while in others they are overused, which can be detrimental to many practitioners' health. Figure C.1 shows a group of women in Asia using spontaneous energetic reactions in their practice.

FIGURE C.1: SPONTANEOUS REACTIONS IN ASIA

It is always going to be difficult to guide somebody safely into the practice of spontaneous energetic movement through a book. It really requires an experienced teacher to monitor and lead a student into this aspect of the training due to the sheer unpredictability of how each person can react to increased energy flow through the body. In general, where there is a specific reaction that takes place in accordance with a stage of development, we have included this in the book. This is because certain movements can be seen as clear milestones of progress – signposts along the way. What we have not discussed are the random movements that can also take place at any time you are working with or generating extra energy movement throughout the meridian system. In many cases we have met practitioners from other styles who have already had these experiences and yet have not known what they were. Sometimes this caused them fear, and in the majority of instances they tried to hold the movements in, because they believed them to be the start of some large energetic imbalance. In very few cases have we found people who actively allowed the process to happen and simply watched to see what would happen if their energy was given the space to move freely.

Spontaneous energetic reactions also vary in usefulness for men and women in Nei Gong practice. This is because of the manner in which energy moves within both genders. In men, energy naturally moves outwards away from the core, and for this reason they can generally handle the level of the spontaneous reactions if they become quite intense. If men enter into a period of large, shaking movements with their arms waving in the air (all possible reactions!), it is not really a problem. They will generally enter a phase like this when the Dan Tien begins to drive more energy through the body. After a short period of time the information within the energy body will have changed and they will begin to calm down again. For women, though, this can be quite different. If women enter into periods of large, spontaneous shaking movements, this can cause a reversal of their energetic flow. As the reactions drive energy outwards from the core of their body, it can begin to drain them and so damage the level of their health. It is better if female practitioners aim to smooth these movements out and make them much softer. This is not accomplished by forcing the movements to subside using willpower or physical tension, but rather through deepening the breath, relaxing the mind and giving the gentle mental instruction to 'relax' to their energy system. When women manage to do this, they will find that the faster and more erratic movements begin to change into softer, flowing movements that are far more gentle and graceful to watch. This then enables them to enter into this phase of their energetic development without running the risk of causing energetic draining.

As stated above, however, to enter safely into this kind of training you should seek out an experienced teacher. We have included information on this part of the process because many practitioners will have experienced these reactions in the past themselves and not known what they were. They are part of Nei Gong practice, a normal and common stage to pass through, but they are not the goal of the practice. As with any reaction or experience, they should not be focused upon; they should be acknowledged and allowed to pass through you so that you enter into the stages of development that come long after the spontaneous energetic reactions have completed.

PROGRESSION INTO NEI DAN TRAINING

Beyond the stages outlined in this book are the deeper aspects of Daoist training. Realistically, although you may touch upon some of these levels through Nei Gong training, it is Nei Dan meditation that is required to fully move into the advanced aspects of the internal arts. The standard process we were taught was first to learn how to stand and move efficiently, and then to move on to learning how to sit properly. This is the stage of moving into a study of seated meditation.

By the time a woman moves on to seated Nei Dan practice, she should have established a solid foundation in the standing and moving exercises outlined in this book. There are differences between male and female practice in the practice of Nei Dan, but they are not as strikingly different as some of the practices for women in Nei Gong. If you would like more information on the practice of Daoist Nei Dan, please refer to the book *White Moon on the Mountain Peak: The Alchemical Firing Process of Nei Dan* by Damo Mitchell. This book has detailed instruction in the advanced stages of Daoist training for both male and female practitioners.

If we look back at the internal process outlined in Chapter 1, we can see how Nei Gong and Nei Dan fit together:

1. Conditioning and preparation of the physical body

2. Regulation of breath and mind

3. Regulation of the menstrual cycle

4. Extraction of Jing from Tian Gui

5. Awakening the energy system

6. Awakening of the Heart centre

7. Attainment of internal vibration

8. Conversion of Qi to Shen

9. Conversion of Shen to Dao

From this list it is possible to see how the first seven stages can be achieved through Nei Gong, while the final two stages require Nei Dan practice. Of course, Nei Dan also has foundation stages of its own, and so there is a certain degree of crossover between the two systems.

The reason that Nei Dan is required for the later aspects of Daoism is that direct work with Shen itself requires moving into work with the congenital aspects of the three treasures. Jing, Qi and Shen as concepts are enough for people to understand if they wish to work with awakening the energy system, but there are also the congenital aspects of these treasures which exist as lights within the depth of our consciousness. Nei Dan is a practice deep enough to take a sincere practitioner into direct contact with these 'substances' so that they can be alchemically changed. This then gives us contact with the source of our own being and can, theoretically at least, lead us towards becoming a spiritual immortal – the highest attainment of the Daoist arts.

We will end this book here with the hope that it has given women, as well as men who teach women in their classes, an overview of the energetic workings of the female body. Nei Gong for women is a very specific practice which should take into account the unique energetic and spiritual characteristics that every woman has inside of her, and we hope that we have contributed a little extra knowledge to the internal arts community. If it helps even a handful of women to develop more of an understanding of their practice, then it has been a successful writing project.

Appendix 1

MENSTRUAL IMBALANCES

In Chinese medical thought, there are various internal conditions that can have a direct effect upon the Uterus and menstruation. The names of these conditions are taken from contemporary Chinese medicine and we have included them here as an appendix in order to help women gain insight into the health of their menstrual cycle. We did not include this information in the main body of the text as we did not wish to aim the book solely at those with knowledge of Chinese medicine.

On top of the brief advice given here, we strongly urge you to visit a qualified and experienced Chinese medical practitioner who should be able to assist you with any of these conditions. Try to find a practitioner who comes with good recommendations.

Internal Cold Affecting the Uterus

Internal Cold within the Uterus can result in some or many of the following symptoms:

- Pain in the lower abdominal region which is made worse in cold weather
- Dark menstrual blood
- Dark clots in the blood
- Scant amounts of menstrual blood
- Abdominal cramping which is alleviated by application of warmth to the lower abdomen
- Loose bowels
- A feeling of being bloated in the lower abdomen – sometimes this is simply an internal sensation while at other times you can physically bloat
- Chronic weight gain around the lower abdomen and hips
- Cold abdomen and lower back
- Low sex drive and poor fertility
- Ache or bruised sensation in lower back and knees

To help resolve these issues, ensure that you eat only warm, cooked meals. Drink hot drinks such as tea and warm water. Cut out all cold food and certainly avoid frozen food such as ice cream. Cold drinks will also contribute to the worsening of this condition. Try always to keep your abdomen and lower back warm, particularly when you are outdoors or where there may be a draught. Try to add some warming spices such as ginger into your diet. At night it can be useful to put a hot water bottle on to your lower back or abdomen, and consider making a hot footbath part of your daily routine for a period of time.

It should be noted that this kind of condition can be due to numerous causative factors including diet and emotional imbalances. Although it is always going to be difficult to give an exact reason for a condition like this without a full diagnosis by a qualified Chinese medical practitioner, it should be noted that a common cause of this type of imbalance is long-term use of oral contraceptives. According to Chinese medical theory, oral contraceptives damage the relationship between the Kidney Fire and the Uterus, which results in the development of internal Cold of this kind.

Practising the mysterious crucible Mudra on a regular basis should also help to alleviate this condition. Make this exercise a part of your daily practice routine.

Excess Internal Heat

At the opposite end of the scale, internal Heat within the body can also affect the Uterus. This Heat can be within the Uterus itself, the Blood or other organs associated with the functions of the Uterus. This can result in some or many of the following symptoms:

- Heavy periods with an excessive amount of menstrual blood

- Menstrual blood of an overly deep or bright red colour

- Sensations of uncomfortable warmth in the body, particularly in the lower abdomen

- An overly active mind – during the day or at night when trying to sleep

- Constipation

- Yellow urine that has a strong smell to it

- A thirst for drinks that cannot be satisfied

- An obsession with sex that is difficult to satisfy

- Dislike of being in warm climates

To help deal with this internal imbalance, try to eat foods that are cooling such as green leafy vegetables. Avoid spiced foods, strong flavours and an excess of meat. Drink herbal teas that are cooling in nature such as peppermint. Ensure that you have a regular practice such as Qi Gong, Yoga or deep breathing and try to stay away from overly stressful situations.

A key causative factor in a condition such as this (aside from diet) is emotional stress. Extremes of emotion and chronic states of mental tension will really exacerbate this kind of condition and so it is imperative that a woman with these symptoms learns to relax.

Liver Qi Stagnation Affecting the Uterus

In Chinese medical thought, the Liver controls the free flow of Qi throughout the body. If this function of the Liver is compromised, then it can have an effect upon many organ systems of the body including the Uterus. In this case the following symptoms may manifest:

- Irregular menstrual cycle

- Scant amounts of menstrual blood

- Purple tinge to the menstrual blood

- Clots in the blood that are often purple

- Swelling and pain in the breasts just prior to menstruation

- Abdominal pain just prior to menstruation

- Low mood and depression around menstruation

- Emotional swings around menstruation

- Swelling and discomfort around the diaphragm area of the torso

Although there are many reasons why any internal condition can arise in a person's body, this particular condition is often closely related to feelings of stress, anger and pent-up frustration. In modern times, these feelings often arise in women who feel unable to express themselves in some way; this can be in their personal or professional life. Explore these issues within yourself and then work to change any situation that may be contributing to this stress. Ensure that you have a regular Qi Gong practice to help smooth out the Liver's Qi and work towards developing your ability to moon-gaze, as this will help to regulate the function of the Uterus.

It is particularly important in this condition to cut out smoking, drugs, alcohol and coffee, all of which will only add to the problem.

General Qi Deficiency

A general deficiency in the quality of your energy will result in feelings of exhaustion and low mood. This lack of Qi strength will often result in the following menstrual symptoms:

- Overly heavy periods with excessive menstrual blood

- Pale colour to the menstrual blood

- A pale complexion

- Chronic tiredness which is worse around menstruation

- Loose bowels, particularly just prior to the onset of menstruation

- Abdominal swelling

- Aching sensation in the lower back

- Inappropriate sweating which can come on without any physical exertion

The first thing here is to ensure that you are getting enough rest; this needs to be for the mind and not just the body. Many people will rest their body by sitting down in a comfortable chair but then stress the mind with watching movies. The mind must also be rested to restore the strength to your Qi. Make sure you have a healthy sleeping pattern and that you do not stay up too late at night. Your diet can be a major factor in this condition, so ensure that you eat healthily and at regular times.

Use gentle forms of practice to restore the strength to your body and focus upon the core in particular. If the core of the body is strengthened, then the Qi becomes less 'slack'; this will in turn start to tackle overall conditions of deficiency.

Avoid cold food and drinks, sugar and processed food, overwork and stress. Ensure that you have enough quiet space in your life to enable your batteries to recharge.

Damp/Phlegm Affecting the Uterus

Damp and Phlegm are two Chinese pathogenic factors that are challenging to clear from the body. They are internal conditions which can result from numerous causes. They generally come with some or many of the following symptoms:

- Scant amount of blood when menstruating

- Menstrual blood often has a slight brown tinge to it

- Vaginal discharge between menstruation

- Menstruation stops and starts over a few days

- Sensations of heaviness in the lower abdomen and limbs

- Chronic weight gain, particularly in the lower abdomen

- Feeling of tightness in chest, which can make breathing tight

- Chronic tiredness

Ensure that your diet is as healthy as possible. Food is one of the best medicines in tackling this kind of condition. There are many books in print on Chinese medical food therapy, and it would be worth investing in a few of these in order to help tackle any bad habits with regard to your diet.

You should avoid cold and frozen foods, sugary food, dairy products, processed foods of any kind and certainly soft drinks. Mental stress and overthinking can also contribute to this kind of condition, so your daily practice routine should include lots of exercises focused upon deep breathing and mental relaxation.

Blood Deficiency Affecting the Uterus

If there is a deficiency within the energetic strength of the Blood, then the following symptoms can arise:

- Pale colour to menstrual blood

- Scanty periods or, in extreme cases, amenorrhea

- Menstruation can start and finish in as little as one or two days

- Pale complexion and lips

- Feelings of dizziness

- Dry eyes and blurred vision

- Palpitations

- Chronic feelings of tiredness

- Low spirit and depressed mood

Blood deficiency is another condition that can be tackled quite effectively through your diet. Try to include some of the following foods in your diet: dark green leafy vegetables, seaweed, spirulina, sprouts and lots of whole grains. Fruits such as goji berries, black grapes and blackberries are helpful too. If you are not a vegetarian, then red meat can help; try to make it organic, though, and consider making a meat and bone soup as this can serve as a powerful Blood tonic. Once again, avoid all cold foods and drinks while you are attempting to rebalance this issue.

Appendix 2

THE TEN LUNAR MONTHS
OF PREGNANCY

B elow is a brief discussion of the developmental stages involved in the ten lunar months of pregnancy. We have included this information because pregnancy is something that obviously affects the majority of women at some stage in their life. Each lunar month is divided into the inner and outer processes. The inner processes are the various interplays of the congenital energy body that take place during each lunar month of foetal development. The outer processes are the foundations of different aspects of a child's health which are established during each lunar month. Note that the sequence for the development of an unborn child is very different in Daoist theory to the Western model. Remember that this is because the ancient Chinese model is focused almost entirely upon the energetic health at each stage of development rather than the growth of the physical body. An example of this would be that during the seventh lunar month the energy around the child's bones is established. Although an unborn child has obviously developed the physical structure of the bones prior to this time, it is only during the seventh lunar month that the potential of their health is consolidated.

The following table summarises the inner and outer processes during each lunar month of a woman's pregnancy. These months are then discussed in more detail below.

Month	Inner Process	Outer Process
0	Extension of Ming through into the realm of manifestation	The potential for the creation of life is established
1	Yin and Yang meet male and female essence	The movement of Liver Blood affects the physical foundation of the foetus
2	Four directions form around the lower Dan Tien	The consolidation of the foetus Qi starts to take place
3	Governing and Conception meridians form, the two poles are established and the Yang souls appear within the body	The emotional basis of the developing child is formed

4	The rest of the congenital meridians manifest and the seven Yin souls are generated	The basis of the health of the child's ability to process and shift fluids through the body is formed
5	Appearance of the congenital lights of the five elements	The health of the child's limbs and physical body is established
6	Appearance of the Zang and Fu organs	The spirit of the organs reaches outwards to develop the health of the remaining aspects of a child's physical structure
7	Opening of the seven points on the vertical branch of the Thrusting meridian, the seven orifices and the middle and upper Dan Tien	The physical structure of the body begins to develop a stronger connection to the bone structure; the strength and vitality of a child's bones are developed
8	The acquired Jing begins to govern the child's developmental processes and the eight Qi take their acquired position	The health of the skin is established. It is also said the aesthetic beauty of a child is developing at this stage!
9	Alignment of consciousness and spirit in preparation for entry into the world	The child's emotional demeanour is developed with regard to how relaxed its temperament will be; whether the child will naturally react with stress or a 'laid back' feeling is partially determined here
10	The focus of the energy system switches from the congenital to the acquired meridians	The child is ready, the energies have been established and it is time for the child to be born

The ancient Daoists placed great importance on the process of being pregnant and so developed a list of guidelines in order to promote the health of the unborn child. Although they could never fully guarantee the absence of congenital defects, they did develop a set of guidelines which would help a mother to give her child the healthiest start in life. These are discussed below by lunar month.

Prior to Conceiving

Many pregnancies are not planned and, of course, in these cases there can be little in the way of planning for a healthy conception. However, in the case of planned conceptions there are several pieces of guidance that potential parents can follow in order to ensure they prepare for the arrival of a new child.

First, both parents should recognise that there has to be a healthy level of energetic resonance in order to help establish a healthy emotional foundation for their child. Both partners must feel a strong energetic and emotional connection to one another in order for resonance to develop. Essentially, this is the energetic basis for love. According to Daoist thought, resonance takes time to develop, and so even if a couple fell in love at first sight, it will take some time for their energetic frequencies to begin vibrating at the same state. For this reason it was classically advised that the couple should have been together long enough for this resonance to have taken place. It is impossible to give exact timescales for this to take place, but you can be sure that it does not happen within the space of a few weeks.

The potential parents should also ensure that they have a healthy emotional relationship with each other. If there are numerous arguments between the couple or one of the couple holds deep resentment for the other, then this is going to have a strong effect on the child's emotional health. The balance of both parents' emotional states helps to develop the foundation of Yin and Yang within the unborn child's spirit. The degree to which the parents relate healthily to each other determines how well Yin and Yang will relate to each other. For this reason it is wise to try to resolve any past issues prior to conception. The healthier the relationship between two people, the better the emotional foundation that is being established for their child.

Both potential parents should spend some time ensuring that their physical and energetic health is as good as it can be. The health of both parents is passed on to their child via the transference of their Jing. The information patterns contained within this energetic substance will go on to form the baseline of their child's health. Although, of course, there will always be weaknesses in both parents, because nobody's health is perfect, you can do your best to get your health to as good a state as possible. Consider taking time to visit a Chinese medicine practitioner in order to help regulate your internal energy prior to trying for a child. The great injustice of Jing, though, is that it is said to pass on family information for three generations. This means that although your health may be good, your parents or grandparents may pass on weaknesses to your unborn child through the lineage of your Jing. This also places responsibility on you to regulate your own health as your Jing will also affect the next couple of generations of your family.

Both parents should adopt a healthy diet for several months prior to trying to conceive. They should also cut out all toxins of any sort including any drugs or alcoholic beverages. In particular, the mother should also try to stay away from any environments where there are toxins around. Smoke-filled rooms should be avoided in order to prevent any damage to your lungs.

Try to avoid stressful situations. Although there are always going to be unavoidable stresses in anybody's life, it is never wise to conceive a child during a particularly difficult period of your life. Consider waiting until your life is a little more settled and there are fewer stresses affecting you. Do not try to conceive if you are working overly hard. This is particularly important for the mother. She should try to establish a healthy balance in her life whereby she is not being overly stressed or overworked. This will all contribute to the baseline of health of the child.

First Lunar Month

During the first lunar month of pregnancy it is particularly important for a woman to avoid eating raw or cold foods. Salads should be avoided along with ice in drinks or any kind of frozen food. Warm, cooked food should be eaten along with warm drinks. Warm water is better than coffee or tea for the first lunar month; coffee should also be avoided throughout the whole of a woman's pregnancy as it runs the risk of damaging the Qi of the unborn child's Heart.

The mother should eat foods that promote the health of the Liver, while at the same time avoiding foods that strengthen the Lungs, as this will restrict the growth of the Liver's energy. There are many books written on Chinese medical food therapy, so it may be wise to invest in one or two of them during your pregnancy.

During this early stage of pregnancy it is of particular importance that a woman avoids feelings of stress, sadness or anger. All of these emotions will negatively affect the balance of the Wood and Metal elemental energy. In particular, feelings of anger will easily transfer to the unborn child at this stage of pregnancy.

Second Lunar Month

During the second lunar month it was classically advised that all sexual stimulation be avoided for the pregnant woman. This is because the Qi of the child is being developed as well as the establishment of the lower Dan Tien. If the mother is overly sexually stimulated during this lunar month, then an excess of base desires will develop within the lower aspects of the child's psyche. These run the risk of developing into sexual deviances or addictions, issues that will hinder a child in the course of spiritual development later in its life.

With regard to food, the same guidelines are given for the second lunar month as for the first. Refer back to the lists of positive and negative foods given in the first lunar month. In addition, avoid fried food, as this runs the risk of developing internal Heat during this lunar month.

Third Lunar Month

Because the basis of the child's emotional standpoint is being developed during this lunar month, it is wise to remain as calm as possible. The mother should avoid any stresses and stay away from anything that may result in a negative emotional state. Quiet breathing exercises are useful during this month in order to help the unborn child to develop as centred a mind as possible. Do not watch unpleasant or emotionally disturbing images on the television such as thrillers or horror films, and try not to read or expose yourself to anything that might be upsetting, as these feelings will be rooted into the child's psyche. It is impossible to look at violent or horror-type images without them leaving an imprint on the mind. Many people think watching violent movies is not affecting them, but of course it is. Everything is a source of information, and this information attaches itself to the energy body via the emotions. During this third lunar month it is particularly important that such images are avoided.

Healthy amounts of cooked vegetables and grains are advised during this lunar month in order to help build the unborn child's health. There are less strict guidelines on food at this time but you should still eat as healthy and balanced a diet as possible.

Fourth Lunar Month

During the fourth lunar month the health of the child's body fluids is established along with the seven Po, the spirits that give a tangible connection to the outside world. It is advised that lots of warm grains are eaten during this month. It can also be useful to eat soups and broths, and in particular chicken soup. These will all help the child develop in as healthy a way as possible.

Emotionally, the most damaging thing at this time is going to be feelings of grief. Any acute senses of loss at this time can negatively affect the health of the child's psyche. The unfortunate thing about this is that you rarely get to choose when you are going to experience feelings of loss or grief. You cannot help when a family member will pass away, a pet will die or a friend will walk out on you. These are all aspects of life that are beyond your control. All you can do is be aware of how these feelings affect you during this time and so try to maintain as calm a state of mind as possible.

Fifth Lunar Month

During the fifth lunar month the unborn child's level of physical strength is being determined. In particular, the strength of the limbs is emphasised. For this reason it is advised that a woman eats very well during this month and ensures that she eats enough to give her child the vitality it needs. The Chinese classical guidance is lots of grain and meat at this time. The energy taken from the meat is necessary for the child's development at this stage. Of course, there are often ethical issues for vegetarians or vegans. We cannot advise you on this as you need to weigh up the strength and importance of your ethical convictions against the classical advice given. If you are a meat eater, then make sure that the meat you are eating at this time is healthy and organic. Do not eat processed meats or cheap, low-quality meat. Look for meat that has been reared in an ethical manner. It may be wise to go to farm shops or specialist food outlets in order to make sure that the meat you eat is healthy and clean.

It is also advised that a pregnant woman does not get up too early during this month and the next. Rest lots, stay in bed late and try to ensure that you preserve your energy; the more you can preserve, the more vitality you will transfer to your unborn child.

Sixth Lunar Month

During this month try to follow the advice from the previous lunar month. This is another month of establishing physical vitality for your child. Eat according to the guidance above and do not get out of bed too early. The only difference is that during this month you should also be engaging in light exercise as well. Brisk exercise that is not too tiring is the best. This can be anything from swimming to brisk walks in the hills. You are trying to develop a balance between resting to store energy and engaging in light exercise to stimulate the body's Qi into a Yang state. The better you can find a balance between these two states, rest and activity, the better a foundation in physical vitality you will build for your child.

Seventh Lunar Month

During the seventh lunar month it is important for a woman to stay in a healthy environment. She should avoid cold, draughty or damp places as all of these energies will be transferred into her body at this time. In addition, she should eat warm foods for the whole month. No uncooked foods should be consumed, and the healthier a woman's diet at this time the better. Avoid sugars and processed foods which will lead to a weakening of the potential of your child's bone health.

A sensible, but slightly unpleasant, food to eat during this month is bone marrow broth. Not the most appetising of dishes for many people, it is very good for helping to develop bone strength.

Eighth Lunar Month

The various formations of internal Qi are stabilising within the child's body at this time as the child is preparing to be born. With only a couple of lunar cycles left prior to entering the world, it is the skin of the child that is soaked in Qi at this time. For this reason it is wise to eat food from the 'five flavours'. This means that a woman should eat a healthy balance of food from each of the elemental categories. For more information on these categories, please refer to any book on Chinese medical food theory. There are many books on the market with lists of food according to these five categories. During the eighth lunar month it is particularly important to try to equalise the food from each of these categories to give the unborn child as varied and balanced a source of energy as possible.

Ninth and Tenth Lunar Months

The spirit of the unborn child is entering its final formative stages at this time. For this reason it is vitally important for the woman to stay away from any external stresses or emotional difficulties. She should rest, try to remain calm and aim to establish as calm a mind for her child as possible. It is almost time for the child to be born and this should be her only focus. It is very important at this stage that she receives as much support as possible from her partner who should be prioritising everything towards maintaining the mother's energetic and emotional health. The woman should not be undertaking any unnecessary work as this will take potential vitality away from the unborn child. This should be maintained up until the birth of the child.

The Partner

These guidelines are to help establish as solid a foundation as possible for a mother's unborn child. You will see that all of the rules are for the mother with regard to what she eats and so on. There was classically little in the way of guidance for the partner of the pregnant woman. Despite this lack of guidance, it should be remembered that we each have an energy field which carries with it vibratory information. This means that if the partner of the pregnant woman does not maintain their health during the pregnancy, this will also have a detrimental effect upon the unborn child. A couple will constantly be transferring Qi from one to another, and this Qi transference wants to be as positive as possible.

Although it is not always possible to follow these guidelines completely for the full ten lunar months, it is important to understand that bringing new life into the world brings with it the responsibility to give that child as healthy a start as possible.

GLOSSARY OF PINYIN TERMS

This is a glossary of Pinyin Chinese terms used in this book and in previous titles by Damo Mitchell. It can be confusing coming into the Daoist arts and encountering so many Chinese names and words. The fact is that direct translation into English can be difficult with many of these terms, but we have attempted to make them as clear and concise as possible.

BA GUA 八卦 The Daoist theory of the eight key energies of the universe. This is the basic tenet of the *Yi Jing* as well as countless other aspects of the tradition.

BAI HUI 百會 (DU 20) An acupuncture point situated on top of the head. It is translated as 'hundred meetings'. In esoteric Daoism, it is also the point where numerous spirits converge and the point where the Chong Mai extends upwards out of the body.

BI YAN HU 碧眼胡 The 'blue-eyed foreigner'; a name for Bodhidharma, the patriarch of Chan Buddhism in China.

CHAN 禪 The form of Buddhism commonly taught in China. A combination of Buddhist and Daoist theory.

DA ZHOU TIAN 大周天 'Large Heavenly cycle', also known as the 'large water wheel of Qi'. This is the primary circulation of energy out of the body which can be achieved through consistent Nei Gong or Nei Dan training.

DAN 丹 The Dan is the 'elixir' which is sought out through alchemical training in the Daoist tradition. Often depicted as red and likened to the ore of cinnabar.

DAN TIEN 丹田 Usually refers to the lowest of the three main 'elixir fields', although there are three main Dan Tien within the body. The primary functions of the lower Dan Tien are the conversion of Jing to Qi and the moving of Qi throughout the meridian system.

DAO 道 The nameless and formless origin of the universe. Daoism is the study of this obscure concept, and all internal arts are a way of experientially understanding the nature of Dao.

DAO DE JING 德道经 The 'virtue of following the way'. The classical text of Daoism written by the great sage Laozi. Also written as *Tao Te Ching*.

DAO YIN 導引 'Guiding and pulling' exercises. These are the ancient exercises developed by the shamanic Wu people to purge the energy body of pathogenic energies.

DAO ZANG 道藏 The *Dao Zang* is the Daoist canon of classical writings which includes more than 1400 pieces of scripture.

DE 德 The congenital manifestation of the transient emotions. De is born from deep within the true human consciousness which is usually buried beneath the various layers of the acquired mind.

DING 鼎 The 'cauldron' of Daoist Nei Dan. This is a location within the energy body where two energetic substances are being combined. Named after the Ding which sits within most Daoist temples.

DUI 兌 One of the eight trigrams of Daoist Ba Gua theory. Its energetic manifestation is metaphorically likened to a lake, although Dui does not directly mean lake.

FENG SHUI 风水 'Wind and water.' This is the Daoist study of environmental energies and the influence of the macrocosm upon the human energy system and consciousness.

FU 符 The magical talismanic drawings of the ancient Daoists. The skilled practitioner of magical Daoism could draw Fu to heal sickness, curse people or perform countless other functions. An almost extinct art in modern times.

GEN 艮 One of the eight trigrams of Daoist Ba Gua theory. Its energetic manifestation is likened to that of a mountain.

GONG 功 The attainment of a high-level skill in any art. To truly attain Gong took a lifetime of dedicated study, especially in the internal arts.

GUA 卦 'Trigram.' These are the eight sacred symbols that make up Daoist Ba Gua theory. They are a way to conceptualise the various vibrational frequencies of the energetic realm and how they interact.

HOU TIAN 後天 The 'post-Heaven' state in which we exist according to Daoist thought.

HUI YIN 會陰 (CV 1) 'Meeting of Yin' is an acupuncture point located at the perineum. It is so named because it is situated within the most Yin area of the human body.

HUN 魂 'Yang soul', the ethereal soul which continues to exist after our death. It is usually housed within the Liver.

HUNDUN 混沌 A term generally translated as referring to 'original chaos'. In Daoist philosophy, it refers to a state which lay dormant within the centre of human consciousness as well as an aspect of the process of creation. It is also the name of a stance used in female-specific Nei Gong training.

JI BEN QI GONG 基本气功 'Fundamental energy exercises.' The primary exercises taught in the Lotus Nei Gong School of Daoist Arts.

JING 精 The lowest vibrational frequency of the three main energetic substances of man. Usually translated as 'essence' and often misunderstood as being human sexual fluids.

JING GONG 精功 'Essence exercises.' The technique of building up and refining our Jing.

JING JIN 經筋 Lines of connective tissue that run throughout the body. These lines serve as 'riverbeds' for the flow of Qi that runs through the meridian system. The term is generally translated as 'tendon collaterals', but it is the authors' opinion that in many respects this term is actually referring to lines of fascia.

JING LUO 经络 The human meridian system which is made up of numerous energetic pathways which regulate the body and transport Qi to and from our organs and tissues.

KAN 坎 One of the eight trigrams of Daoist Ba Gua theory which is usually likened to the energetic manifestation of Water. Especially important in the practice of Nei Dan.

KUA 胯 The area of the body that includes the hip region and inguinal crease. As a term the Kua also refers to the manner in which this region of the body moves and connects into the rest of the body's physical and energetic structure.

KUN 坤 One of the eight trigrams of Daoist Ba Gua theory. Its energetic manifestation is usually likened to that of the planet.

KUN LUN SHAN 崑崙山 In Daoist legend, a mythical mountain which was said to reach up into the Heavens.

LAO GONG 勞宮 (PC 8) An acupuncture point situated in the centre of the palm. Its name means 'palace of toil' due to it being on the human hand which carries out a lot of physical work. In Daoism, this point is very important in venting heat from the Heart and so it is rarely at rest. It is a very important point in Qi Gong practice because it regulates the internal temperature and also allows us to emit Qi in practices such as external Qi therapy.

LAOZI 老子 The great sage. The 'original Daoist' who wrote the *Dao De Jing*. Supposedly, he left this text with a border watchman when he retreated into hermitage in the western mountains of China.

LI 離 One of the eight trigrams of Daoist Ba Gua theory. Its energetic manifestation is usually likened to fire. It is especially important to understand in the context of Nei Dan training.

LIANG YI 兩儀 The collective name for Yin and Yang. Literally translated as the 'two poles'.

LONG DAO YIN 龍導引 'Dragon Dao Yin.' A set of four sequences based upon the preliminary training methods from the martial style of Baguazhang. They twist the spine and open the joints to assist with the energetic purging process.

Lu 爐 The 'furnace' of Daoist Nei Dan. This is the place within the body where expansion is created which generates heat. This heat is then usually added to the Ding in order to create alchemical change.

MING 命 Your predestined journey from life to death. Usually translated as 'fate', but this really does not explain the true meaning of the term.

MING MEN 命门 (GV 4) An acupuncture point in the lower back that is very important in Nei Gong practice. This point is referred to several times in this book and serious internal arts practitioners should work very hard to awaken the energy in this area of their meridian system.

NEI DAN 內丹 The Daoist form of alchemical meditation usually associated with the northern sects of Daoism. Through working with various energetic and spiritual substances within the body, the practitioner seeks states of transcendence and, ultimately, immortality.

NEI GONG 內功 The process of internal change and development which a person may go through if they practise the internal arts to a high level.

NEI JING TU 內经图 The 'chart of the inner landscape'. One of two important alchemical charts carved into a courtyard wall of the 'White Cloud Monastery' in Beijing.

NU DAN 女丹 The practice of 'women's alchemy'. A slightly different process exists for women due to the nature of their energetic systems.

PO 魄 The 'Yin soul' which dies with the human body. Largely connected to our physical senses, the Po resides in the Lungs.

PU 樸 'Simplicity.' Often likened to being like an 'uncarved block'. The ideal state of mind according to the Daoist tradition. This has much to do with shedding the layers of the acquired mind which pull you away from existing in a simple state.

QI 氣 'Energy.' A term that is difficult to translate into English. In Nei Gong theory, it is an energetic vibration which transports information through the energy system.

QI GONG 氣功 Usually gentle exercises that combine rhythmic movements with breathing exercises to shift Qi through the body. The term means 'energy exercises', although it is sometimes translated as 'breathing exercises'.

QI HAI 氣海 (Ren 6) An acupuncture point which sits in front of the lower Dan Tien. In English its name means 'sea of Qi' because it is the point where Qi is generated and from where it flows. Like water returning to the sea in rivers and streams, Qi returns to the lower Dan Tien when it circulates in the 'small water wheel of Qi'.

QIAN 乾 One of the eight trigrams of Daoist Ba Gua theory. Its energetic manifestation is usually likened to the movements of Heaven.

REN 人 In Daoism, Ren is 'humanity'. Humanity sits between Heaven and Earth and is a reflection of their fluctuations and movements. Ren is nourished by Earth and stimulated to development through the actions of Heaven.

SAN BAO 三寶 The 'three treasures' of man, which are Jing, Qi and Shen.

SHEN 神 The energy of consciousness. Vibrates at a frequency close to that of Heaven. It is manifested within the body as a bright white light.

SHEN GONG 神功 This is the arcane skill of working with the substance of consciousness. In Daoism, it is said that a skilled Shen Gong practitioner can manipulate the very energy of the environment.

SHEN XIAN 神仙 The 'Heavenly immortal' is essentially full realisation of the possibility of spiritual immortality, which is the final goal of Daoist Nei Dan.

SHENGMU YUANJUN 聖母元君 Female deity within the Daoist tradition to whom various myths are attributed, the most noted of which are that she was the mother of Laozi as well as his first teacher.

SUN 巽 One of the eight trigrams of Daoist Ba Gua theory. Its energetic manifestation is usually likened to that of the wind.

TAIJI 太极 A Daoist concept of creation which can be translated as meaning the 'motive force of creation'.

TAIYI 太 The 'great pole' of Daoist philosophy is the single point of union which moves out of stillness. It is also the name of a standing posture utilised in advanced female-specific Nei Gong training.

TIAN 天 'Heaven.' Not to be mistaken for the Christian concept of Heaven, this refers to the vibrational frequency of the macrocosm. Within the microcosm of the body, Heaven is used metaphorically to refer to human consciousness.

TIAN GAN 天干 The 'Heavenly stems' is a model of the Yin and Yang divisions that take place in the Wu Xing within the Heavenly realm.

TIAN GUI 天癸 An energetic component involved in the formation of menstrual Blood for women. The term is often translated as 'Heavenly Water'.

TUI NA 推拿 A form of Chinese medical massage which means 'push and grasp'.

WU 巫 The shamanic Wu were the historical ancestors of the Daoists. They served as medicine men, bringers of rain and general mystics to the ancient tribes of China.

WU SHEN 五神 The 'five spirits'. The collective name for the Shen, Hun, Yi, Zhi and Po.

WU WEI 無為 The act of 'non-governing'. An important philosophical concept in the Daoist tradition. This term is often misunderstood to mean that Daoists should 'do' nothing and thus are essentially lazy.

WU XING 五行 The five elemental energies. An important part of Daoist creation theory, psychology and medicine.

WU XING QI GONG 五行气功 'Five Element energy exercises.' They are an important part of the Lotus Nei Gong School of Daoist Arts syllabus.

WUJI 无极 The Daoist concept of non-existence. The blank canvas upon which reality is projected and an important part of Daoist creation philosophy.

XIAN TIAN 先天 The 'before Heaven' congenital state which is all-important in Nei Dan training.

XIN-YI 心意 'Heart-mind.' This is the framework with which we attempt to understand the various aspects of human consciousness. Originally a Buddhist concept, it was absorbed into Daoist teachings.

XING 性 Your 'nature'. This is the expression of the various energetic and spiritual components of consciousness.

XIU ZHEN TU 修真图 The 'chart of cultivating perfection'. A highly influential chart in the Daoist alchemical tradition.

XIWANGMU 西王母 The 'holy mother of the west' is a Daoist immortal and deity associated with the power of the western Heavens, prosperity and immortality. She is often the patron deity of many female Daoist practitioners. She is often associated with the seven-star constellation.

YANG 陽 The Daoist philosophical extreme of movement, masculinity and action. One of the two great points required to manifest existence.

YANG QI 阳氣 In Chinese medicine, this refers to our internal Qi which moves out towards the surface of the body and the congenital meridians. In Nei Dan theory, it can also refer to the state of energy prior to its movement into the realm of existence.

YANG SHENG FA 养身法 Literally 'life-nourishing principles'. This is the Daoist practice of living healthily, which should be studied alongside all internal arts.

YI 意 'Intention' or 'awareness'. An important element of human consciousness to cultivate in Nei Dan training.

YI JING 易经 The 'classic of change'. An ancient Daoist text which is based upon Ba Gua theory. Commonly written as *I Ching*.

YIN 陰 The Daoist philosophical pole of stillness, femininity and quietude. One of the two poles required in order for existence to come into being.

YIN QI 阴氣 Our internal Qi which moves inwards to nourish the organs of the body. Can also be used in alchemical theory to describe the movement of Wuji as it coalesces around the condensed energy of Yang Qi.

YIN TANG 印堂 A meridian point situated between the eyebrows. Translated as the 'hall of impression', it is often equated with the spiritual third eye of the Eastern arts.

YONG QUAN 涌泉 (K 1) An acupuncture point on the base of the foot which means 'bubbling spring'. This is the main point through which Earth energy is drawn into the body.

Yuan Jing 元精 The original essence which exists prior to the beginning of the movement of the acquired essence. It is said to reside in the space between the Kidneys.

Yuan Qi 元氣 The original state of Qi prior to its movement into the acquired realm.

Yuan Shen 元神 The original state of human psyche prior to the movement from the congenital to the acquired. It exists as a brilliant white light within the space of the human Heart-mind.

Yuan Xi 元息 'Original breath.' The breath of life that is passed down into existence from Dao. Yuan Xi is an expression of the movement of Yuan Qi.

Zang Fu 脏腑 The collective name for the Yin and Yang organs of the body.

Zhen 震 One of the eight trigrams of Daoist Ba Gua theory. Its energetic manifestation is often likened to thunder.

Zhen Ren 真人 The 'true person' of Daoism is a high-level state of attainment possible through alchemical cultivation of the inner state.

Zhi 志 An element of human consciousness which is directly linked to the state of our Kidneys. The nearest translation in English is 'willpower'.

Zhuangzi 莊子 An important sage in the Daoist tradition. Zhuangzi was known for his humour and the fact that he poked fun at almost every aspect of life.

Zi Bao 子胞 The 'child container' is the Uterus as well as the energetic matrix associated with this physical organ within the female body.

Zi Fa Gong 自發功 The process of releasing spontaneous energetic movements through the body. This happens as stagnant energetic pathogens are released and the body begins to return to some kind of order.

Ziran 自然 The Daoist philosophical concept of acting in harmony with nature and returning to an original state.

Zuo Wang 坐忘 This can be translated as 'sitting and forgetting'. This is the entering of the silent state during Daoist meditation.

About the Authors

This book was written jointly by Roni Edlund and her partner, Damo Mitchell. Both are full-time practitioners of the Daoist internal arts and together they run the Lotus Nei Gong School of Daoist Arts.

RONI EDLUND

Roni Edlund met her partner, Damo Mitchell, while travelling through South East Asia in 2007. Shortly afterwards, she moved to the UK from her home country of Sweden and has since been practising the Daoist arts with Damo and several of his teachers in Asia. Roni Edlund has a passion for the Yang system of Taijiquan and the Cheng method of Baguazhang as well as her practice of Nei Gong. Alongside this, she also has a degree in acupuncture and Chinese medicine, which she sees as an integral part of her internal studies.

Roni Edlund teaches alongside Damo on larger retreats and events as well as running her own classes and courses around Europe. Many of these courses are specifically for women and cover the material outlined in this book.

DAMO MITCHELL

Damo Mitchell was born into a family of martial artists and thus began his studies when he was four years old. Since this time he has practised the martial and spiritual arts of Asia extensively, practices that he now passes on in the Lotus Nei Gong School of Daoist Arts. Damo has written several other books on the subjects of Daoist Nei Gong and Nei Dan but can only claim to have taken a supporting role in this book because it was the personal experience of Roni Edlund, taken from her practice, that really enabled this book to be written.

For more information on the authors or to find out more about the workshops and classes they teach around the world, please visit their website at www.lotusneigong.com.

INDEX